Conversations with
Terrence McNally

Literary Conversations Series
Monika Gehlawat
General Editor

Conversations with Terrence McNally

Edited by Raymond-Jean Frontain

University Press of Mississippi / Jackson

The University Press of Mississippi is the scholarly publishing agency of
the Mississippi Institutions of Higher Learning: Alcorn State University,
Delta State University, Jackson State University, Mississippi State University,
Mississippi University for Women, Mississippi Valley State University,
University of Mississippi, and University of Southern Mississippi.

www.upress.state.ms.us

The University Press of Mississippi is a member of the Association of University Presses.

First printing 2023
∞

Library of Congress Cataloging-in-Publication Number: 2022047794
Hardback ISBN 978-1-4968-3457-7
Trade paperback ISBN 978-1-4968-4327-2
Epub single ISBN 978-1-4968-4328-9
Epub institutional ISBN 978-1-4968-4329-6
PDF single ISBN 978-1-4968-4330-2
PDF institutional ISBN 978-1-4968-4331-9

British Library Cataloging-in-Publication Data available

For James V. O'Connor,
my first, and still my best,
theatre companion

Select Works by Terrence McNally*

This Side of the Door (Cherry Lane Theatre, 1962)
The Lady of the Camellias (Winter Garden Theatre, 1963)
And Things That Go Bump in the Night (Royale Theatre, 1965)
**Here's Where I Belong* (Billy Rose Theatre, 1968)
Witness and *Sweet Eros* (Gramercy Arts Theatre, 1968)
Noon in *Morning, Noon, and Night* (Circle in the Square on Broadway, 1968)
Next (Greenwich Mews Playhouse, 1969)
Where Has Tommy Flowers Gone? (Eastside Playhouse, 1971)
Whiskey (Theatre at St. Clement's, 1973)
Bad Habits (Astor Place Theatre, 1974)
The Ritz (Longacre Theatre, 1975)
Broadway, Broadway (Forrest Theatre, Philadelphia, 1978)
**The Rink* (Martin Beck Theater, 1984)
It's Only a Play (Manhattan Theatre Club, 1985)
Frankie and Johnny in the Claire de Lune (Manhattan Theatre Club, 1987)
Andre's Mother (Manhattan Theatre Club, 1988)
Hope in *Faith, Hope and Charity* (South Street Theatre, 1988)
The Lisbon Traviata (Manhattan Theatre Club, 1989)
Up in Saratoga (Old Globe Theatre, San Diego, 1989)
Lips Together, Teeth Apart (Manhattan Theatre Club, 1991)
**Kiss of the Spider Woman* (Broadhurst Theatre, 1993)
A Perfect Ganesh (Manhattan Theatre Club, 1993)
Love! Valour! Compassion! (Manhattan Theatre Club, 1994)
Master Class (John Golden Theatre, 1995)
Dusk in *By the Sea, By the Sea, By the Beautiful Sea* (Bay Street Theater, Sag Harbor, NY, 1996)
**Ragtime* (Ford Center for the Performing Arts, 1998)
House (co-written with Jon Robin Baitz; Bay Street Theater, Sag Harbor, NY, 1998)
Corpus Christi (Manhattan Theatre Club, 1998)
**The Food of Love* (New York City Opera, 1999)

Some Christmas Letters (St. Bartholomew's Church, 1999)

**The Full Monty* (Eugene O'Neill Theatre, 2000)

***Dead Man Walking* (San Francisco Opera, 2000)

Ghost Light (Bay Street Theatre, 2002)

***A Man of No Importance* (Mitzi E. Newhouse Theater, Lincoln Center, 2002)

The Stendhal Syndrome (Primary Stages, 2004)

Crucifixion (New Conservatory Theatre Center, San Francisco, 2005)

Dedication or The Stuff of Dreams (Primary Stages, 2005)

Some Men (Second Stage Theater, 2007)

Deuce (Music Box Theatre, 2007)

Unusual Acts of Devotion (Philadelphia Theatre Company, 2008)

***Catch Me If You Can* (Neil Simon Theatre, 2011)

Golden Age (Manhattan Theatre Club, 2012)

And Away We Go (Pearl Theatre Company, 2013)

Mothers and Sons (John Golden Theatre, 2014)

***Great Scott* (Dallas Opera, 2015)

***The Visit* (Lyceum Theatre, 2015)

***Anastasia* (Broadhurst Theatre, 2017)

Fire and Air (Classic Stage Company, 2018); revised as *Immortal Longings* (Zachary Scott Theatre, Austin, TX, 2019)

* Date given marks the New York premiere unless the play did not have a New York premiere. Most of McNally's plays produced at the Manhattan Theatre Club later transferred to Broadway.

** Opera libretto or book for musical

Contents

Introduction   xi

Chronology   xxxix

The Quiet and Scandalous World of Terrence McNally   3
Neal Weaver / 1974

Terrence McNally: Scripts Together, Worlds Apart   12
Larry S. Ledford / 1991

Measuring the Times: Terrence McNally Straddles the Sexual Divide   15
Otis Stuart / 1991

Terrence McNally   20
John L. DiGaetani / 1991

Terrence McNally   29
Joy Zinoman / 1991

The Playwright's New Directions: Terrence McNally, Exploring
Parts Unknown   52
Judith Weinraub / 1994

On a Roll   57
Richard Alleman / 1995

Terrence McNally: The *Theater Week* Interview   62
Carol Rosen / 1995

Love! Valour! Compassion!   73
Melissa Burdick Harmon / 1997

Love! Valour! McNally!   78
Alan Frutkin / 1997

Terrence McNally   82
David Savran / 1998

Love! Valour! Musicals!   101
Nelson Pressley / 2002

Writers and Their Work: Terrence McNally   107
Gregory Bossler / 2002

Gay for Play: Prolific Dramatist Terrence McNally Riffs on
Queer Theatre   120
Eddie Shapiro / 2005

Terrence McNally '60 Prepares for Another Broadway Opening   122
Laura Butchy / 2007

Living Life by the Beat of His Own Libretto   131
Peter Marks / 2010

McNally's Aria   135
Randy Shulman / 2010

A Playwright's Status Report: McNally's *Mothers and Sons* Gauges
a Changed America   142
Patrick Healy / 2014

Break Down the Barriers: An Interview with Terrence McNally   146
Raymond-Jean Frontain / 2018

Index   159

Introduction

The career of five-time Tony Award recipient Terrence McNally is remarkable for both the range of its accomplishments and the depth of its contradictions. There are four reasons why this is so. First, he cannot be typed in terms of a particular theatre movement or group. Initially active in the burgeoning Off-Broadway theatre movement in the 1960s, McNally is—with Sam Shepard and Lanford Wilson—one of the few playwrights of his generation to have successfully made the transition to Broadway and, in the process, passed from avant-garde to mainstream acclaim. (The confusion that critics had typing him early in his career is suggested by the fact that his first play, *And Things That Go Bump in the Night*, which was produced *on* Broadway, was for many years included in an influential anthology of *Off*-Broadway plays.¹) Yet in the late 1990s and 2000s, as Broadway productions became too top-heavy for their own good, he made a transition again, this time with ease to smaller, more intimate stages in the midtown theatre district, and he worked regularly and effectively with regional theatres.

Second, McNally saw—or, more properly, did—it all in terms of his dramaturgy as well. Initially celebrated as the author of dark, absurdist social satires and political protest plays like *Botticelli* and *Next*, he gradually forsook a politically confrontational theatre style to engage in more broadly farcical comedy in plays like *The Ritz* and *It's Only a Play*. However, following the emergence of the AIDS epidemic in the mid-1980s, his plays grew to be more lyrical meditations upon the causes of human isolation, the underlying causes of hatred and prejudice, and the need for interpersonal connection (*Frankie and Johnny in the Clair de Lune*; *Lips Together, Teeth Apart*; *A Perfect Ganesh*; *Love! Valour! Compassion!*; *Unusual Acts of Devotion*). Yet following the premiere of *Master Class* in 1995, his plays became increasingly concerned with the redemptive power of art, the human drive to connect with other people through theatre, and the relationship of sexual vitality to artistic creativity (*Dedication or The Stuff of Dreams, Golden Age, Immortal Longings*). His range was such that there is no such thing as a characteristically "McNally play" as there is a distinctively Wildean, Shavian, Albee-esque, or Pinteresque mode of drama.

Third, as a playwright who was deeply engaged by music, McNally strad-dled the divide between music and theatre circles. He wrote the book for multiple musicals, as well as the librettos for two major operas. He may be the only American playwright whose actual voice was more familiar to opera fans than to theatregoers, inasmuch as for nearly thirty years (1979–2008) he was a member of the Texaco Opera Quiz panel that fielded questions during the weekly "Live from the Met" radio broadcasts.

Finally, and perhaps most paradoxically, McNally was a gay man who was never in the closet; who introduced self-respecting gay characters in his plays as early as 1964; who authored several of the most important Ameri-can plays produced in response to the AIDS pandemic; who was a tireless speaker on behalf of gay civil rights issues; and whose civil unions with, and/ or marriages to, Gary Bonasorte and (following the latter's death) Tom Kirdahy attracted national notice. Yet to the dismay of some gay activists, he declined to be identified as a "gay playwright."

Despite that refusal, he is recognized as one of the most important playwrights of his generation—if not, with Tony Kushner, the most accom-plished American gay playwright since Tennessee Williams.

Biography

Michael Terrence McNally was born November 3, 1938, in St. Petersburg, Florida, to Hubert and Dorothy (Rapp) McNally, a pair of transplanted New Yorkers who ran a seaside bar and grill called The Pelican Club. (Ironically, while trying early in his career to appear more precocious, McNally misrep-resented his year of birth as 1939, a piece of misinformation that has been widely reprinted since.) His only sibling, Peter, was born six years later.

McNally described his parents as convivial people who enjoyed social-izing, but who tended to drink to excess. After a hurricane destroyed their establishment in St. Petersburg, the family returned initially to Port Ches-ter, New York, then moved to Dallas when the playwright was eleven, and three years later to Corpus Christi, where Hubert managed a Schlitz beer distributorship. McNally's earliest full-length play, *This Side of the Door*—produced in an Actors Studio workshop in 1962 featuring newcomer Estelle Parsons—deals with a sensitive boy's battle of wills with his over-bearing father, a theme that pervades a number of McNally's early, mostly unpublished plays and that the playwright acknowledged is partially auto-biographical. But whatever the nature of the tension between McNally and his father as the boy was growing up, McNally also spoke of his parents generously volunteering to listen to an important football game in the driveway on their car radio so that their pubescent son would not miss a Saturday afternoon opera broadcast on the better radio in the parlor.

McNally's parents enjoyed Broadway musicals and would leave on the coffee table the *Playbills* from their occasional trips to New York. When McNally was around eight years old, his parents took him to see *Annie Get Your Gun*, starring Ethel Merman. On a subsequent outing McNally saw Gertrude Lawrence in *The King and I*. Both performances made a lasting impression on him. In 1979, when Merman announced her retirement from the stage, McNally was writing a column for the *New York Guide* and pointedly told her in an open letter that "Queens do not abdicate."[2]

McNally was introduced to opera while in the middle grades at Christ the King School in Dallas by an Ursuline nun who brought recordings of Puccini duets to class on Friday afternoons. He subsequently discovered the Saturday afternoon "Live from the Met" radio broadcasts and, in advance of each week's performance, would make small figures of the characters that he could move about on a proscenium stage constructed from a shoe box as he followed the broadcast. In high school he bussed tables at a Peter Pan Cafeteria to earn the money to buy opera records.

At W. B. Ray High School in Corpus Christi, McNally was mentored by Maurine McElroy, a gifted English teacher who regularly invited a select group of students to her home after school for classical music and conversation. She was the first person to encourage McNally to write (although, because the young McNally did not understand that Ira was a man's name, his first effort—written in a juvenile hand on lined notebook paper preserved in the Harry Ransom Humanities Research Center in Austin, Texas—dramatized how composer George Gershwin met and married his supposedly *female* lyricist, who, as music aficionados well know, was in actuality his *brother*). And, when the time came for McNally to apply to colleges, McElroy encouraged him to concentrate on schools outside Texas to ensure that he developed as broad a view of the world as possible. Eventually, McNally would dedicate *Apple Pie* and *Frankie and Johnny in the Clair de Lune* to her, and in several of his plays he praises her by name for her ability to instill in young minds a love of Shakespeare. When she died in 2005, he supplied the inscription for her tombstone: "Not just an English teacher, but a life teacher."

In 1956, a seventeen-year-old McNally matriculated as a journalism major at Columbia College, the undergraduate arm of Columbia University, from which he graduated Phi Beta Kappa with a B.A. in English in 1960. His years there were part of Columbia's golden age of instruction, and his teachers included such extraordinary figures as Moses Hadas for classical civilization, Meyer Schapiro for art history, Eric Bentley for drama, and Lionel Trilling for literature. But he was particularly influenced by Andrew Chiappe, the mesmerizing lecturer in a popular two-semester course on Shakespeare in which students read every one of the bard's plays in the approximate order of their composition.[3] In his senior year, McNally wrote the campus variety show, which featured music by fellow student Edward L. Kleban (who would go on to share with others the Pulitzer Prize for *A Chorus Line*), and was directed by Michael Kahn (who would later serve as the artistic director of the Folger Shakespeare Library's theatre in Washington, DC).

During his college years, McNally returned to Texas in the summers to work as a cub reporter for the local newspaper, the *Corpus Christi Times-Caller*. His career in journalism came to an abrupt end, however, when he reported that during his interview with political maverick (and future president) Lyndon B. Johnson, the senator sat idly thumbing through a magazine featuring naked women as he took a call from his wife.

McNally's interest in journalism was quickly replaced by his growing interest in music and theatre. Upon arriving in New York, McNally had begun attending theatre and opera on a regular basis. Student-discounted prices made it possible for him to attend several plays a week. In a late interview, he warmly recalled the community that formed among those who waited in line for Standing Room tickets at the Metropolitan Opera, where he attended Maria Callas's explosive American debut in *Norma*. His Manhattan social sphere would eventually extend to the gay bars that operated in Greenwich Village, where patrons might spend an evening drinking and singing with a down-on-her-luck Judy Garland. He movingly memorialized both Garland and the gay piano bar culture of the 1960s in the Stonewall scene of *Some Men*.

While still an undergraduate, McNally's interest in theatre and music brought him an invitation to the party that followed the opening night performance of Marc Blitzstein's *The Cradle Will Rock* at the New York City Opera. Leaving the party, he shared a cab with Edward Albee. Having just premiered his groundbreaking Off-Broadway drama *The Zoo Story*, Albee was about to become the single most influential playwright in America. The nineteen-year-old college student soon moved in with the twenty-nine-year-old playwright. They lived as a couple for nearly five years—that is, during the period when Albee wrote and/or first saw produced such groundbreaking plays as *The Sandbox, The American Dream,* and *Who's Afraid of Virginia Woolf?* Albee biographer Mel Gussow claims that Martha's praise of her imaginary son's fine blond hair that became "fleece" in the summer sun and his ambivalently "blue, green, brown" eyes are Albee's affectionate inscription of his boyish lover in what remains his most famous play.[4]

After McNally and Albee's relationship had waned, McNally entered into a long-term relationship with handsome, talented, but deeply closeted actor Robert Drivas. McNally credited Drivas with reigniting his passion for writing after his first professionally produced play, *And Things That Go Bump in the Night,* was savaged by critics. McNally would subsequently write *Witness* (1968), *Sweet Eros* (1968), and, most importantly, *Where Has Tommy Flowers Gone?* (1971) for Drivas. In 1973 Drivas joined McNally at Yale University on a fellowship, during the course of which McNally wrote a farce titled *The Tubs* about a straight man who inadvertently takes refuge on a stormy night in a Mafia-owned gay bathhouse. When the play premiered on Broadway, retitled *The Ritz* and directed by Drivas, it was the surprise hit of the season. Drivas also directed McNally's Obie Award-winning *Bad Habits* (1974). Although McNally and Drivas broke up as a couple in 1976, they remained close friends until Drivas died of AIDS-related complications ten years later.

McNally subsequently partnered with actor Dominic Cuskern, who originated the role of the Conductor in *Prelude & Liebestod* as well as the title role in *A Perfect Ganesh,* and with Gary Bonasorte, a playwright and founding member of the Rattlestick Theater Company, with whom McNally fell in love in 1993 but lost to an AIDS-related illness in November 2001. McNally began living with Tom Kirdahy, a public interest attorney, in 2001; the couple married on December 20, 2003, in Dover, Vermont; repeated their vows in Washington, DC, on April 6, 2010, after gay marriage became legal in our nation's capital; and repeated their vows once again on June 26, 2015, on the steps of New York City's Town Hall in a ceremony officiated by Mayor Bill de Blasio (Kirdahy's college roommate) after marriage equality became the law of the land. Kirdahy has served as a producer for most of McNally's plays since *Some Men* in 2007. In addition to his long-term relationships with male partners, McNally had an affair with fellow playwright and sometime collaborator Wendy Wasserstein between 1987 and 1990. According to Wasserstein biographer Julie Salamon, McNally inspired the character Geoffrey, a bisexual theatre director, in Wasserstein's *The Sisters Rosensweig* (1993).[5] Still, McNally identified exclusively as gay.

McNally's respect for the communal nature of theatre is evident in his work habits. Early in his career, he collaborated with Leonard Melfi and

Israel Horovitz on three trilogies of one-act plays (*Morning, Noon, and Night*, 1968; Cigarettes, Whiskey, and Wild, Wild Women, 1973; and *Faith, Hope and Charity*, 1988) in which the three playwrights shared a cast, a set, and a general concept, but wrote independently of one another. He continued the practice with Joe Pintauro and Lanford Wilson (*By the Sea, By the Sea, By the Beautiful Sea*, 1996) and, with a slight variation, with Jon Robin Baitz (*House*, 1998). He also took part twice in The Twenty-Four Hour Plays festival in which playwrights write one-acts, which are then cast, rehearsed, and performed all within twenty-four hours (*The Sunday Times*, 2006; and *Teachers Break*, 2008). From 1985 until 1998, McNally's plays were initially produced at the Manhattan Theatre Club (MTC), which he credited with allowing him the freedom to pursue new ideas without worrying about their commercial appeal.[6] Although McNally and artistic director Lynne Meadow suffered a falling-out following MTC's initial (but subsequently reversed) decision to cancel its production of *Corpus Christi*—complicated by her rejection of McNally's *Dedication*, which she had commissioned to open the recently refurbished Biltmore Theatre (later renamed the Samuel J. Friedman Theatre)—they recombined forces in 2011 with a Tony-nominated revival of *Master Class*. In 2012, MTC sponsored the New York premiere of McNally's *Golden Age*.

McNally said that he preferred to write with the voice in his head of the actor who will play the part and that he was happiest working with those actors who "hear my voice and get my humor."[7] Not surprisingly, he collaborated repeatedly with some of the finest stage actors of the day: Robert Drivas, James Coco, Doris Roberts, Charlotte Rae, Kathy Bates, F. Murray Abraham, Nathan Lane, Christine Baranski, Richard Thomas, Faith Prince, Anthony Heald, Zoe Caldwell, Audra McDonald, Brian Stokes Mitchell, Marin Maizie, Marian Seldes, Angela Lansbury, Chita Rivera, Tyne Daly, John Glover, Fred Weller, Bobby Steggert, and Micah Stock. While there may not be such a thing as a typically McNally play, there may well be a "McNally actor"—one who is adept at comedy, yet able to shift suddenly and seamlessly to haunting pathos.

McNally's extraordinary productivity was affected, but not hindered, by the occurrence of lung cancer in November 2001 and its recurrence in May 2007. (The incidence of esophageal cancer and tuberculosis drives the plots of *Dedication* and *Golden Age*, respectively.) In 1999, McNally stepped down as vice president of the Dramatists Guild, where for eighteen years he'd proven a powerful voice for the right of the playwright to control his or her text and for the preservation of Manhattan's landmark theatre buildings, as well as a leader in the theatre community on issues related to AIDS research and social services for individuals infected with HIV. In 1998, McNally was awarded an honorary degree by The Juilliard School for service to the arts in America. (In 1993–1994, he revived—in conjunction with colleague John Guare—the school's moribund play-writing division.[8]) On the occasion of McNally's seventieth birthday, Sardi's restaurant (in the heart of New York City's theatre district) unveiled its caricature of the playwright. In spring 2010, the John F. Kennedy Center for the Performing Arts in Washington, DC, dedicated all three of its stages to revivals of *The Lisbon Traviata* and *Master Class* in tandem with a production of a Kennedy Center-commissioned new play, *Golden Age*, under the title "Terrence McNally's Nights at the Opera."

The honors continued to multiply. In 2011 he received the Dramatists Guild of America Lifetime Achievement Award. On April 23, 2018, a documentary film biography titled *Every Act of Life* (dir. Jeff Kaufman, Floating World Pictures) premiered at the Tribeca Film Festival, followed by an all-star panel discussion refereed by retired *New York Times* drama critic Frank Rich. A month later, on May 20, McNally was inducted as a member of the American Academy of Arts and Letters, becoming (with Eric Bentley, John Guare, Tony Kushner, and David Mamet) one of only five living playwrights at the time to be so honored. And on June 9, 2019, he was honored with a Lifetime Achievement Award by the American Theater Wing at the annual Tony Awards ceremonies. On March 24, 2020, he died of complications from COVID-19.

"Unwitnessed, Unheard, Alone"

The premiere of Edward Albee's *The Zoo Story* on January 14, 1960, is generally credited with kicking into high gear the vibrant avant-garde American theatre movement that challenged the staid and more heavily commercial values of Broadway. As playwright John Guare recalls, in the 1960s, "we all wrote our own version of *Zoo Story*. Albee spawned an entire generation of park bench plays. Theatre for years became littered with park benches. To show you were avant-garde, you needed no more than a dark room and a park bench."[9]

McNally initially followed Albee's lead, but with a significant difference. For, as willing as Albee was to challenge social norms and theatre conventions, he insisted on keeping his own sexual orientation private and did not acknowledge the possible homosexual attraction shared by his *Zoo Story* characters until he wrote *Peter and Jerry* in 2007. McNally, conversely, began the action of his first professionally produced play, *And Things That Go Bump in the Night* (1965), in the moments *after* Clarence and Sigfrid have met in a park and gone to the bunker-like home of the charismatic Sigfrid to have sex. Unbeknownst to Clarence, Sigfrid's mother and sister photograph the men's bedroom activities, only to turn the images into a slide show subsequently used to humiliate Clarence. Fleeing his tormentors, the young man is electrocuted on the security fence that the family has erected around its property. As in *The Zoo Story*, Clarence and Sigfrid's encounter in the park culminates in the violent death of one of the men. Yet, whereas it would take the iconoclastic Albee forty-seven years to put homosexuality squarely on stage, the twenty-six-year-old McNally did so—much to the rabid dismay of New York's conservative theatre critics—in his first Broadway play.

McNally's early plays were a part of the social protest movements of the late 1960s and early 1970s, particularly the antiwar movement. *Tour* (1967) dramatizes the disengagement of a middle-class American couple as they view from the air-conditioned security of their automobile the poverty and suffering of a Third World nation in the throes of a revolution—an effective correlative for American disdain for the Vietnamese people whom American armies were supposedly fighting at the time to defend from communist barbarians. Likewise, in *Botticelli* (1968), two American soldiers make a game of the names of the great figures in Western civilization to pass time as they stand guard against the enemy in the jungle; their veneer of cultural sophistication functions as a foil to the brutal indifference with which they mow down an emaciated Viet Cong soldier who ventures into a clearing looking for food. And in *Bringing It All Back Home* (1970), McNally's most Albee-esque play, the delivery of a son/brother's coffin from the Vietnam battlefield exposes the emptiness of the American Dream that the war is supposedly being fought to protect.

Collectively these early plays form a dark satire on mid-twentieth-century American moral complacency. *¡Cuba Si!* (1968), written to be performed by Academy Award-nominated actress Melina Mercouri at a rally at Madison Square Garden protesting the military junta that had taken place in her native Greece, satirizes the disdain that contemporary America—a country born from a revolution—now has for the very idea of the same. Yet, as the play's militant female freedom fighter tells a news reporter, "if everyone in the world doesn't care about the revolution, then there will never be one."[10] Likewise, in *Witness* (1968), which McNally termed "a comedy of violence,"[11] a public opinion survey taker and a window washer stumble into a high-rise apartment on the day that a presidential motorcade is scheduled to pass in the street below; they prove unable to prevent an assassination that echoes John F. Kennedy's in Dallas five years earlier. And in *Where Has Tommy Flowers Gone?* (1971), McNally celebrated—and rued the self-destructive extremes of—the American youth movement's conviction that "blowing this country up so we can start all over again" is the only way to create an America they respect.[12]

Violence pervades McNally's early plays, particularly in terms of sexual relations. In *Sweet Eros* (1968), a young man pours out his heart to the naked woman whom he's gagged and bound to a chair, as though the only form of interpersonal connection that one can establish in a violent world is through force. And in *Let It Bleed* (1972), a young couple, while showering after having sex, grows convinced that an intruder lurks on the other side of the shower curtain—a haunting anticipation of the opening scene of McNally's opera libretto for *Dead Man Walking* nearly thirty years later. In *Let It Bleed*, the emotional and physical nakedness that one must allow in order to experience love also leaves one vulnerable to suspicion and fear.

Surely the best of McNally's early plays, and the one that earned McNally his greatest early acclaim, is *Next* (1968) in which a married, middle-aged, overweight businessman is surprised to be summoned for a pre-induction physical. Assuming that the Army will rectify its error once the medical officer sees how unfit he is for service, Marion passes from mortification at having to strip and reveal his ungainly physique, to outrage at the absurdity of his situation, and, finally, to blind terror in the face of an implacable, totalitarian agency that has no respect for human life or individual dignity.

The vulnerability of protagonists like the young lovers in *Let It Bleed*, Clarence in *And Things That Go Bump*, and Marion in *Next* reflects a young playwright's uncertainty about how one may meet the demands of a brutal world that does not value—as Clarence offers as his mantra—"Florence, Shakespeare, and [the chance to connect with] someone in the park."[13] The sensitive person is in danger of dying "unwitnessed, unheard, alone"[14] (as, ironically, Ruby fears in *And Things That Go Bump*)—unheard except, of course, by the young playwright who attempted to give such persons a voice.

"I Can't Believe This Whole Night"

In 1969, when asked to adapt *Next* for the screen, McNally confided to an interviewer that he would do so without leaving New York for Hollywood:

"I write well. I am careful about selecting words. I care that my characters express themselves well. That's not what Hollywood wants. When I was in Hollywood and read some scripts, I was struck dumb by how little dialog is in them."[15] Ironically, McNally would spend part of the period 1979–84 in southern California at the behest of Norman Lear, the successful producer of such groundbreaking television situation comedies as *All in the Family*, *Maude*, *The Jeffersons*, and *One Day at a Time*.

The sitcom pilot episodes that McNally wrote during this period would not have made for average television fare. Like Burt Shevelove, Larry Gelbart, and Stephen Sondheim's *A Funny Thing Happened on the Way to the Forum* (1962), McNally's "XXIII Skidoo" was set in classical Rome and was influenced by the comedies of Plautus and McNally's namesake, Terence. Another, "The Education of Young Harry Bellair, Esq." (the pilot on which McNally collaborated most closely with Lear), was set in early eighteenth-century London and appropriated the conventions and character types of Restoration comedies of manners. A third, "Positively Tenth Street," took place in the same West Village neighborhood in lower Manhattan that McNally had inhabited since graduating college (and which in 2008 he would celebrate in *Unusual Acts of Devotion*). What these scripts have in common—and presumably the reason that none was optioned by studio executives—is that they rely heavily upon sharp, witty dialogue at a time when slapstick sitcoms like *Happy Days* and *Three's Company* ruled the airwaves.

McNally's experience in Hollywood, however, allowed him to draw upon a brighter palette of emotional colors for his plays by developing his skills as a farceur. McNally's comic talent had been on display in the one-act play that he contributed to the anthology production *Morning, Noon, and Night* (1968). *Noon* is a sexual farce in which five strangers are lured at lunchtime to an apartment in lower Manhattan by a personal advertisement in a *Village Voice*-style newspaper. Each expects to have his or her idiosyncratic—and, needless to say, incompatible—desire fulfilled by a mysterious pansexual named Dale. McNally's original script for the play veered into tragedy as the lone gay man, Kerry, commits suicide by jumping from a window after he has been humiliated by the others, much as Clarence runs from Ruby and Sigfrid's house and is electrocuted on their fence in *And Things That Go Bump*. But in the final version, after the others leave, disappointed by the failure of Dale to appear, Kerry lingers in the apartment, only to have his sexual optimism rewarded by the arrival of yet another man looking for Dale. The audience does not know if Kerry will finally enjoy his hoped-for tryst with another gay man or whether a new round of screwball misunderstandings is about to commence.

The revised ending of *Noon* marked a breakthrough of sorts for McNally. He would continue for the next fifteen years to focus upon broadly drawn, even amiably freakish, characters as he learned to use farce to hold at bay his nightmare of a violent universe in which the gentle and the good—and, by extension, the gay—cannot long survive. *Bad Habits* (1974) satirizes American reliance upon psychotherapy. In Act I ("Ravenswood"), one therapist encourages patients to indulge their every whim, while in Act II ("Dunelawn") a therapist of a different school preaches the most repressive kind of self-denial. And in *Whiskey* (1975), McNally satirized America's fetishization of alcohol consumption by focusing upon a troop of country and western performers, each of whom is named for a particular label ("Tia Maria," "Johnny Walker," "Southern Comfort," "Jack Daniels") and who die together in an alcohol-fueled fire. The edge of the satire is softened in the final scene as the dead performers look down from heaven on the national memorial service hypocritically being held in their honor.

But it would be in *The Ritz* (1975) that the artistic consequences of McNally's evolving philosophy of life were placed most dazzlingly on display. *The Ritz* repeats the basic elements of McNally's early plays in that the naive and socially ineffective Gaetano is pursued by an implacable foe in the form of his hateful mafioso brother-in-law, much as Clarence and Marion are tormented by Ruby and the Army physician, respectively. Gaetano's radically different fate, however, depends upon the fact that he inadvertently stumbles into a gay bathhouse where the socially marginalized have formed a community that celebrates and supports identity difference. Thus when, like Clarence, Gaetano is forced to dress in women's clothing and is mocked for it, his cross-dressing does not alienate him from others because he does so in the company of two newfound friends who seek to help him escape his implacable foe; and, rather than fleeing from his tormentors, Gaetano eventually stands up to his brother-in-law and grows so bold as to knee him in the groin. Likewise, Gaetano is initially, like Marion, self-conscious about his weight. But in the carnivalesque world of the bathhouse, where physical appetites are celebrated rather than made into a source of shame, Gaetano becomes the object of desire of the club's notorious "chubby chaser." Even though the sexual predilections of the bathhouse patrons are every bit as extreme as those on display in *Noon* and *Bad Habits*, there is no mention in *The Ritz* of the need for psychotherapeutic treatment. The bathhouse community does not simply tolerate the eccentricities of its members, but warmly supports them, much as the bathhouse regulars conspire to allow Talent Night hopeful Googie Gomez to believe that she is a legitimate performer rather than the worst singer and dancer ever to darken the stage.

Significantly, whereas an early version of the play concluded with the sadistic mafioso being carted off to the steam room to be gang-raped (poetic justice of sorts, but a continuation of the violence initiated by the thug), *The Ritz* concludes with the irrepressible Chris (clearly a descendent of Kerry in *Noon*) returning to his sexual adventuring in the baths. In farce, Eros proves stronger than Thanatos: the desire to connect outweighs the impulse to destroy.

In farce, McNally found the means by which his harried protagonist can retain his dignity in an unsympathetic and threatening world. And it bears noting that, in *The Ritz*, McNally—who, from the late 1980s through the mid-1990s, would write a series of plays about the importance of physical and emotional connection—offered the first real community that appears in his canon. Sexual desire is no longer a source of confusion or shame, as it is in *Bad Habits*; characters are "cured" of their painful self-consciousness not through the machinations of a therapist, but by being accepted by other people.

"I don't believe this whole night," hapless Gaetano says at the end of his evening of screwball madness.[16] Neither could McNally's audience. For the first time in Broadway history, homosexual desire was represented on stage not as evidence of personal unhappiness, as in *The Boys in the Band* (1968), but as something joyous. Over the course of four hundred performances, largely heterosexual, middle- and upper-middle-class theatregoers flocked to look at actors, naked but for a towel, making jokes about Crisco parties and steam room orgies. Broadway's closet door was blown open by the gales of laughter emanating from the Longacre Theatre every evening.

Farce opened a new avenue for McNally that proved remarkably therapeutic, not only for his characters but for the playwright himself, as evidenced in the final play of this second period of his development. *Broadway, Broadway* (1978) failed in its Philadelphia tryout, largely because Geraldine Page had been miscast as a ditzy novice producer hosting in her Manhattan town house the opening night party for a play that critics will pan before the night is over. And even though this play did not make it to Broadway, the New York stage that season was in the economic doldrums, and there was no other show coming into town that might take its place at the theatre. So "Broadway, Broadway: A New Play by Terrence McNally" remained on the marquee of a dark theatre for most of the season, a daily reminder to McNally of his failure. In several of the interviews reprinted in this collection, McNally described this time as the lowest point in his career. Not surprisingly, following the failure of *Broadway, Broadway*, McNally left New York to reinvent himself, as we have seen, in Hollywood.

On his return, however, he rewrote *Broadway, Broadway* as *It's Only a Play* (1985), the title a reminder to everyone in the theatre to keep professional matters in perspective. While the play proves a rich satire of the Broadway scene, it functions ultimately as a testimonial to how artists, however egomaniacal, come together as a creative community able to rise from the ashes of failure. Perfectly cast this time (Christine Baranski took the part of the inept yet naively well-intentioned producer, Julia Budder), it proved a great success. Over the course of a manic evening, an assortment of neurotic artists (director, lead actress, playwright, and the playwright's best friend, who is a television actor) pass in and out of Budder's second-floor bedroom, where they retreat to snort cocaine, phone their agent, and/or hide from the mob of mercurial sycophants at the party taking place downstairs. *It's Only a Play* is a psychodrama of sorts: in order to help himself get over the failure of *Broadway, Broadway*, McNally upped the ante in a farce about a failed play—much as twenty years later he would write the book for the musical *A Man of No Importance*, which is about an Irish bus conductor's being pilloried for directing a parish production of Oscar Wilde's biblically inspired *Salome*, after McNally himself had been pilloried for his own biblically inspired *Corpus Christi*.

The plays of this second major period of McNally's career proved so witty that, in her study of new American dramatists, influential theatre historian Ruby Cohn thought to group McNally with Neil Simon as a master of one-liners.[17] But Cohn failed to recognize that, beginning with *The Ritz*, an emotional expansiveness is manifest in McNally's theatre, one that seems antithetical to the pained outcry against social injustice and self-deception that characterizes the early plays. Clearly, McNally had to make this psychological advance before he could move on to his next deeply painful, yet ultimately transcendent, period.

"We Gotta Connect. We Just Have To. Or We Die."

McNally's world—and, as a consequence, his theatre—changed dramatically in the mid-1980s due to the frighteningly rapid spread of the Human Immunodeficiency Virus (HIV), that resulted in Acquired Immune Deficiency

Syndrome (AIDS). The theatre and music worlds in which McNally moved would be decimated by the epidemic, and McNally spent much of his time from the mid-1980s through the mid-1990s eulogizing friends and colleagues at memorial services, speaking at rallies in favor of increased support for HIV research, and writing short plays like *Some Christmas Letters* and *Andre's Mother* to be performed at fundraisers to help persons with AIDS.

The losses that he witnessed personally culminated in the 2001 death of his partner, Gary Bonasorte. But perhaps the loss that had the greatest impact on McNally's theatre was the death in 1986 of former lover and continuing close friend Bobby Drivas from AIDS-related causes, followed eight months later by that of another close friend, actor James Coco, from heart disease. Shortly after delivering the eulogy for Coco at his memorial service, McNally embarked on a previously scheduled two-week tour of India. The trip had a profound effect on him at this difficult time in his life. Writing in *Horizon* following his return, McNally marveled at "the beauty of [the Indian] people who delight in the spirit and presence and wonder of each other. If Indians know something we don't, it is perhaps this sense that the greatest treasure on this planet is one another."[18]

This quiet reveling in the joy of human interaction permeates the plays that he would create across the next decade. Immediately upon his return, he threw himself into writing a play about an emotionally needy short order cook's attempt to win over a psychologically scarred coworker. He conceived and wrote *Frankie and Johnny in the Clair de Lune* (1987) in only a matter of weeks. "We gotta connect. We just have to. Or we die," Johnny implores the emotionally defensive Frankie.[19] And although AIDS was not the obvious subject of the play, audiences—who had only recently learned that HIV was transmitted through bodily fluids—gasped when, after the sexually ambivalently named Frankie has cut her finger preparing him a snack, Johnny tenderly sucks the blood from her finger.

"I still don't quite know where *Frankie and Johnny* came from," McNally later wrote, continuing:

> I do know I began it shortly after I had lost my two best friends and dearest collaborators in the theatre, Robert Drivas and James Coco. Friends seemed especially precious and life unbelievably fragile. I had always thought they would be in my personal and professional life forever. . . . *Frankie and Johnny* is more a poem about feelings than a true story about anyone I know. I missed Bobby and Jimmy a lot. I still do, I always will, but I missed them less while I was writing *Frankie and Johnny.*[20]

The desire for, and accompanying impediments to, connection with another person are at the heart of every play that McNally wrote during this richly productive third period of his career. In *The Lisbon Traviata* (1989), Stephen and Mendy share an obsession with opera diva Maria Callas's ability to sing so movingly of love and death. But fear of the "dark, mean, and extremely dangerous streets" that lie outside their comfortable apartment "at the height of our very own Bubonic Plague"[21] drives Stephen to kill his long-frustrated partner, Mike, as Mike attempts to leave him for a younger man. The enjoyment of opera may help ease the pain of loneliness, but obsession with a diva may also intensify one's isolation by preempting intimacy with another person.

McNally's next three plays form an informal trilogy that addresses how the fear of difference renders life-sustaining intimacy impossible and, more specifically, that challenges the inhumanity manifested in 1980s and early 1990s America towards victims of AIDS. In *Lips Together, Teeth Apart* (1991), two married heterosexual couples spend the Fourth of July weekend at the Fire Island house that one of the women has inherited from a gay brother who recently died of an AIDS-related illness. Their fear of using his swimming pool lest they catch the virus that killed him, unspoken for most of the play, bespeaks a paranoia about sexual difference that is shown to infect even the most intimate of heterosexual relationships.

Conversely, *A Perfect Ganesh* (1993) offers a vision of an alternative social-religious system in which the emotionally wounded and physically damaged are ministered to by a god who, unbeknownst to them, moves in their midst to help them overcome the obstacles to intimacy that they themselves have created. The play suggests how racial and sexual differences must be accepted as a part of life if one is to live fully and religiously.

And in *Love! Valour! Compassion!* (1994) McNally offered one of the most moving responses to the AIDS epidemic by an American writer. Following the activities of eight gay men across three holiday weekends in the summer, the play neutralizes the fear of death with a comic extravagance too poignant to qualify as farce. Dressed in ghostly white tulle tutus, toe shoes, and feathered headdresses, six of the eight men rehearse for a benefit performance of Tchaikovsky's *Swan Lake*. Joining hands, they create a visual parody of the medieval Dance of Death. Yet rather than weep at their misfortune, they dance so intently that they eventually collapse in laughter at their own absurdity.

At the climax of the play, one of the HIV-positive friends panics after seeing his lover through a health crisis. "Who's gonna be there for me when it's my turn?" he asks. His interlocutor assures him that "We all will. Every one of us."[22] And indeed, that promise is kept symbolically in the last moment of the play as the men strip naked and join hands to step down into a moonlighted lake, quietly swimming out of the audience's view: they enter the waters of death and advance together to meet the unknown. No longer need a gay man fear that he will die "unwitnessed, unheard, alone," as Clarence was tragically forced to do. Instead, in McNally's world, one can now be certain that one is part of a community of other gay men in whose company, and with whose support, one can brave those things that go bump in the night.

McNally continued to develop the theme of the urgency of connection even after the development of protease inhibitors in 1995 made AIDS a more effectively managed syndrome. In *Corpus Christi* (1998), he retold the biblical narrative of the life and passion of Jesus Christ in terms of the self-discovery, social ostracization, and murder of a gay teenager named Joshua in McNally's hometown of Corpus Christi, Texas, during the 1950s, when McNally himself came of age. Conservative social critics were outraged by McNally's transforming the biblical Wedding Feast at Cana into a gay marriage, Jesus's cure of a leper into Joshua's compassion for a young man in the advanced stages of an HIV-related illness, and Jesus's association with Mary Magdalene into Joshua's befriending a gay hustler. Coincidentally (and all the more horrifically), the play premiered within a week of the brutal murder of gay college student Matthew Shepard, who was beaten, stripped naked, and tied crucifixion-style to a barbed wire fence in sub-freezing temperatures outside Laramie, Wyoming, where he was left to die "unwitnessed, unheard, alone."

Nearly a decade later, McNally returned to his examination of the life-or-death importance of human interconnection, and the insecurities that create hindrances to satisfying human relationships, in three plays written closely together. *Some Men* (2007) is structured as a series of vignettes of American gay life from 1922 to the present framed by the events at a gay wedding. The play readily admits to the difficulties of maintaining a satisfying relationship in the gay world: sexual chemistry may not be present when other elements of attraction are; personal insecurities such as fear of social disapproval or reluctance to limit oneself to one partner become barriers to engagement; and gay self-loathing may prove a bell jar that stifles the most promising relationship. Yet, at the play's end, what has seemed initially to be a pastiche of loosely connected, historically organized scenes is revealed to contain multiple connections among characters of different generations that could not have been anticipated by the audience. Far from living separate, disconnected lives in different cities and decades, the "some men" of McNally's title function as colored pieces of glass in the constantly changing kaleidoscope of modern gay life: names and circumstances may differ, but a desire for connection makes all gay men one.

An unsuspected unity is similarly on display in *Deuce* (2007), which focuses on two former women's tennis doubles champs who are reunited late in life as guests of honor at a US Open tennis match. McNally's tennis metaphor effectively depicts how two people with radically different modi operandi and performance styles may still function as an organic unit.

And in *Unusual Acts of Devotion* (2008), five neighbors escape the stifling heat of their respective apartments on the tarred rooftop of their six-story apartment building on New York City's lower West Side one evening in summer. "Nobody can take care of themself," hard-eyed Mrs. Darnell stoically observes, "we just think we can."[23] She echoes a sentiment voiced elsewhere in the play by the younger, more optimistic Nadine and the older, more world-weary Josie: "We can make each other happy so easily and we so seldom do. Put on a CD. Close the window. Open the window. Love someone. Love someone who loves you back."[24] The unusual acts of devotion referred to in the title range from Leo's massaging Mrs. Darnell's legs to Chick's monitoring the diabetic Leo's glucose level more conscientiously than Leo himself does, to cantankerous Mrs. Darnell's offering her life to save her younger neighbors.

In the plays of this third major stage of McNally's development, the playwright had come 180 degrees from his early work. As in *Let It Bleed,* a threat lies immediately outside the intimate world of the play that threatens to destroy human happiness. (At the start of *Unusual Acts,* for example, the audience sees an interloper climb onto the roof and hide behind a water tank where his presence is periodically reaffirmed by the ominous glow of a cigarette in the darkness. As the action advances, music playing on the radio is periodically interrupted by news bulletins concerning the police search for a serial murderer on the loose in the neighborhood.) But, unlike in those early plays, McNally's later characters respond to the threat of oblivion, not in terror, but with love, valor, and compassion, thereby allowing for truly unusual acts of human devotion.

At the height of the AIDS pandemic, while fellow gay playwrights Larry Kramer and Tony Kushner raged against the dying of the light, McNally was able to release his anger and model in his plays a transcendence through human compassion of the pain of mortality and flux—a transcendence made the more surprising by the depth of his own grief.

"Sing for Your Supper. Sing for Your Salvation."

McNally emerged in the 1990s as one of the most successful playwrights in America, winning four Tony Awards in a scant six years: back-to-back awards for Best Drama for *Love! Valour! Compassion!* and *Master Class* and the award for Best Book for a Musical for both *Kiss of the Spider Woman* and *Ragtime.* The latter are a reminder of the flip side of McNally's career as one of America's premiere librettists.

Ironically, McNally's early involvement with the musical did not bode well. In 1961, having graduated the previous year from Columbia, McNally was hired to tutor the two teenaged sons of Nobel Prize-winning novelist John Steinbeck as the family embarked on a round-the-world cruise.[25] Six years later, when Steinbeck's *East of Eden* was optioned as the basis of a musical, the novelist insisted that McNally write the book. *Here's Where I Belong* (1968) proved a disaster, closing the same night that it premiered and losing its substantial investment, thereby earning from *Variety* the sobriquet "the costliest one night stand on Broadway."[26] McNally was so frustrated by changes made to his book without his permission that he insisted his name be removed from the program.

His second musical outing proved equally trying, although for very different reasons. In 1984, he was hired to write a new book for an existing score by John Kander and Fred Ebb, who were dissatisfied with the efforts of their original librettist, Albert Innaurato. McNally's involvement with *The Rink* (1984) not only reversed the traditional pattern of collaboration in which the book is completed before the composer and lyricist begin work on the score, but he was expected to fashion an original story that showcased the talents of stars Liza Minnelli and Chita Rivera, who were already under contract and ready to begin rehearsals.

Fortunately, McNally's collaboration on *The Rink* with Kander and Ebb, and with star Rivera, proved only a prelude to their most successful collaboration, *Kiss of the Spider Woman* (1993), for which McNally adapted the novel of the same title by Manuel Puig. Focusing upon the clash between the harshness of life and the seductive yet deadly allure of fantasy, McNally explored a theme that would dominate his plays during the next decade: the ambivalently liberating and destructive nature of role-playing.

McNally collaborated with Kander, Ebb, and Rivera one final time in a musical made of Friedrich Dürrenmatt's dark satire of passion and greed, *The Visit*. Originally conceived as a vehicle for Angela Lansbury, who was forced by her husband's declining health to withdraw before rehearsals began, the play was well received during its tryout in Chicago. Unfortunately, it was scheduled to come to New York the month following the September 11, 2001, terrorist attacks on the World Trade Towers. Fearing the musical too dark for the time, the producers canceled the opening. Competing commitments among the principals further delayed a Broadway production. The play eventually opened in New York in 2015 in a brilliantly pared-down production staged by John Doyle, but was forced to close early when a previously undiagnosed brain tumor made it impossible for co-star Roger Rees to continue in his role.

McNally collaborated successfully with other songwriting teams as well. In 1989, he translated to the musical stage E. L. Doctorow's novel *Ragtime*, in conjunction with composer Stephen Flaherty and lyricist Lynn Ahrens. As one of the show's senior producers observed at the time, the project was dead in the water until McNally found a way to organize for the stage Doctorow's numerous interlocking narratives.[27] With Flaherty and Ahrens he also adapted for the musical stage a film script by Barry Devlin, *A Man of No Importance* (2002), about a sexually repressed, middle-aged gay bus conductor who discovers truths about himself and about the nature of community after he is ostracized by church authorities for undertaking a local production of Oscar Wilde's *Salome*. This team's final collaboration, *Anastasia*, was originally intended to premiere in St. Petersburg on the anniversary of the Romanov executions, a plan preempted by tensions in US-Russian relations. It opened instead in April 2016 on Broadway for a successful two-year run.

Like *A Man of No Importance*, McNally's *The Full Monty* (2000, music and lyrics by David Yazbek, adapted from the British film of the same title) dramatizes the struggle to achieve self-acceptance, this time focusing on a group of unemployed, lower middle-class working men who resort to stripping to support their families and boost their deflated egos. McNally seemed to have been attracted to *Catch Me If You Can* (2011, music by Mark Shaiman, lyrics by Scott Wittman)—originally a memoir by a wildly successful forger and con man pursued for years by the FBI—because of its inherent theatricality. The essential untruthfulness of performance allows Frankie, the con man protagonist, to access a deeper inner truth than he could otherwise as he successfully impersonates an airline pilot and emergency room doctor, among other professionals. Unfortunately, concerned that McNally's anatomy of the psychological implications of role-playing might demand too much of a Broadway audience, the producers hired a second, uncredited writer to make the show more commercially appealing. As a consequence, McNally was faulted by reviewers for corny jokes not of his making.

Who remembers the name of the author of a musical's book, McNally asked in a 2002 *New York Times* article written shortly after he'd been invited to a party celebrating "Kander and Ebb's *Kiss of the Spider Woman*." "It will always be Bizet's *Carmen*, not Mérimée's; Jerry Herman's *Mame*, not Lawrence and Lee's," he said.[28] The librettist is invariably the most easily forgotten member of a show's creative team. Thus, McNally's continued involvement with musicals and operas was evidence of his enjoyment of the communal nature of theatre—of brainstorming with others to flesh out an initial idea, of writing new pages to resolve a problem that becomes apparent during rehearsal, of renouncing the claims of ego and doing what is best for the project.

One musical work for which McNally's libretto has been singled out for special praise is *Dead Man Walking* (2000, music by Jake Heggie), which has become one of the most frequently produced American operas of the past twenty years. Based on the memoir by Sister Helen Prejean, a Roman Catholic nun who ministered in prison to a man convicted of brutally raping a young woman as well as murdering both her and her boyfriend, the opera—like McNally's book for *A Man of No Importance* and his libretto for another opera, *The Food of Love* (1999, music by Robert Beaser)—translates into music the values of love, valor, and compassion on which McNally focused so movingly in his plays in the 1990s.

"Where We Really and Truly Are"

McNally collaborated again with Jake Heggie on *Great Scott* (2015), a comic opera about the making of operatic art written expressly for Joyce DiDonato and Frederica von Stade, the principal female performers of their *Dead Man Walking*. The opera, which dramatizes the professional difficulties and personal sacrifices demanded of the artist, is in keeping with the themes of the plays of the fourth and last period of McNally's development. Since *Master Class* in 1995, McNally's plays increasingly became an extended meditation upon the transformative powers—and dangers—of theatre.

"Theatre is a deep reflection of the human community," McNally wrote in his foreword to the print version of *A Man of No Importance*. "Theatre is not a place to hide from the world but instead the very place where we may finally discover our true selves."[29] As a consequence, theatre should be where audiences go in the hope of being transformed. Unfortunately, too often both audiences and actors use theatre to escape into fantasy from the unsatisfying, quotidian "real" world.

McNally's understanding of the conundrum of the playwright was dramatized in an early, undated, untitled, and apparently never-performed work in which a twenty-year-old playwright named Bill steps to the edge of the stage to address his audience directly: "A playwright," Bill says, "must face the truth. If he does not face the truth his play is false and nowhere is it easier to spot a liar than in the theatre." But Bill also acknowledges that "the theatre is full of magic—it's always fascinated me—and I take advantage of that magic as often as I can. Absolutely anything can happen when you're in a theatre."[30] The trick is for the playwright to employ theatre's magic only in the service of truth, rather than allowing it to shorten the actor's vision or distract the audience's attention from the work of transformation waiting to be done.

There was always a metadramatic element to McNally's theatre. In *And Things That Go Bump in the Night*, for example, Ruby dresses in the torn, soiled costumes that she wore when she sang on the opera stage years earlier; she directs the evening's events as though they're a scripted drama. And in *The Lisbon Traviata*, Stephen "performs" his parting from—and murder of—Mike as though he were Don Jose at the close of Bizet's *Carmen*.

But it is in *Master Class* that McNally initiated an ongoing meditation on the nature of theatrical truth and on the sacrifices made by the artist, as well as on what a society loses when it does not enjoy a vibrant cultural scene. As Callas teaches student performers how to interpret the arias they've selected to perform during a master class at Juilliard, the play reveals how closely Callas's own personal challenges mirrored the circumstances of the heroines whose roles she sang on stage, which proved the one place where Callas could be most fully herself. The failure of the student performers to sing with the intense commitment that Callas brought to her roles stems from their reluctance to explore their deeper selves; they prefer instead to concentrate on creating a professional persona and launching a career. Conversely, Callas's loneliness is revealed as the price one must pay for a life of exhaustive self-examination and relentless pursuit of truth.

The two one-act plays that make up *The Stendhal Syndrome* (2004) both address the experience that a tour guide, leading a group of American tourists to view Michelangelo's *David*, explains occurs "when art speaks to something deeper in us than perhaps we understand."[31] The first audience for Wagner's *Tristan und Isolde* fainted from the intensity of the emotions that his music aroused, she says—much as the tourists in her group finally fall silent in the presence of Michelangelo's sculpture and as Margaret and Katharine do visiting the Taj Mahal in *A Perfect Ganesh.* Similarly, *Prelude & Liebestod* offers the thoughts of an orchestra conductor, his wife, and a gay man who hopes to seduce the bisexual conductor after he conducts Wagner with his wife and the gay man in the audience. "I'm only alive when I come," the conductor acknowledges in an interior monologue; that is "the way I want to be alive: ecstatic, half-conscious, eyes closed, brain flaring, words, thoughts inadequate"[32]—when he ejaculates *and*, the play makes clear, when he is engaged with music.

Two additional plays in this group form a diptych of sorts. In *Dedication or The Stuff of Dreams* (2005), the manager of a struggling children's theatre hopes to gain possession of a once-glorious but long-shuttered and now-dilapidated opera house in upstate New York. His negotiation with the crusty, terminally ill property owner becomes a debate over the ambivalent power of theatre either "to take us away from where we really and truly are" or to allow us to dream and soar above the mortal coil that is human existence.[33]

Similarly, *And Away We Go* (2014) is a historical kaleidoscope in which a performance of Aeschylus's *The Oresteia* in Periclean Athens morphs into a rehearsal of Shakespeare's *The Tempest* in Jacobean London, which in turn is transformed into the green room during a performance at Paris's Théâtre Royal on the eve of the French Revolution, the first reading of Chekhov's *The Seagull* by Stanislavski's Moscow Art Theatre, and the closing night performance of the American premiere of Beckett's *Waiting for Godot* at the Coconut Grove Playhouse in Florida in 1956. Exploring the creative tensions and interpretive conflicts that produce great art, the play celebrates the resilience of thespians and the electrifying experience of live theatre.

Finally, two of McNally's last plays, *Golden Age* (2012) and *Immortal Longings* (2019; originally produced as *Fire and Air* in 2018), explore the overlapping drives toward spiritual transcendence and carnal satisfaction inherent in artistic creation and performance. *Golden Age* juxtaposes the quotidian goings-on backstage with the sublime music being performed on stage at the Paris premiere of what would prove to be Vincenzo Bellini's final opera, *I Puritani.* An autumnal quality infuses the play as Bellini's blood-spewing cough suggests that his tubercular end is near and that he shall neither be able to return to his beloved Sicily nor complete the opera of Shakespeare's *King Lear* that he is impatient to begin writing. When asked what *I Puritani* is about, Bellini answers "forgiveness"—much as McNally's play, in the manner of Shakespeare's great romances, exhibits a calm, even transcendent, acceptance of human weakness and mortality. Neither Bellini nor, apparently, McNally himself had reason to fear any longer those things that go bump in the night.

Similarly, taking its title from Cleopatra's staging of her own death in Shakespeare's *Antony and Cleopatra*, *Immortal Longings* explores Ballets Russes impresario Sergei Diaghilev's inability to separate his ambition to create the most extraordinary ballets from his need to possess his premier danseur, Vaslav Nijinsky. Diaghilev's travails to fund his company's productions and to parry the attacks of his critics coalesce with his anxiety to retain the affections of the man who is both his muse and his principal antagonist. For McNally, love and artistic creativity were the result of the same powerful need to bridge the distance between the ideal to which one aspires and the reality in which one is forced to live.

Conclusion: The Problem of Being a Gay Playwright

In early 1993, during the talk-back that followed a workshop performance of *A Perfect Ganesh*, activist Larry Kramer challenged McNally for writing about two wealthy middle-aged matrons vacationing in India at a time when, Kramer argued, the AIDS epidemic was such a dire emergency that every gay artist in America needed to be shouting himself hoarse calling for social justice. Shortly thereafter, McNally was criticized by *The Advocate* for calling himself a "playwright," rather than a "gay playwright."[34]

McNally responded in a 1996 op-ed piece in the *Los Angeles Times* titled "Gay Theater? No, Just Life," in which he argued that continuing to identify oneself as a "gay playwright" when no heterosexual colleague felt the need to identify himself publicly as a "straight playwright" was tantamount to promulgating discrimination against gays and lesbians. He wrote:

> Gay theater doesn't exist anymore. There is good theater and there is bad theater. Gay playwrights either write a play as worthy of your (or mine) interest as Mr. Arthur Miller or they don't. You can't get away with a bad "gay" play any more than you can with serving up lousy food in a "gay" restaurant.[35]

A playwright who happens to be gay, he suggested, is only advertising the mediocrity of his work if he expects audiences to come to it simply because it is a "gay" play.

This is not to say that McNally no longer believed in a playwright's advancing a political agenda through his work; his own agenda was simply not as aggressively in evidence in his later plays as it was in his early ones. "Theater is a place to change hearts," McNally noted in his interview with Eddie Shapiro in this collection, "and you change minds by changing hearts first. A homophobic person's heart has to be spoken to before his mind. Change the heart and then people change their minds when they go into the voting booth." Thus, while McNally's *Some Men* is one of the most moving depictions of the pleasures and pains of gay relationships to grace the boards in recent years, it is anything but a jeremiad in favor of gay marriage.

McNally's later plays combine to make a "theatre of empathy" in which audiences emerge from the theatre more aware of what happens to humans both as individuals and as a society when people act without compassion for others. As a playwright, McNally said, his primary purpose is to "find what connects us":

> When theatre works, I find it deeply moving, it can be very funny, very bold, very dramatic, touching, you feel connected to people around you in a way. Whether there are ninety-nine seats or fifteen hundred, when a play works well, there's a sense of community and you feel connected to your fellow humans. That's how it should be.[36]

As such, theatre is essential to human survival, for, as Johnny tells Frankie, "we gotta connect. We just have to. Or we die."

■ ■ ■

This introduction has been adapted from an essay titled "Terrence McNally: Theatre as Connection" that was first posted on glbtq.com on April 1, 2013. I gratefully acknowledge the efforts of graduate assistants A. J. Underwood and Alex Harvey, who retyped the original interviews and helped secure some of the copyright permissions; of English department administrative assistant Melissa Eubanks, who repeatedly found a way to force a peevish operating program to cooperate in formatting my computer script; and of Santino DeAngelo, who tracked down several of the more-difficult-to-locate copyright holders. A fellowship from the Harry Ransom Humanities

Research Center at the University of Texas in Austin allowed me to examine the contents of the McNally Archive, in which I first read several of the interviews gathered in this volume.

McNally was a generous interviewee. He was invariably frank and open, except when he sought to protect the privacy of others. And he never publicly voiced his disagreements with others. (For example, it was only in the last years of his life, when he sat for a series of interviews with Jeff Kaufman for the documentary *Every Act of Life,* that he spoke on record about his parents' resentment of his homosexuality, or about the lack of support that he received from his lover, Edward Albee, when first writing plays.) He invariably took his interviewer's questions seriously, which is why printed interviews with him contain so little evidence of his outrageous sense of humor.

Two cautions must be offered the reader of this volume at the outset. First, having myself interviewed McNally numerous times while writing *The Theater of Terrence McNally: Something about Grace* (2019) and editing *Muse of Fire* (2021), a collection of McNally's writings about theatre, I've had ample opportunity to appreciate his extraordinary recall of the most minute details of every theatre and opera performance he ever attended, yet vague recall of the facts of his own life. For example, in various interviews over the years, while never varying the singers or the arias that he heard, he described his first exposure to opera as having occurred in the fourth, fifth or sixth grade. Similarly, he variously said that his relationship with Edward Albee lasted five, six, or seven years. Apart from his misrepresenting the year of his birth in order to appear more precocious at the start of his career (a misrepresentation he was exasperated not to be able to correct after it became part of the print record), he was not attempting to deceive, but was simply vague about details that were not important to him. Appreciating that I needed to provide a reliable overview of his life as part of the introduction to this volume, he put me in touch with his younger brother, Peter, for details of their family's history, and with Molly Jones, a good friend whom he met in his early years in New York and who possessed a superb recall of his various apartments and the members of their social circle.

A second consideration to be taken into account from the start is McNally's gift as an anecdotalist. He warmed quickly to people and oftentimes colored or heightened the details of a story for that particular interlocutor. For example, when telling the story of his interviewing then-Senator Lyndon Baines Johnson while McNally was a college-aged cub reporter in Corpus Christi, Texas, in 1957-58, he variously reported the senator's idly paging through a copy of *Playboy* while taking a phone call from his wife. As the years went on and Americans grew less shocked by public mention of a soft-core magazine like *Playboy*, McNally changed the title in his telling to *Hustler* or *Screw* (which were not even published in the late 1950s) in order to communicate the shock value of the incident. Rather than footnote factual discrepancies in the interviews, I allow McNally's misstatements to remain part of the record but insert a bracketed "sic" to alert the reader to the discrepancy.

The interviews are reprinted here with only minor editing to correct the misspelling of proper names and for syntactical clarity. Because some of the original interviews were edited to conform to that magazine's or newspaper's house style and others were not, stylistic inconsistencies may appear from chapter to chapter, particularly in terms of McNally's preferred spelling of the word as "theatre," which some of the original publications were careful to respect and others ignored.

RJF

Notes

1. Albert Poland and Bruce Mailman, eds., *The Off Off Broadway Book: The Plays, People, Theatre* (Indianapolis: Bobbs-Merrill, 1972), 44–81.

2. Terrence McNally, "Terrence McNally Letters: Ethel Merman Come Home!," *New York Native*, June 11–17 1979, 15.

3. Raymond-Jean Frontain, "Trafficking in Mere Humanity: Shakespeare, McNally, and the Reach of 'This Wooden O,'" *Explorations in Renaissance Culture* 36, 1 (Summer 2010): 93–118. On Chiappe's pedagogy and its influence on McNally, see 96 and 113–14.

4. Edward Albee, *Who's Afraid of Virginia Woolf?*, in *Collected Plays*, 3 vols. (Woodstock, NY: Overlook Duckworth, 2004–5), I.297; and Mel Gussow, *Edward Albee: A Singular Journey* (New York: Simon and Schuster, 1999), 107.

5. Julie Salamon, *Wendy and the Lost Boys: The Uncommon Life of Wendy Wasserstein* (New York: Penguin, 2011), 293.

6. "Playwrights need a home where they are fed, nourished, and challenged. I am lucky to have found one at MTC." "A Few Words of Introduction," in *Three Plays by Terrence McNally* (New York: Plume/Penguin, 1990), x.

7. Raymond-Jean Frontain, "Break Down the Barriers: An Interview with Terrence McNally," in this collection, 154.

8. On McNally's involvement with the program, see Leide Snow, "Teaching the Impossible," *Theater Week*, October 17–23, 1994, 17–22. John Guare recalls his collaboration with McNally at Juilliard in his "Introduction" to McNally's *Fifteen Short Plays* (Lyme, NH: Smith and Kraus, 1994), ix.

9. Quoted in Gussow, *Edward Albee*, 129.

10. *¡Cuba, Si!*, in Terrence McNally, *Fifteen Short Plays* (Lyme, NH: Smith and Kraus, 1994), 91.

11. "Author's Note," *Sweet Eros and Witness* (New York: Dramatists Play Service, 1969), 30.

12. *Where Has Tommy Flowers Gone?*, in Terrence McNally, *Collected Plays, Volume II* (Lyme, NH: Smith and Kraus, 1996), 95.

13. *And Things That Go Bump in the Night*, in McNally, *Collected Plays, Volume II*, 51.

14. *And Things That Go Bump in the Night*, 13.

15. "Eye," *Women's Wear Daily*, April 13, 1969, Section 1, 14.

16. *The Ritz*, in McNally, *Fifteen Short Plays*, 302.

17. Cohn compares McNally to Simon to the former's disadvantage: "Co-opting existential anxieties, Neil Simon's characters evoke Broadway laughter. Less anxious and less coherent, Terrence McNally's characters present an unconventional surface; they may utter obscenities, shed their clothes, indulge in sexual deviation, and yet they do so with charm, and without offence. Bound to Broadway, McNally sacrifices the intensity he achieved at the age of twenty-two [*sic*] in *Things*." Ruby Cohn, *New American Dramatists 1960–1990*, 2nd ed. (New York: St. Martin's Press, 1991), 22.

18. Terrence McNally, "A Fortnight in India," *Horizon*, September 1987, 2.

19. *Frankie and Johnny in the Clair de Lune*, in *Three Plays by Terrence McNally*, 136.

20. "A Few Words of Introduction," in *Three Plays by Terrence McNally*, xi.

21. *The Lisbon Traviata*, in *Three Plays by Terrence McNally*, 85.

22. Terrence McNally, *Love! Valour! Compassion!* (Garden City, NY: Fireside Theatre, 1995), 132.

23. Terrence McNally, *Unusual Acts of Devotion*, Philadelphia Theatre Company Rehearsal Script, November 5, 2008, 100. Unpublished TS supplied by Terrence McNally.

24. McNally, *Unusual Acts*, 117.

25. On McNally's friendship with Steinbeck and collaboration on the musical version of *East of Eden*, see Raymond-Jean Frontain, "McNally and Steinbeck," *ANQ: American Notes and Queries* 21, 4 (Fall 2008): 43–51.

26. McNally's clippings files archived in the Harry Ransom Humanities Research Center (HRC) at the University of Texas at Austin contain a story from *Variety* titled "Mitch Miller (UA) 550G Legit Flop Now / The Costliest '1-Nite Stand on B'Way.'" The story, presumably published after the play's opening and closing night performance on March 3, 1968, is unsigned. The clippings service did not note the date of the issue or the page number, and I have been unable to find issues of *Variety* before 1972 in any database.

27. "It's only because you [McNally] sat down three years ago and cracked this thing, found the means to unfold it on the stage," that *Ragtime* made it to a Broadway opening, one producer wrote. Another opening night message of congratulations praised McNally for finding "a structure that maintains the relative weight of the stories in the novel so exactly. No wonder Mr. Doctorow is pleased." Because each note is signed only with a first name and one of those signatures is illegible, I have been unable to identify either author. Both notes may be found in the HRC McNally Collection, Box 43, Folder 4.

28. Terrence McNally, "Random Thoughts of a Librettist, or Quick! Who Wrote the Libretto for *Aida*?," in *Muse of Fire: Reflections on Theatre*, ed. Raymond-Jean Frontain (Vancouver, BC: Fairleigh Dickinson University Press, 2021), 65.

29. Terrence McNally, "Introduction," *A Man of No Importance* (New York: Stage and Screen, 2003), i.

30. Unpublished typescript, page I-2. Harry Ransom Humanities Research Center, University of Texas at Austin, McNally Archive, Box 58, Folder 1. In response to my query, McNally recalled that the working title of the play may have been "The Playwright" (e-mail communication March 3, 2019). Such a title would suggest that McNally saw the play in the same vein as Moss Hart's *Act One* (1959), which—as he noted in several of the interviews reprinted in this collection—he considered one of the most effective depictions of a life spent writing for the theatre.

31. Terrence McNally, *The Stendhal Syndrome* (New York: Grove Press, 2004), 27.

32. McNally, *Stendhal Syndrome*, 60.

33. Terrence McNally, *Dedication or The Stuff of Dreams* (New York: Grove Press, 2006), 97.

34. Alan Frutkin, "Love! Valour! McNally!," in this collection, 78.

35. Terrence McNally, "Commentary: Gay Theater? No, Just Life," *Los Angeles Times*, December 8, 1996, 3.

36. David Savran, "Terrence McNally," in this collection, 99.

Chronology

1938 Michael Terrence McNally is born November 3 in St. Petersburg, Florida, to Hubert and Dorothy (née Rapp) McNally, transplanted New Yorkers who run a seaside bar and grill. His only sibling, Peter, is born six years later.

1946–49 After the family bar and grill is destroyed in a hurricane, the McNallys return to Dorothy's hometown of Port Chester, New York. The family later moves to Dallas, Texas. While McNally is in fifth grade, an Ursuline nun at Christ the King School introduces him to opera. He spends Saturday afternoons listening to "Live from the Met" on the radio and attends his first two Broadway shows (*Annie Get Your Gun*, starring Ethel Merman, and *The King and I*, starring Gertrude Lawrence), which make a lasting impression.

1949–56 The family relocates a final time to Corpus Christi, Texas. During his years at W. B. Ray High School (1952–56), McNally is mentored by Maurine McElroy, an extraordinary English teacher who regularly invites select students to her home to read poetry and listen to classical music.

1956–60 After being encouraged by McElroy to attend college out of state, McNally wins a scholarship to attend Columbia College as a journalism major, returning to Corpus Christi in the summers to work as a cub reporter for the *Times Caller*. In New York City, McNally begins a lifelong practice of attending the theatre and opera several nights a week. After meeting twenty-nine-year-old Edward Albee, the nineteen-year-old McNally moves in with the budding playwright. They will remain a couple for nearly five years.

1961–62 While working as a stage manager at the Playwrights Unit of the Actors Studio, McNally is recruited by director Molly Kazan to travel with and tutor the two teenaged sons of Nobel Prize-winning novelist John Steinbeck and his third wife, Elaine, as the family embarks on what is expected to be a year-long cruise around the world. Following their return to New York, Steinbeck suggests that McNally write the book for *Here's Where I Belong*, an ill-fated musical adaptation of Steinbeck's *East of Eden*.

1964–65   Early versions titled *Bump* and *There Is Something Out There* are workshopped by Albee-Barr-Wilder in New York and by the Guthrie Theater in Minneapolis before *And Things That Go Bump in the Night* opens on Broadway on April 26, 1965. Dismayed to see an unapologetically gay character on the Broadway stage rather than relegated to Off-Off-Broadway where they thought he belonged, critics vehemently disparage the play. But committed producers keep it running for two weeks, allowing McNally to learn from his actors and from the audience's response what was and was not working.

During the play's development process, McNally separates from Albee and becomes lovers with Bobby Drivas, the actor playing Sigfrid. McNally writes his next several plays for Drivas, tailoring *Where Has Tommy Flowers Gone?* (1971) to showcase Drivas's talents. Drivas will go on to direct McNally's *The Ritz* and *Bad Habits*, as well as star in Albee's *The Man Who Had Three Arms* (1983) and will remain one of McNally's closest friends until Drivas's death from AIDS-related causes in 1986.

1969   *Next*, written for good friend and actor James Coco, becomes McNally's first critical and financial success. It is directed by Elaine May, whom McNally credits with giving him a crash course in playwriting.

1975   *The Ritz* premieres January 20 at the Longacre Theatre in New York City and runs for four hundred performances. Richard Lester's 1976 film version retains the original cast but fails to capture the manic high spirits of the stage production.

1978   *Broadway, Broadway*, McNally's attempt to turn to comic fodder the failure of *And Things That Go Bump* thirteen years earlier, fails during its tryout in Philadelphia, preempting its scheduled opening in New York. McNally will later rewrite the play as the highly successful *It's Only a Play*.

1978–84   McNally commutes between New York and Hollywood as he collaborates with television producer Norman Lear on *The Education of Young Harry Bellair, Esq.*, a situation comedy set in early eighteenth-century London that draws upon the conventions of the Restoration comedy of manners. Although *Education* and several other pilots fail to find network support, McNally's adaptation of John Cheever's "The Five Forty-Eight" for PBS (1979) earns critical acclaim, and his *Mama Malone* runs on CBS in summer 1984.

1985–95   Following the successful run of *It's Only a Play*, McNally embarks on a decade-long collaboration with the Manhattan Theatre Club (MTC). MTC will premiere a string of McNally hits— *Frankie and Johnny in the Clair de Lune* (1987), *The Lisbon Traviata* (1989), *Lips Together, Teeth Apart* (1991), *A Perfect Ganesh* (1993), and *Love! Valour! Compassion!* (1994)—making for one of the most successful pairings of playwright and theatre company in twentieth-century American theatre history.

The emerging AIDS epidemic infuses McNally's work with an extraordinary poignancy. The loss of Bobby Drivas in 1986 to AIDS and, a year later, the fatal coronary of close friend and collaborator James Coco prove the immediate impetus for McNally's extended meditation on the nature of, and impediments to, human connection that extends across several plays. At the same time, a trip to India immediately following Coco's memorial service introduces McNally to a religious view of life that sanctifies loss as an essential part of humanity, allowing him to create the lyrically transcendent endings that characterize the plays of his MTC period. McNally's 1982 commitment to sobriety likewise alters the tone of his plays, which come to demonstrate a warmer and more compassionate acceptance of human weaknesses.

1985–2001   As vice president of the Dramatists Guild, McNally is active in theatre community events to raise awareness of the toll that AIDS is taking on the arts community and in protests to save three Beaux-Arts theatre buildings threatened with demolition to make way for Times Square's Marriott Marquis Hotel and Theater. Both concerns extend to his creative work as well, which become meditations on the nature of loss and artistic depletion. Thus, in plays like *Some Christmas Letters, The Last Mile*, the Tony Award-winning *Love! Valour! Compassion!*, and the Emmy Award-winning *Andre's Mother*, McNally becomes a major voice during the AIDS epidemic. And in *Ghost Light* and *Dedication*, he examines America's failure to preserve its theatre heritage.

1993   McNally wins the first of his four competitive Tony Awards for his book for the musical *Kiss of the Spider Woman*. Subsequent Tony Awards will be for *Love! Valour! Compassion!* (1995), *Master Class* (1996), and the book for the musical *Ragtime* (1998). Earlier. McNally had won the Hull-Warriner Award—notable because it is bestowed by dramatists upon their fellow dramatists—in 1974 for *Bad Habits*, in 1987 for *Frankie and Johnny in the Claire de Lune*, and in 1989 for *The Lisbon Traviata*. In addition, over the years he wins four Drama Desk Awards, two Lucille Lortel Awards, and two Obie Awards.

1996   Inducted into the American Theater Hall of Fame.

1998   Awarded an honorary degree by The Juilliard School for "invaluable contributions to the theatre."

1998–99   Controversy over McNally's retelling in *Corpus Christi* the story of Jesus's life and ministry in terms of a gay teenager's coming of age in 1950s Texas is fanned by a *New York Post* columnist and by protests organized by the Catholic League for Religious and Civil Rights. McNally responds to the controversy surrounding *Corpus Christi* in his book for the musical *A Man of No Importance* (2002), which concerns a conservative church community's censoring an amateur theatre group's production of Oscar Wilde's *Salome*, and in *Crucifixion* (2005), which addresses the sexual hypocrisy of the Roman Catholic Church. (*Crucifixion* is honored as Best New Script by the San Francisco Critics Association.)

    McNally's relationship with MTC is strained after the theatre rejects *Dedication or The Stuff of Dreams*, which had been commissioned to inaugurate its recently refurbished Broadway theatre, the Samuel J. Friedman (formerly the Biltmore). A reconciliation occurs in 2011 when MTC moves the Kennedy Center production of McNally's *Master Class*, starring Tyne Daly, to Broadway. But MTC's production of *Golden Age* in 2012 proves disappointing, resulting in a second hiatus in the playwright and theatre company's working relationship.

2000   *Dead Man Walking*, based on the 1993 memoir of the same title by Sister Helen Prejean, with music by Jake Heggie, premieres at the San Francisco Opera and quickly becomes one of the most frequently produced English-language operas around the world. In 2015, McNally will write the libretto to a contemporary comic opera scored by Heggie, *Great Scott.*

2001   The first manifestation of cancer results in the removal of a portion of one lung in December. Although McNally had stopped smoking in 1981, a recurrence of cancer results in the removal of a portion of his second lung in 2007.

2003   After living together since 2001, McNally and social activist lawyer Tom Kirdahy enter into a civil union in Dover, Vermont, on December 20. After the District of Columbia declares gay marriage legal, the couple are married in Washington on April 6, 2010, with actors Tyne Daly, John Glover, and Malcolm Gets, as well as Kennedy Center president Michael Kaiser, as their witnesses. And after the US Supreme Court makes gay marriage legal across America, they repeat their vows on the steps of New York's City Hall in a ceremony conducted by Mayor Bill de Blasio on June 26, 2015. Beginning in 2007, Kirdahy becomes increasingly active producing McNally's plays.

McNally had previously registered a domestic partnership with Gary Bonasorte, a founding member of the Rattlestick Theater Company, with whom he lived from 1993 until Bonasorte's death from AIDS-related causes in 2001. A self-described "serial monogamist," McNally also enjoyed long-term relationships with actor Dominic Cuskern (1976–81) and playwright Wendy Wasserstein (1987–90).

2008   On McNally's seventieth birthday, legendary Broadway theatre restaurant Sardi's unveils its caricature of the playwright.

2010   The John F. Kennedy Center for the Performing Arts honors McNally by staging his three plays about opera (*The Lisbon Traviata, Master Class*, and *Golden Age*) simultaneously on its three stages.

2011   Receives the Dramatists Guild Lifetime Achievement Award.

2013   Returns to his alma mater, Columbia University, to address the graduating class on Class Day. McNally's speech movingly reviews the changes in American gay life and social consciousness since his own graduation in 1960.

2015   To honor the fiftieth anniversary of McNally's Broadway debut, Grove Press collects eight of McNally's plays under the title *Selected Works: A Memoir in Plays.* McNally contributes an introductory essay to each play in which he recalls the circumstances of its composition, the conditions of American theatre at the time, and his personal engagement with the play's issues. McNally receives the Lucille Lortel Lifetime Achievement Award from the League of Off-Broadway Theatres and Producers.

2018   McNally is inducted into the American Academy of Arts and Letters as one of only five living playwrights at the time. A documentary of his life and career titled *Every Act of Life* (dir. Jeff Kaufman) premieres at the Tribeca Film Festival.

In honor of McNally's eightieth birthday, New York City Mayor de Blasio declares November 4 "Terrence McNally Day." The official proclamation praises McNally for having served "as a civil rights activist, championing marriage equality and tackling issues that impact the LGBTQ community and people with HIV/AIDS" and concludes: "Through his thought-provoking and witty plays, musicals and operas, Terrence has engaged and uplifted generations of diverse audiences in New York and far beyond, and at age 80, the untiring artist is still creating new works."

2019   Presented a Lifetime Achievement Tony Award during the American Theater Wing's annual Tony Awards ceremonies.

2020   Dies of complications stemming from the coronavirus on March 24 at his winter home in Sarasota, Florida.

2021   Efforts by the Broadway community to honor McNally are forestalled by the continuing coronavirus crisis. Finally, on November 1, McNally's admirers fill the Gerald Schoenfeld Theatre where such close professional collaborators and personal friends as Audra McDonald, Christine Baranski, Nathan Lane, F. Murray Abraham, Joe Mantello, Chita Rivera, John Glover, Tyne Daly, Brian Stokes Mitchell, Jake Heggie, Don Roos, Graciela Daniele, John Benjamin Hickey, Matthew Lopez, Michael Urie, Lynn Ahrens, and John Kander offer tributes and perform scenes from McNally's plays. On November 3, the New York City Cultural Landmarks Commission unveils a plaque affixed to McNally's long-term residence at 29 East 9th Street, in the heart of Greenwich Village, celebrating the contributions of the playwright, librettist, and social activist. That evening all of the Broadway marquees go dark in his honor.

**Conversations with
Terrence McNally**

The Quiet and Scandalous World of Terrence McNally

Neal Weaver / 1974

Originally published in *In Touch* 2, no. 1 (October 1974): 34–37, 77–79.

The place was the Playwrights Unit at the Actors Studio in New York City. The time, December 1962. The occasion: a workshop production of a play called *There Is Something Out There* by a blond, baby-faced, twenty-four-year-old playwright named Terrence McNally. (Later the title was to be changed to *And Things That Go Bump in the Night*.)

The house was packed with the cream of the New York theatre's actors, playwrights, and directors. Expectations seemed high. A large invited audience had attended the dress rehearsal the night before, and reports were enthusiastic. Veteran director John Stix had put the production together, and assembled a cast of very capable actors, headed by Madeleine Sherwood, Ben Piazza, Barbara Dana, and Hal England. Terrence himself was a source of interest in that he had earlier worked as a stage manager at the Studio and was therefore known to many of the members. And there was also the fact that he was sharing an apartment with Edward Albee, who was then riding the crest of his Broadway success with *Who's Afraid of Virginia Woolf?* To further intrigue the audience, there was a rumor going around that one of the studio's actors had accidentally walked in on a rehearsal of the production and discovered the cast engaged in shooting pornographic photographs! (As it turned out, the photos were props for the show, and they were a good deal less than pornographic, but the rumor served to make the audience both eager and a little nervous.)

Whatever the audience expected from this clean-cut, innocent-looking young playwright, they got more than they bargained for; the play's later title may have come from a Scottish prayer, but the plot and the characters were straight out of Krafft-Ebing.

The play concerned a spectacularly bizarre family, headed by a flamboyant ex-opera singer named Ruby (Miss Sherwood), which includes her son, Sigfrid, a sort of metaphysical hustler, and her teenaged daughter, Lakme, whose pet occupation is recording on tape and film her brother's dealings with his pickups, male and female. When the brother brings home an idealistic and masochistic young protest marcher named Clarence, the whole family gears for action. Brother lures him to bed, while sister photographs and tapes the encounter. While the film is developing, Clarence is subjected to all manner of humiliations, including having all his clothes stolen, so that he is reduced to putting on a dress of Ruby's. At length, Ruby joins the game, and Clarence is invited to see a slide show. He politely accepts, blithely unaware that he is to be the star of the show. But when the slides are projected before the assembled family (those much-talked-about rehearsal photos!), Clarence is so mortified, distressed, and embarrassed that he dashes out of the house and is electrocuted when he collides with the electric fence that surrounds the house.

Today, in New York City, the play would probably not raise an eyebrow. But at that point in time, plays that examined homosexuality and the nuances of sadomasochistic behavior were few and far between. During the performance, the atmosphere was electric. (I happened to be the stage manager for the production, and so had an excellent vantage point to observe the proceedings from the light booth. And I must say, the play had shocked me. But I'd had several rehearsals to get used to it and decide for myself that there was a real writer at work.)

Still, at the intermission, which preceded the critique and discussion of the play, there were few indications of the storm that was about to break. It's true: a couple of the more conventional-minded female members of the studio were pacing about nervously, looking very threatened, and telling anyone who would listen, "I don't *need* this sort of thing." But the discussion started innocently enough. Terrence sat at the front of the room, waiting expectantly for comments—and parliamentary procedures were maintained for a while.

But it soon began to be clear that the play had upset and angered a number of people. There were others who liked the play or at least were rational in their responses. But rationality didn't stand a chance in the hullabaloo that ensued. Someone asked actress Madeleine Sherwood how she felt about the play. She leapt to her feet and launched into an impassioned speech about how she hated the play, and hadn't wanted to do it, and how sick and tired she was of playwrights who portrayed women—and especially mothers—as villains and castrating bitches. But on the other hand, she said, it *was* a spectacular role, and not the sort of thing she was likely to be offered a chance at in the commercial theatre, so she agreed to do it. Another actress (not involved in the performance) leapt to her feet, blazing with rage and with tears streaming down her cheeks. She obviously viewed the play with absolute loathing, but she was not coherent enough to make it clear just why.

Edward Albee was muttering grimly that it was a mystery to him why, in the year 1962, the word "homosexual" couldn't be mentioned in public without creating mass hysteria.

And at the front of the room, Terrence sat, looking at the audience with a rather diffident perplexity, seemingly baffled by the furor he'd unleashed.

Everybody was getting into the act now, and we were fast approaching a general melee, when Broadway director Alan Schneider (he'd just directed Albee's *Virginia Woolf*) managed to make himself heard above the din.

"Ladies and gentlemen, I am shocked! I am shocked! That a group of supposedly sophisticated, creative people—actors, writers, and directors—members of my profession—should heap abuse on a fellow artist simply because he chooses to depict a particular aspect of human behavior!" He talked on, spreading oil on troubled waters, and shaming his hearers, if not into good sense, at least into good manners or silence. And the meeting broke up.

When *And Things That Go Bump in the Night* was produced on Broadway in 1965, under the direction of Michael Cacoyannis, with Eileen Heckart as Ruby, the operatic mother; Robert Drivas as the hustler son; Susan Anspach as the shutter-happy daughter; and Marco St. John as Clarence, the victim, the controversy was greater still. During previews, audiences loved the show. But the critics attacked with a vengeance, and there were tales told to the effect that on the second night the audience was so angry it stormed the stage and tried to pull the set down. According to Terrence, nothing quite that violent happened, but there were incidents:

"In the middle of the second performance, a man jumped out of his seat, ran down to the stage, grabbed Eileen Heckart's train, and screamed, 'Stop this play! It's obscene! It's offensive!' At the end of every performance, the audience was split fifty-fifty. Half of them were shouting, 'Bravo!' and the other half were booing. We even had pickets in front of the theatre, urging people to come and see the show. A lot of people thought I'd paid them to be there, but they were total strangers. I don't know who they were. One night I went out to speak to them. They asked me who I was. I told them I was the playwright, but they didn't believe me."

To keep the show alive, producers Ted Mann and Joseph E. Levine decided to put all tickets on sale for $1. The theatre was packed with people, many of whom had never been to the theatre before. (Ultimately, more than twenty thousand people saw the show, counting preview audiences.)

In 1968, Terrence scored another *succés de scandale* with *Sweet Eros* in which Robert Drivas played a young kidnapper who was afraid of being loved, but [was] lonely, and therefore was holding Sally Kirkland as his prisoner. The *scandale* was due to the fact that Sally spent most of the show tied to a chair wearing nothing but a bit of Max Factor pancake. (And *Sweet Eros* is still upsetting people: just this year the cast of a Boston production was hauled into court on obscenity charges.) But as a result of all the furor, few critics paid much attention to what the author was really up to.

And so it has gone. This young, serious-minded playwright with the incredibly innocent face seemed to have a knack for shaking people up and shocking his audiences. But he's no pornographer. And it wasn't only the subject matter of his plays that disturbed. It was his whole view of the world that a lot of people weren't ready for: a clear-eyed, critical view that penetrated current hypocrisies and stripped off a lot of comfortable masks. There's a speech in *Things That Go Bump* that sort of sums it up: "We deal with what's left us . . . not what we'd like to add to the mythology. It's a subtraction process and if the answer is zero . . . that's okay, too." It might be the credo of a whole generation of young writers who were committed to finding out what was true and what was not, and were determined not to fall back on reassuring popular clichés about what people "ought to be."

It wasn't until *Next* was produced Off-Broadway that the world began to catch up with Terrence, and a new young audience had appeared capable of relating to his vision. He'd had other plays, Off-Broadway as well as on television, and his works were proving successful in schools and regional theatres. But *Next* was the first real commercial hit. That production, directed by Elaine May (on a double bill with her own play, *Adaptation*) and with James Coco as the embattled hero, finally made him an "established" playwright.

This year, his new play, *Bad Habits*, proved so successful Off-Broadway that it was transferred to Broadway. And another play, *Tubs*, produced last season at the Yale Repertory Theatre, is tentatively scheduled for a Broadway opening in November.

The baby-faced playwright has come of age. (And he's probably damn glad of it: it must be disconcerting for a working playwright to find lady columnists referring to him as a "cutie-pie"!)

Terrence McNally, like the hero of his play, *Where Has Tommy Flowers Gone?*, was born in St. Petersburg, Florida, on November 3, 1939 [*sic*]. His parents were expatriate New Yorkers, who soon moved on to Corpus Christi, Texas, so he doesn't remember Florida at all.

"I had a high-school English teacher—a remarkable man [*sic*] who was most influential in my life. He was interested in me, and encouraged me. Prior to that I'd intended to go to the University of Texas. But I was inspired to come east. My best friend and I both applied at both Yale and Columbia. We were both accepted at both places. But it seemed ridiculous for us, having been close friends all through high school, to come all that way to be roommates in college. We wanted to open ourselves up to new influences. So we flipped a coin. He got Yale and I got Columbia."

But at Columbia, his interest was journalism, not theatre: "I certainly didn't want to be a playwright. Ever since I was a kid, I used to write little stories and started newspapers. I think if journalism had been more interesting to me when I first started out in it . . . but my jobs were always straight news stories and I was always more attracted to the features."

Still, it was at Columbia that he gained his first playwriting experience: "I read one day in the school paper that they were looking for someone to write the varsity show. I took a shot at it and it worked. That was in 1960. The show was called *A Little Bit Different*. There was a pony ballet in it, so you can imagine how serious it was. Then when I was graduating, I got a $6,000 grant for being the best English major of the year. I took that money and went off to Mexico and started to write seriously."

There was also a period when he went back to Corpus Christi, and worked as a journalist on the Corpus Christi *Caller-Times*.

Eventually he wound up back in New York again, where he obtained the job as stage manager at the Actors Studio. The late Molly Kazan, wife of director Elia Kazan, and at that time moderator of the studio's Playwrights Unit, asked him if he'd like a job as tutor for the two teenaged sons of a friend of hers who were planning a trip around the world and needed an older companion. The friend turned out to be John Steinbeck, and Terrence took the job.

"They knew their way around better than I did. And I looked younger than they did. But the boys were great, and the trip, which lasted a year, was fantastic."

Somehow, despite all of this activity, he was able to finish his first play, called *This Side of the Door*, as well as *There Is Something Out There*.

By chance, the performance at the Actors Studio shared a bill with a play directed by John Strasberg, son of Lee Strasberg, the Studio's guiding light.

Italian film director Franco Zeffirelli was in New York getting ready to go into rehearsal for his Broadway production of *Camille*, based on the novel by Alexandre Dumas, fils, in which the Strasbergs' daughter Susan was to star. Therefore, they invited Zeffirelli to the performance to see John's work—but he also saw Terrence's, with the result that Terrence was hired as an "adapter" of *Camille*.

"I usually leave that out of the biographies. Franco was looking for someone with a 'young American approach' to do rewrites. It all happened in a weekend. I got $200 and billing for it. It was done to get experience."

Camille turned out to be one of the most spectacular flops of the season. It was not only panned; it was practically hooted.

Shortly thereafter, I happened to be speaking to actress-writer Mary Mercier who I knew had been present for the massacre Terrence had received at the Studio after *There Is Something Out There*. "Poor Terrence!" I said.

"Why do you say that?" she asked.

"Well, to be stuck with a spectacular flop like *Camille* right on top of the shellacking he got at the Studio."

"Darling, I was in *Camille*. Don't feel sorry for Terrence. Terrence is stronger than anybody. Terrence will outlast us all!"

In any case, Terrence didn't have much time to grieve. Director Alan Schneider had been impressed with *There Is Something Out There* when he saw it at the Studio, and recommended Terrence to Dr. Arthur Ballet of the Office for Advanced Drama Research at the University of Minnesota. Dr. Ballet wrote to Terrence, offering to produce the play in Minneapolis at the Tyrone Guthrie Theater. The play opened there in February of 1964, under the title *And Things That Go Bump in the Night*, with a cast that included Leueen MacGrath, Robert Drivas, and Joseph Chaikin. As before, the play had its violent partisans and detractors.

After nearly a year of delays, and negotiations with two different sets of producers, the play opened on Broadway. And that was really a devastating experience. As Terrence later described it, "Two of them [the critics] went so far as to demand that I be electrocuted on that fence in the second act. The others contented themselves with rock throwing and some name calling. People asked me how I felt. I told them. Others treated me as if my entire family had been exterminated by one grisly blow of fate. I accepted their condolences. My younger brother, Peter, who had come from Texas fully expecting to see his big brother carried through the streets of New York in Roman style, said unflinchingly, 'Well, there's no place to go but up.' He was right, too."

Nevertheless, the impact of that failure turned him off writing for the theatre for more than a year.

"I was very much in debt, so I took a job editing an alumni magazine at Columbia for about a year."

Meanwhile, plans were afoot for a Broadway musical version of John Steinbeck's novel *East of Eden*. As a result of his previous connection with the Steinbeck family, Terrence was asked to write the book for the show, which was called *Here's Where I Belong*. But it was not where Terrence belonged. By the time the show tried out in Philadelphia, he saw that it was hopeless, and severed his relations with it. His name was removed from the show before its opening (and closing) night.

Then, at last, his luck began to change. He won a Guggenheim Grant that gave him the financial independence to go back to writing seriously. *Sweet Eros/Witness, Tour* (as part of a show called *Collision Course*) and *Noon* (the middle section of *Morning, Noon, and Night*) were written shortly thereafter. "By then I think I really wanted to be a playwright. . . . while I had the Guggenheim, I wrote *Next*. And that's when I started making money. It's a modest income, but I'm happy I can support myself as a writer. It's that simple. I think I'm very lucky."

Now, with the success of *Next* and *Bad Habits* under his belt, Terrence lives in a small cheery apartment in New York City's Greenwich Village, which he shares with a cairn terrier named Charles. Charles, however, was absent for our interview, having hogged the spotlight when a reporter for the *New York Post* came to call. Of the apartment, Terrence says, "It's not really my style. It used to be Jimmy Coco's. He gave it to me as a present after *Next*. But it was a delight to be able to just move in and not have to worry about renovating. And it's a tremendous improvement over some of my past apartments. There was one place that had only DC current. What a thing to do to a person! For three years I couldn't listen to music because I couldn't play the phonograph. Or even use the vacuum cleaner or the TV set. I used to call people up and say, 'Can I see the news at your house?'"

I remembered stories about the Off-Broadway production of *Morning, Noon, and Night*—a package of three one-act plays by Israel Horowitz, Terry, and Leonard Melfi, respectively, which had been directed by Ted Mann of the Circle in the Square. Rumor had it that Horowitz had become so agitated over rewrites that he took a poke at the director and was subsequently barred from rehearsals. And I'd also heard that Terrence had completely rewritten the *Noon* section just before opening. I asked for his account of the proceedings.

"I was hardly ever at rehearsals because I was involved with the production of *Sweet Eros* and *Witness* at the same time. But I finally got to see a matinee just before the opening. And I took my friends Jimmy Coco and Bobby Drivas with me."

(Coco and Drivas are close professional associates as well as friends. Coco appeared in both *Witness* and *Next*, and Drivas played leading roles in *And Things That Go Bump in the Night*, *Sweet Eros*, and the title role in the more recent *Where Has Tommy Flowers Gone?*, in addition to directing the current Broadway production of *Bad Habits*.)

"Originally I'd had the homosexual character throw himself out the window at the end. But when I saw it, it was very apparent to me that the ending wasn't working as I'd intended. At first I wanted to blame the actors. But Jimmy and Bobby didn't agree. They reminded me of *The Odd Couple*, where Felix is always saying, 'I'm going to jump out the window!' But if he actually did jump, you'd hate Neil Simon. Fortunately, I had the sense to listen to my friends, and wasn't stubborn. I rewrote the scene that night— and it went in the following night, just in time for the opening. When Clive Barnes saw it, the actors had bits and pieces of the script taped all over the set because there hadn't been time enough to learn the new lines. Charlotte Rae's phone conversation at the end was plastered to the top of the table so she could read it. . . . If you have bright friends, be willing to listen to them. If I've improved at all as the result of my experience, it's that I've learned how to work with other people in the theatre."

In talking with Terrence, and in hearing stories from others, the one thing that always seemed most remarkable about him is his equanimity. In a profession full of flamboyant tempers and temperaments who veer toward hysteria with every crisis, he seems downright placid.

"Well, you sort of have to be if theatre is what you want. No one's making anyone work in the theatre. You can quit anytime you want to. . . . I've had a lot of plays that were happy experiences. And certainly I've never had one bad enough to make me want to stop writing plays. There's been only one person I've met in the theatre I truly didn't like. And after all, a play is a play. It's not the end of the world to have a play produced. Every day something new happens. And as with everything else, a play will either work out or it won't."

(One actor who has worked with him says that Terrence isn't serene at all. That inside his placid exterior, he's positively seething. And there may be something in it. After all, the passions and the violence in his plays have to come from somewhere!)

The interview was drawing to a close. The mother of an actress in the Broadway *Bad Habits* had just suffered a heart attack, so an understudy was going in. Another actor was doing a television job. Director Robert Drivas was out of town, so it was up to Terrence to get to the theatre to keep an eye on the replacements.

As we parted and headed in our separate directions, I remembered Mary Mercier's comment, "Terrence will outlast us all!" And she wasn't far wrong. When that first performance of *There Is Something Out There* occurred in 1962, he was the fresh-faced kid, the novice, the unknown among the name writers of the Studio. And the names of that time—Jack Gelber, Jack Richardson, Edward Albee, William Archibald, Arthur Kopit—where are they now? One dead, some apparently no longer writing, none having escaped a certain eclipse of their literary reputations. And Terrence is just now really coming into his own!

You've got to watch out for those quiet ones.

Terrence McNally: Scripts Together, Worlds Apart

Larry S. Ledford / 1991

Originally published in *Stages: The National Theatre Magazine*, November-December 1991, 4–5. Reprinted by permission.

Don't try to pigeonhole Terrence McNally. He refuses to fit into the mold of anything he has written before. "The Picassos of the world are allowed to go through blue periods, neo-classic periods, and abstract periods," he says, "but somehow playwrights are supposed to stay in our blue period or our green period and sometimes I just want to work in charcoal, sometimes I want to paint in oil. I want to keep trying new things."

"I like the fact that Shakespeare mixes humor and tragedy, rich people and poor, smart people and dumb people," McNally continues. "To me Shakespeare is like living in New York City. There is this explosion of different people and sights and sounds and smells. I can't be one of those playwrights who say, 'I just want to focus on the middle class.'"

Native Texan Terrence McNally has not ridden the express to success. He had the good fortune to have had his first play produced on Broadway (which almost never happens today), but from *And Things That Go Bump in the Night* through *Where Has Tommy Flowers Gone?* and *Bad Habits*, to his first super hit *The Ritz*, last season's *The Lisbon Traviata*, and this year's *Lips Together, Teeth Apart*, his rise to international recognition has been one of slow steady progress.

In recent years he has established a wonderful working relationship with Lynne Meadow and her Manhattan Theatre Club, one of the most successful production companies in New York, where his work has been nurtured and given the kind of support that playwrights dream of. With top directors and the best actors in American theatre to work with and the time required to rehearse and rewrite, MTC came into McNally's life when they were needed most. "After *It's Only a Play* (it was called *Broadway, Broadway* at the time) closed in Philadelphia," he remembers, "I was in a real slump, one that lasted a couple of years. And then these people [from MTC] came along and said, 'We'd like to do a revival of it.' And it really gave me my second wind as a playwright."

It's Only a Play was actor James Coco's last play; it is the production in which McNally met actress Christine Baranski for the first time; and it began his collaboration with director John Tillinger. During previews of that play, Meadow said to McNally that she would produce his next play sight unseen. McNally, still seeming in awe, recalls, "Nobody had ever said anything like that to me—shown such faith or trust—and it really released something in me. *Frankie and Johnny in the Clair de Lune* was the result.

"That was the best Christmas gift I ever got because for the first time in my life I wasn't peddling, auditioning, trying to get a play on. I knew I had a place to have it done.

"And," he adds, "Manhattan Theatre Club has such a good reputation that really good actors and directors and designers want to work there. Clearly, the quality of productions at that theatre are Broadway standard." McNally concedes that his one regret is "only that it is not a dream ensemble of actors that you get to work with over and over again. That's why I write plays for specific actors."

The actors he has in mind are not always available, of course, but when the cast of his current hit *Lips Together, Teeth Apart* assembled for rehearsals last March, the playwright was thrilled. With an ensemble that included Christine Baranski, Swoosie Kurtz, Nathan Lane, and Anthony Heald, who wouldn't be?

"You write your best," he says, "when actors of that caliber are involved. But getting a company like that together isn't often likely." He adds with sadness, "Chekhov had a company, as did Shakespeare, as did Molière. Most of the great playwrights had a company to write for. I think that's one of the worst things that has happened in the American theatre: that no one has been able to provide a company of actors."

The latest McNally script, on MTC's production schedule for next April, is *A Perfect Ganesh*. For the only time in our interview, he is reluctant to talk. "I'm loath to talk about new plays," he says. "I'm sure the title isn't going to give people as much trouble as *Lips Together, Teeth Apart* though." He laughs. "People were calling it 'Legs Together, Tits Apart'; 'Teeth Together, Mouth Open.'"

"This they think is my first Jewish play," he chuckles, "but Ganesha is the Indian god of good fortune. He is part boy, part elephant, and he travels on a mouse. Right now it looks like it is going to be a three-character play. It's about two women traveling in India." And that's about as far as he would go on that subject, other than to say, somewhat cagily, that he has written it for two of the greatest actresses in the English-speaking theatre and hopes they will show up.

McNally has just made his second venture into the world of motion pictures, with his first film since the adaptation of his hit farce *The Ritz. Frankie and Johnny*, which stars Michelle Pfeiffer and Al Pacino, has just been released by Paramount, and McNally is very happy with it. "It's very different from the play," he says, "with only about twenty percent of the original in the film. There are other characters and everything has been opened up to accommodate the medium." Asked about the cast, he answers, "The role of Frankie was written for Kathy Bates and she was wonderful in it, but wait until you see Michelle. She is absolutely wonderful. I was moved to tears when I saw the final film."

Don't try to pin a label on Terrence McNally.

He has written a play set to the music of Richard Wagner (*Prelude & Liebestod*), a play that blends high comedy with melodrama (*The Lisbon Traviata*), pure tragedy (*Andre's Mother*), dramatic social comedy (*Lips Together, Teeth Apart*), and books for two musicals (*The Rink* and *Kiss of the Spider Woman*).

No single description fits, except, perhaps, his own. "I would like to hear it said that there is no typical play by Terrence McNally," he says. "Plot is never a high priority for me, and neither is philosophy; people are. It's the mystery of the human experience that makes good playwriting."

For McNally, good theatre says to an audience, "Here are some interesting people. Sit in a dark room and watch them."

And we do.

Measuring the Times:
Terrence McNally Straddles
the Sexual Divide

Otis Stuart / 1991

Originally published in *The Village Voice*, September 3, 1991, 92–94. Reprinted by permission.

"I'm glad I never saw my brother dance with another man. And now I never will."
—Sally in *Lips Together, Teeth Apart*

Terrence McNally is writer of the moment again, this time for what has become his signature specialty, straddling the sexual divide.

Last year, McNally celebrated his twenty-fifth anniversary as a working playwright. *And Things That Go Bump in the Night* opened on Broadway in 1965 to bad reviews qualifying for the *Guinness Book of World Records* and sent its author straight to a nine-to-five job for two years. A quarter-century later, McNally can look back on a career as eclectic as any in our theatre and images it would never have known without him: James Coco in the army in *Next*, a silent Sally Kirkland nude for the virtual entirety of *Sweet Eros*, a gay bathhouse reinventing the Greek in farce [*sic*] for *The Ritz*, and *The Rink*, the musical that finally won Chita Rivera a Tony.

This year, burning his candle at both ends, stage and film, McNally is back in gear on a scale he hasn't known since the mid-'70s, when *Bad Habits* and *The Ritz* were back-to-back Broadway hits. His latest, *Lips Together, Teeth Apart*, at the Manhattan Theatre Club, is the rarest of theatrical species, SRO at high summer. The film version of *Frankie and Johnny in the Clair de Lune*, with Michelle Pfeiffer and Al Pacino no less, has just wrapped for an October release.

"I've had a kind of nonhistory with Hollywood so far," McNally says, fresh from Los Angeles and a look at the rough cut of *Frankie and Johnny*. "I know how to send my plays around, but I'm too old to devote a year to a screen-play and then wait for it to get done. Movies can take years to get made and then are so far from the original impulse that they've become relocated, re-imagined, and a vehicle for Whoopi Goldberg.

"*Frankie and Johnny* moved very quickly. The finished product is very much what I wrote. Basically, I put the play in a drawer. I wouldn't go to see a movie where two people sat around and talked for two hours, in real time. In the film they're not alone in her room as much. You meet people in the restaurant, friends of Johnny. Nathan Lane is in it as Frankie's buddy. New York is a character. Very little dialogue from the play remains, but the expe-rience should be the same. It's about the same themes.

"Even more than *Frankie and Johnny*, what's attracted me to film lately was *Andre's Mother* on *American Playhouse*. More people probably saw that piece than all my other work combined. Probably because of what it was about, I got incredibly moving letters, mostly from mothers in North Dakota and Wyoming and Texas. Some of them were signed, like, 'George's mother.' I found out that something about film really reaches people. I'm still a creature of the theatre, though. I see work by someone like Martin Scorsese, who is a great director, and he's moviestruck in the way I'm stage-struck, still."

The images that have brought McNally back into the theatrical mainline could hardly differ more from the manic McNally of the '60s and '70s, mae-stro of one-act Armageddon. Frankie the waitress who's seen it all and her short-order [cook] Johnny, the affluent opera queens of *Lisbon Traviata*, and the mismatched yuppie couples of *Lips Together* use anything—sex, opera, one-liners—to get a grip on the world. The anarchists and bedlam-ites of the earlier plays were more often out to blow it all up. Like the sense of paradox that has animated his people all along, however, the difference between the real-world concerns of the latter-day McNally and the combus-tible hyperbole of the early days is the key to their common denominator.

McNally has become a concrete chronicler of his times. His interest in writing dates from an Eisenhower-era adolescence in Corpus Christi, what he's described as "a cross between *American Graffiti* and Bach's Mass in B Minor." Despite an early full-length play, a Gershwin bio based on liner notes in which George marries his sweetheart Ira, McNally's first interest was in journalism, his first job on a newspaper. An interview with then-Senator Lyndon Baines Johnson suggested a future elsewhere. The junior reporter spent less time on oil rights than the details *chez* LBJ, the copy of *Screw* [sic] on his desk, the phone call from Lady Bird.

McNally the playwright has held onto that sense of reportage, and his work to date virtually catalogues the past three decades of New York theatre, uptown and down. The *Morning, Noon, and Night* trilogy is a near roll call of the 1960s' new playwrights, McNally in tandem with Israel Horovitz and Leonard Melfi. *Bad Habits* and *The Ritz*, one structurally and the other thematically, synopsize the '70s free-for-all, just as *Frankie and Johnny* and *Lisbon Traviata* synopsize the anomie of the '80s. *Lips Together* brings the circle round to one of the touchiest territories of the '90s, the lost border between gay and straight, with all its attendant anxieties.

"Anybody could be a playwright in the '60s," McNally remembers. "It was no big deal to get a play on. The first play I ever wrote was produced on Broadway, which would be fairly inconceivable now. The spirit of New York was theatre then, and it isn't anymore. It's become about restaurants. The '80s were about business, and Donald Trump set the tone, not Abbie Hoffman. It was us against them back then. Your attitude about the war was a simple dividing line. It was very black and white, and I think the lines have gotten blurred. Who is us? Who is them? Who am I? Unless you write a play for a specific audience now, you don't know who's sitting out there, whereas in the '60s I knew who came to my plays. We were all against what we saw as the establishment.

"Now we've become the establishment. A theatre like Manhattan Theatre Club has become what used to be Broadway. When I first went to work for Manhattan Theatre Club, we had a room with fluorescent lighting and Samsonite chairs. Now MTC has an annual budget of $4.4 million. The biggest change of all is that there's virtually no activity on Broadway. And I don't mean Broadway as a measure of status. I mean it as the best real estate in the country for putting on plays. Imagine John Lee Beatty's set for *Lips Together* in a Broadway theatre with 20 feet of blue surrounding it. The house would float. I want Broadway for the real estate. Thirty years ago *Substance of Fire* would have been done on Broadway with Henry Fonda. *Lips Together* would have been a Broadway show with Deborah Kerr. Now, the established voices have taken over what was once the venue for new voices. So where do those guys go?

"To take a chance on a new play is producing, and you've got to be very brave to do that now. What signifies the times to me was that when *[Lips] Together* got a terrific review from Frank Rich, no one thought, 'Ah, let's move it.' The thought was, 'Let's wait and see what David Richards says next week.' Nobody's dreaming in theatre right now."

The McNally of *Frankie and Johnny*, *Lisbon Traviata*, and *Lips Together* has managed the measure of his times onstage and off. Being a gay writer isn't what it used to be, and as the last of the first generation to debut as gay playwrights, McNally has sent the fingers of his successors straight to the PC. His work falls midway between the respective territories of his gay peers who've made it into the working mainstream.

He's one-half repartee and diva fixation, a past master of the generically gay milieu embodied by Charles Ludlam and Harvey Fierstein. (Harold Clurman placed McNally among "the most adept practitioners of the comedy of insult.") McNally's charted both gay cliché, in *The Ritz*, and gay fact, in *Lisbon Traviata*. But like Edward Albee, he's also drawn the reverberations and mirror reflections gay life has struck off straightdom. His work is replete with Albee's ambiguous echoes and missionary positionings.

Both McNallys are potentially problematic in a politically correct world. For some, *Lisbon Traviata* was, at best, a throwback to the era of high culture sissies and, at worst, the rebirth of the gay psycho. By the same measure, *Frankie and Johnny* and *Lips Together*, which contain not a single gay character, can be seen as the return to the era of the invisible homosexual.

"*And Things That Go Bump in the Night* was reviewed as a play by a gay playwright with an enormous amount of innuendo. Every review certainly mentioned 'his good friend Edward Albee.' The inference was that this is a play by a sociopath, i.e., a homosexual. John Simon's review is a classic. It's called 'Come Back, Albertine.' He's still bringing up Edward. He mentioned him in his review of *Lips Together*.

"I just read a review of *Lips Together* in *Theater Week* that made me very angry. The fascism of this politically correct agenda really angers me. The play was reviewed as a politically incorrect gay play because I enforced every stereotype, like that gay men listen to opera or show tunes. Well, that's not quite true. They also listen to Schubert and Billie Holiday and 'Moonglow.' Go to Fire Island and every house is playing music rather loudly.

"The reviewer then said that I reinforce the idea that gay men have promiscuous sex because the guys are having sex in the bushes. Well, gay men have sex. One of the ways you are gay is having sex with another man. These people want gay men as Ozzie and Harriet, the kind of people who go around dusting and are very tasteful and vaguely liberal.

"*Lisbon Traviata* was criticized for saying homosexuals are homicidal. That's not accurate. One man, because he loved someone very passionately, was driven to murder. That doesn't say that all gay men are murderers. I think gay men are capable of murder. They're also capable of love and generosity and pettiness, like everyone else, and that's what I want as a writer, to be able to write characters as I see them.

"I'd never want to write a play that was a statement. My early plays were like that and that's one of the things that was wrong with them. I don't write plays to do service to gays, but I certainly don't think I'm doing them a disservice either. Theatre is not about writing role models. I'm always told how funny my gay characters are. I hope the straight ones are funny, too. Humor is not a homosexual prerogative."

Terrence McNally

John L. DiGaetani / 1991

Originally published in John L. DiGaetani, ed., *A Search for a Postmodern Theater: Interviews with Contemporary Playwrights* (Westport, CT: Greenwood Press, 1991), 219–28. Reprinted by permission.

The playwright Terrence McNally was born in St. Petersburg, Florida, on November 3, 1939, [*sic*] and was raised in Corpus Christi, Texas. He first came to New York City to attend Columbia University, where he received his bachelor's degree in 1960 with a major in English. Since then he has continued to live in New York, though his plays have sometimes premiered elsewhere. His first experience with writing for professional theatre occurred with *And Things That Go Bump in the Night*, which was staged in New York in 1965. *Next* premiered in Westport, Connecticut, in 1967 but was staged successfully in New York two years later. *Botticelli*, a television play McNally wrote, was televised in 1968. *Where Has Tommy Flowers Gone?* (New Haven, Connecticut, and then New York in 1971) did very well Off-Broadway. *Bad Habits* played on Broadway in 1973. His biggest success—as a play on Broadway and as a film—was *The Ritz* (1975). *It's Only a Play* appeared Off-Broadway in 1982 and was restaged two years later. McNally also wrote the book for the musical *The Rink*, which was staged on Broadway in 1984. More recently, his *The Lisbon Traviata* appeared Off-Broadway in 1985, followed in 1987 by the very successful *Frankie and Johnny in the Claire de Lune*. His *Lips Together, Teeth Apart* appeared in New York in 1991.

McNally has received two Guggenheim Fellowships, in addition to a Rockefeller grant and a citation from the American Academy of Arts and Letters. He has been a member of the Dramatists Guild since 1970, and has been vice president of the Guild since 1981.

DiGaetani: I have enjoyed those of your plays that I have been able to see here in New York, especially *The Lisbon Traviata*. I was interested in the presentation in that play of the character of the fanatical opera fan.

McNally: I thought that was a rather fresh character for the stage. The play also concerns the obsession with the cult of personality, which is why Maria Callas is such a symbol in the play. But she could also have been Marilyn Monroe or Judy Garland or any of those women that fanatical fans make famous. The most famous ones, I guess, were Bette Davis and Joan Crawford. I think the general population think Bette Davis is a fine actress and some people think that Maria Callas was an interesting singer, but the obsession and the cult of personality are something specific to opera fanatics. I'm not a psychoanalyst, but I have observed the behavior.

I also think in the play Maria Callas represented a standard of romanticism that is missing now. Both men in *The Lisbon Traviata*, when they talk about new singers and complain that they lack personality, are lamenting the loss of romanticism. I don't think we live in a very romantic age, but Stephen is a romantic character, and it is romantic characters who are driven to acts of violence. I also think personally that Maria Callas is so superior to any other singer, and that we are also talking about a decline of standards. The Metropolitan Opera House that I go to today is not the same theatre I used to go to in the sixties, when there were at least five sopranos of greatness and five tenors worth hearing. I think the pickings are much slimmer now. There are some great singers still, of course, but suddenly the sixties does look like a golden age. So I think the characters in *The Lisbon Traviata* are bemoaning the loss of that age. They also mourn for the loss of a relationship, for Mendy's love for Stephen is always unrealized, and Stephen is losing Mike. They all love the wrong person. Also, Stephen in the play is a man who is forty years old. *The Lisbon Traviata* is not a play about a twenty-year-old whose heart is broken. It's about a man who feels his life crumbling when Mike, his lover, leaves him. I think a man can feel that way when his wife leaves him, a wife can feel that way when her husband leaves her, a child can feel that way when a parent abandons him through death or a divorce. I think that pain of separation is a very real feeling.

DiGaetani: Are you a Maria Callas fan yourself?

McNally: Oh, yes, I am. To me she is the ideal singer. The rudeness about other singers in the play is pretty much my own opinion.

DiGaetani: Some of those remarks were nasty, especially the one about Beverly Sills. I remember one aria heard during the play, with the response: "Nice try, Bubbles."

McNally: But actually, I love Sills, and that remark wasn't meant to be cruel. I think most of the singers come off pretty well.

DiGaetani: There's a bitchy quality in the play.

McNally: I hope so! There's a bitchy quality in opera queens. The world of opera is an archaic world with a queen-bee star figure. I mean, singers are not creating new roles; they're recreating endlessly Tosca, Norma, Aida. So we start comparing Tebaldi's Tosca to Callas's to Milanov's to Birgit Nilsson's. I don't consider myself an opera queen, but I'm a passionate operagoer and I go to new operas as well. However, most opera fans haven't seen many operas; they have seen maybe ten operas in their lives. They're seeing *Tosca* for the fiftieth time with the fiftieth Tosca, so this audience is comparing. I also care passionately about opera as theatre, and I'm so disappointed that there's so little sense at the Metropolitan Opera of opera as theatre. I saw *Dialogue of the Carmelites* on television recently, and that's my vision of what opera should be.

DiGaetani: It was done at the Met, don't forget.

McNally: I know, but I wish that style characterized the majority of the productions there as opposed to the kind of mindless spectacles that go on there.

DiGaetani: You're referring no doubt to the Zeffirelli *Turandot*?

McNally: No. Actually, I liked the Zeffirelli *Turandot* all right. It was some of his other productions I disliked. His *La Bohème* managed to dehumanize the opera; whenever I see *La Bohème* and don't cry, something is wrong. To make *Bohème* an unmoving experience! I think something is seriously wrong when the physical production and the sets are so enormous that Mimi's death doesn't reach me, and I criticize Zeffirelli for overproducing an intimate opera like *La Bohème*. *Turandot* can withstand such treatment, but I think *La Bohème* is a fragile, intimate piece.

DiGaetani: I think Zeffirelli wanted to de-sentimentalize the opera, and he did.

McNally: Yes, but it's as if you see the whole opera from a long shot. If it were a film, you'd say, "Can't we have one closeup, one medium shot?" If the opera is always viewed from a long shot it becomes visually boring and you lose the opera's intimacy.

DiGaetani: How do you work? Do your plays start with ideas?

McNally: I saw Arthur Miller's *All My Sons* the other night. The themes of the play are more important than the characters. The son's an idealist, his father's a hopelessly compromised, corrupt person, and the mother is a woman who doesn't want to face reality. We don't know much more about them than that, and the ideas are what you take home. But I start with characters who interest me, and situations like "What would Stephen do if he catches them in bed?" Really the catalyst—very few people seem to notice it—the real turning point for me in *The Lisbon Traviata* is during the first act when Stephen is stood up by a character we never meet, Hal, one of the most important people in the play. In the first act the only reason Stephen is putting up with Mendy and the inane conversation is because Stephen thinks he's going to be with Hal that night, and then Hal stands him up. Clearly, he's had a better offer. I don't really think something's come up at the restaurant, as Hal states, and I don't think Stephen believes the excuse. *The Lisbon Traviata* is a play about sexual jealousy, which is a form of passion. The play is one I am especially proud of. It's not perfect, but I care a lot about it.

DiGaetani: What about *Frankie and Johnny in the Claire de Lune*?

McNally: It's a serious play about relationships, which tells you absolutely nothing. What's different is that the people in it are blue-collar. The play is about a waitress and the consequences of a one-night stand with a short-order cook in the restaurant they both work at.

DiGaetani: It sounds like in many ways your most recent work is trying to avoid comedy. You became so famous as a comic writer because of *The Ritz*.

McNally: *It's Only a Play* was a very serious comedy, but it worked more seriously as people thought afterwards about what it had to say about the state of the American theatre, fame, and money. But it was perceived as a ha, ha, ha comedy. I love the fact that I have the ability to make people laugh, but I liked the gasps at the end of *The Lisbon Traviata*, too. Tonight at this theatre they're doing a new play of mine; it's a forty-five-minute one-act play called *Prelude and Liebestod*. Music obviously plays a large part in the work. This play takes place during a performance of the *Prelude and Liebestod* from Wagner's *Tristan und Isolde*. The play presents the sexual fantasies of people in the audience—a lot of interior monologue while the music is being played.

This theatre, Circle Rep, is presenting the play in its lab, so it's an in-house project; the play is not advertised to the public. When the director said he wanted to do it, I said I'm about to go into rehearsal with a professional production, and that involves big responsibilities on my part, so I won't be able to take part in this production. The director then said, "I don't think it needs any more work from you." So I'm just going to see it for myself cold tonight and see if he was right.

DiGaetani: One of the worst parts about being a playwright must be waiting for reviews.

McNally: That's what *It's Only a Play* is about. The play takes place between 9:30 and 11:30 of an opening night, with the characters waiting for Frank Rich's review.

DiGaetani: I really liked that play, but *The Ritz* was your biggest commercial success. In that play there seemed a lot of tension between the Italian characters and the homosexual setting. Did you think in those terms? Italian culture is very homophobic, especially southern Italian culture, and part of the comedy of that play results when these Italian characters find themselves in a gay bathhouse.

McNally: That sounds more schematic than it actually is. I write lots of Italian characters. But I did want a character named Gaetano, and his nickname is Gay.

DiGaetani: The first act reminded me of the opening of Puccini's *Gianni Schicchi*, beginning with a death scene and a corpse onstage.

McNally: Well, the early influences on me were operatic. I came into the theatre through opera, really. There was no theatre where I grew up in rural Texas, but I could hear opera broadcasts on the radio on Saturday afternoons. So I guess I think operatically. My plays are filled with long speeches—arias, really—and I love trios and quartets with overlapping dialogue. Sometimes I write a scene and think, actually this is a trio or duet. I think there's a real musical structure to my plays, which of course nobody ever notices and I never get the credit I think I will for! But leitmotifs and themes do recur in my plays. If I have any sense of structure, it comes from knowing music. I'm not a formally trained playwright, but I love opera, and opera reminds me of Italians, whom I think of as very volatile. But I like Italians. Obviously, I like Gaetano and his wife, but I don't like her brother. There are a lot of ethnics in that play, like Googie Gomez. I've done several Latin characters. One thing I don't want to write about is WASPs. Actually, since I come from south Texas, I probably am a WASP, even though I was raised a Catholic.

DiGaetani: But your name is Irish!

McNally: But I was like a WASP in that society because it was pretty much Anglos or Latins. There was always the conflict and a dividing line in my hometown. South Texas isn't the South as the South is, but south Texas was Latin versus Anglo as opposed to Black and white, which you get in most of the South and East. In Texas that was the big racial, cultural, social, and economic dividing line. But I'm very comfortable around Latin people, though I personally am not very exuberant. This Latin affection of mine is my projection of my boisterous self, I guess. I find it very liberating to create Latin characters who throw themselves on the ground and beat their chests.

DiGaetani: You don't do things like that?

McNally: In real life I'm rather cold.

DiGaetani: Some of the critics have compared *The Ritz* to a Feydeau comedy with a gay twist. Is that the way the play seemed to you?

McNally: I've never read Feydeau. I don't think I've ever seen a Feydeau play, but what I did in *The Ritz* was consciously put everything I'd enjoyed as a child and as an adult in the theatre. I got in a hiding-under-the-bed scene, a recognition scene when a long-lost nephew turns up, and even mistaken identities and chases. All those things I enjoyed as a kid in movies and plays. I think one of my favorite Broadway shows was *A Funny Thing Happened on the Way to the Forum*. A lot of my play was a tribute to vaudeville as I understand it—that very physical and low comedy which I adore. I loved *Sugarbabies* for the same reasons. I love either Maria Callas or Bert Lahr, but I have more trouble with middle-class comedy.

DiGaetani: What made you become a playwright?

McNally: I was going to become a journalist. I went to the theatre a lot and liked it, and when I was a graduating senior, I read in the school paper that no one had turned in a varsity show, which was an original musical, a great Columbia tradition. Rodgers and Hart wrote varsity shows when they were at Columbia, and Hammerstein wrote a varsity show when he was there a year or two after them. A lot of famous Columbia alumni who went into the theatre wrote a varsity show. I'd been given a full scholarship to Columbia and I felt I'd never been a very good student in terms of giving anything back to Columbia, so I thought I'd try to write the varsity show that year. I wrote this silly show and people liked it. Then I graduated and went off to Mexico to write the great American novel, but while I was there, I also wrote a one-act play. I sent it to the Actors Studio and it got accepted, and suddenly I started writing plays. The next thing I wrote was what I consider my first real play, *And Things That Go Bump in the Night*, which got staged on Broadway and closed two weeks later. Then I got a Guggenheim and with it I wrote *Next*, which was the first play of mine that earned me some money and was successful. It ran about two and a half years Off-Broadway and was done in a lot of theatres around the country. Ever since *Next* I have earned my living as a writer, and somewhere in there I said, "I guess I'm a playwright." But I still like journalism a lot.

DiGAetani: Were you a journalism major at Columbia?

McNally: I was an English major. At Columbia I thought I'd write fiction. I even won a prize and went off to Mexico to write the great American novel, as all English majors are going to do. I never finished it, and I can't even find it, but I did write that first play. It did get staged Off-Off-Broadway, as *This*

Side of the Door; it was painful for me to watch. I felt like I was telling the secrets of my family in that play, and that didn't make me feel good.

DiGaetani: But all writers do that, don't they?

McNally: [Eugene] O'Neill said that if you really want to write a play about your family, you've got to wait until you get older. I was too young.

DiGaetani: Thomas Mann got into a lot of trouble with his family for the very same thing.

McNally: My family never saw my first play, but they did see *And Things That Go Bump in the Night*, which they still thought was about them. My mother always thinks every character is her!

DiGaetani: And in a way she may be right.

McNally: Not really. She's certainly not in *The Ritz* or *The Lisbon Traviata*.

DiGaetani: What kind of work do you plan to do in the future? Would you like to work on a text for an opera?

McNally: Yes, but I'm not a poet. I think good librettos should be terser and with more elevated language than I am comfortable writing. I tend to overwrite, then in rehearsal I get rid of the verbiage, but I think a libretto needs to start where I leave off, if you know what I mean. Maybe one day I'll get the right idea for a libretto. Bernstein was one of the few composers I could get excited about working with. In addition, John Kander, the composer I worked with on *The Rink*, also has real opera potential. In the meantime, I finished my newest play, *Frankie and Johnny in the Claire de Lune*. What do you think of when you hear "Claire de Lune"?

DiGaetani: Debussy.

McNally: The title also means "moonlight." Music figures prominently in this new play. The music from Debussy's "Claire de Lune" is heard in the play at one point. I have also just finished a screenplay on the life of Puccini. Whether or not it gets produced remains to be seen. A star would have to be involved for my screenplay and ideally that will happen. I'm very proud of the screenplay and have had very good reaction to it as literature. Now whether people are going to want to put up $30 to $40 million to make the film! . . . I have been long interested in Puccini. He wrote romantic music, but as a person he was a thoroughly modern man.

DiGaetani: He was also a depressive. He had a horrible marriage with Elvira. In my book on Puccini I present him as a depressive and an intellectual.

McNally: I see him as a misogynist who had great problems with women. I think he was the original macho man.

DiGaetani: He was very dependent on women.

McNally: I think the only woman who ever measured up was his mother.

DiGaetani: And she died on him.

McNally: I think he was very clear in his complicated feelings toward women. They're either whores or saints.

DiGaetani: To get back to your work, what are the major difficulties of writing for the theatre?

McNally: There are a lot of difficult things about maintaining a career in the theatre these days, which adults don't like to go through. Earning a living can be very tiring, and this is not a time when people are eager to support the theatre. I ran into a playwright at the opera last night and he seemed so angry and bitter and defeated and depressed, and that's just not a healthy way to feel if you're going to be creative. What inspired Verdi and Puccini was success and a receptive audience. Those Italian audiences were hungry for a new Puccini opera, hungry. I don't think audiences are hungry for anybody's plays right now, so these are difficult times for playwrights. I also think you need a kind of passion to work in the theatre. It's involvement with other people, it's raising your voice, it's loving, it's hating, it's risking. I don't think there's any rejection a writer experiences more painful than an audience indifferent to his work. A novelist doesn't know if readers like his work, except for the reviews and book sales. But a playwright sees audiences walk out of the theatre or hears the cruel, cruel exchanges at intermissions. You really have to have a thick skin but still be sensitive. I think you have to be stagestruck to be a playwright. I think playwrighting is the most exciting way to write, to explore what it means to be alive and human—using other people, collaborating with them. They can break your heart, actors and directors, but they can also inspire you.

In New York City there are going to be very difficult times for playwrights, and I don't think that's so true around the rest of the country. As the playwright in *It's Only a Play* waits for the *New York Times* reviews, his friends say to cheer him up, "But there's regional theatre." He says, "Don't give me regional theatre! This is my regional theatre—New York. The regional theatre you're talking about is plays that couldn't get done in New York, performed by actors who couldn't get jobs in New York, performed before audiences who wish they lived in New York." That's how I feel. I don't want to be a playwright in Tulsa or Corpus Christi or Wyoming. I live here, and this is my regional theatre. I like this building, Circle Rep, or the Manhattan Theatre Club, and I like Broadway. I care about Broadway as the most perfect real estate for theatre in this country. New theatres put up now, often on college campuses, are too large; they're not well designed for the relationship between stage and audience and the actors. On Broadway, playhouses exist for the presentation of plays, and I'm worried that all that irreplaceable real estate will be torn down.

DiGaetani: That would be horrendous. And what about other playwrights?

McNally: I think there are a lot of good playwrights around, but audiences and critics often don't notice them. This town is not nurturing theatre in the right way. I don't mean Be Kind to Imperfect Plays Week, but there's an enthusiasm for the theatre that has been lost—partially due, no doubt, to the prices of theatre tickets. Even now it costs $50 for a couple to see an Off-Broadway play. People say, "That doesn't matter since *Cats* is still selling out at $50 per ticket," but that's only one show. Yes, Broadway will always survive on one or two big musicals a year, but there has to be room for an audience to take a chance on a play. We have set up this system so that only the greatest play ("greatest" in the most inflated, ignorant sense of the word) can survive, so unless my new play is perceived as "better" than my last play, it fails, and that's stupid. Part of the problem is audience expectations. The play has to be the greatest play Tennessee Williams ever wrote; it can't be another play by Tennessee Williams in which he examines new issues. There's an example of a man who, just because he didn't top himself, was deemed a failure. Small musicals, serious plays, where are they going to play? Not every play was meant to run ten years.

DiGaetani: Could part of the problem be that for middling entertainment people are used to watching television or going to the movies?

McNally: I think that we have more ambitious entertainment in the theatre now. One of the things that makes New York great is theatre, and if this town is going to cavalierly run it out of town, the quality of life will diminish in New York. I don't think theatre will ever totally go in this city, but for New York theatre to be only a theatre of *Cats* and *Les Misérables* . . .

DiGaetani: That would be miserable.

Terrence McNally

Joy Zinoman / 1991

Originally published in *The Playwright's Art: Conversations with Contemporary American Dramatists*, edited by Jackson R. Bryer (New Brunswick, NJ: Rutgers University Press, 1995), 182–204. © 1995 by Rutgers, the State University. Reprinted by permission of Rutgers University Press.

Terrence McNally was born in 1939 [*sic*] in St. Petersburg, Florida, and grew up in Corpus Christi, Texas. After graduating from Columbia University, he worked at the Actors Studio. His first play, *There Is Something Out There* (later revised as *And Things That Go Bump in the Night*), was produced in 1962. Other plays include *The Lady of the Camellias* (adapted from a play by Giles Cooper; 1963), *Next* (1967), *Tour* (1967), *Botticelli* (1968), *Sweet Eros* (1968), *¡Cuba Si!* (1968), *Witness* (1968), *Noon* (1968), *Last Gasps* (1969), *Bringing It All Back Home* (1969), *Where Has Tommy Flowers Gone?* (1971), *Bad Habits* (1971), *Whiskey* (1973), *The Ritz* (1973), *It's Only a Play* (1985), *Frankie and Johnny in the Claire de Lune* (1987), *The Lisbon Traviata* (1989), *Lips Together, Teeth Apart* (1991), and *A Perfect Ganesh* (1993). He has written books for the musicals *The Rink* (1985) and *Kiss of the Spider Woman* (1992) and has adapted *The Ritz* and *Frankie and Johnny* for the movies. His book for *Kiss of the Spider Woman* won the 1993 Tony Award, *Bad Habits* won Obie and Dramatists Guild Hull Warriner awards, and McNally has also received two Guggenheim Fellowships, a citation from the American Academy of Arts and Letters, and the William Inge Award. This interview took place on November 13, 1991.

Interviewer: How did you become a playwright? There are so many easier ways to live.

McNally: I think it was to torment my parents. It made my father very nervous. I always liked writing, and for quite a while I thought I was going to be a journalist. But I think in my heart of hearts I always really wanted to be a playwright. I'm a great believer in taking young people to quality theatre if we're going to have a theatre that endures in the future, because our audiences are dwindling. My parents took me to New York to see *Annie Get Your Gun* with Ethel Merman when I was about five years old, and then when I was about ten or eleven, they took me back to see Gertrude Lawrence in *The King and I*. I think these stayed in the back of my mind as something very, very special, and no movie ever affected me so much. Gertrude Lawrence died about a week after I saw the show, and I cried terribly; to this day, she and Yul Brynner dancing is more vivid than a play I saw last week, including some of my own. It just made this incredible impression on me, so it was always there.

My parents were both New Yorkers, though I pretty much grew up in Corpus Christi, Texas. They used to go to New York once a year to see friends and family, and they would always leave theatre programs on the coffee table for the next six months or so. People don't leave movie stubs on the coffee table; they don't even leave most novels on the table—so the theatre in our house was always something special. Although my parents maybe saw one play a year or two, [plays] were always something very, very special; so I knew about it. I remember how affected my father was by *Death of a Salesman* and how much he loved *South Pacific* and *Kiss Me, Kate*. He would play those albums over and over and over. Growing up in Corpus Christi there was very little theatre. We had a little amateur theatre, and the only play I remember seeing was *Picnic* because our speech teacher was playing the Rosalind Russell role. We were dying to see her rip the guy's shirt off and say, "Marry me, marry me!" Her name was Miss Birmeister, and the only reason we went to see this play was to see her do this big sexy scene.

Eventually I went off to college, to Columbia, when I was seventeen, and I started going to the theatre right away. I really enjoyed it; I think I saw every single play on Broadway. You used to be able to sit in the last row of a Broadway theatre for, I think, $1.90 or some pretty low price. I thought theatre was great entertainment, but I still was going to be a famous journalist. Part of my disillusionment with journalism began in Texas when I was working for our local newspaper. I was very aware of those cameras right there and tape. You're furiously writing the facts down while these other people are videotaping or audiotaping everything. You're driving back to the paper knowing that it's going to take you an hour to write the story, you're not going to get home until one o'clock in the morning, and it's already on the radio and TV. I didn't think I wanted to earn my living competing with a camera.

I also did an interview with Lyndon Johnson, who was in Corpus Christi when he was a senator. He was talking to Lady Bird on the phone and he was flipping through the new issue of *Playboy*, which I put into my story because I thought it was very, very theatrical. Well, he didn't. He called the editor of the *Corpus Christi Caller Times* and said, "Who the hell was this kid you sent?" It was for a summer job in college when I did this interview with him. I loved the drama of him talking to Lady Bird about something boring domestically while he was flipping through *Playboy*. I had to get that into my story. The editor didn't think it would cause much of a fuss, but it did. I think then that I got my first taste of drama, getting an audience, readers, excited; and I liked that.

Then I was about to graduate from Columbia, and they needed something called the Varsity Show. Columbia was probably one of the last universities to put on an all-male show (Columbia College was all male in my day), and they didn't have a writer for it. Rodgers and Hammerstein had written one, Rodgers and Hart had written one, and it was a great tradition; but the school paper said, "There's going to be no Varsity Show this year unless someone writes it." So, sort of like Judy and Mickey saving the day, I decided I would write the Varsity Show. The guy who wrote the music and lyrics was Ed Kleban, who went on to write *A Chorus Line*, and it was directed by Michael Kahn, who is now the head of your Shakespeare Theatre here in Washington. It's the one poster I have in my office; I treasure it. The best thing about it is it says "Book by Terrence McNally, Lyrics by Ed Kleban"—no director. Michael went all over campus with a magic marker writing "Directed by Michael Kahn," so this poster is a true collector's item! They say, "Where's your poster for *Frankie and Johnny* or *Lips Together*?" And I say, "No, this is the one that inspires me!"

At any rate, I graduated, and I went off to write. I thought all I could write was a novel, so I wrote about forty pages of this pretty dreadful novel, and then I wrote a play which I sent in to Actors Studio. I got a letter from a woman named Molly Kazan, who was Elia Kazan's wife. I'm giving a very long answer, I'm sorry. It's how things happen in life. In the movies you come to New York and you stand at the Statue of Liberty and shake your fist at the skyline and say, "I'm going to conquer you, you bitch." I don't think many writers have ever done that. Molly Kazan said, "You show an aptitude for dialogue but not much sense for stagecraft," because I had a scene where a woman was drenched in water and then there's a quick blackout, lights up, and she's in a totally different dress. She said to me, "Do you realize if you pour a bucket of water over a woman, her hair is going to get wet, her makeup will run, her dress will be ruined? You cannot have the lights come up a second later and it's a year later and she's totally changed herself. I think you should come here and just be a stage manager. Have you ever been backstage?" I said, "No." "Do you know any actors or directors?" I assumed she didn't count the Varsity Show at Columbia as a genuine experience, so I said no, and she said, "Here's this job."

So I was stage manager for two years at the Actors Studio. People say, "What was that like?" And I say, "Very menial work: sweeping up and stuff like that." But I kind of eavesdropped a lot, and I saw people like Kazan working with actors. In the Playwrights Unit, some very wonderful plays were developed, like *The Zoo Story* and *The Night of the Iguana*. It was really exciting, and I learned a lot just by being there, because that was my only practical theatre training. I was once asked to act, and I sure got over that bug. I was in a play with Jane Fonda; she and I were brother and sister, and Keir Dullea was my older brother. I thought I was not very good but okay. The day we did it, my knees were literally shaking. I threw up. I came out, my eyes were blinking, I had tics, and it was the most horrible two hours of my life. But I think it's a good way to learn about playwriting—to be an actor and to think moment to moment the way an actor must. I wrote my first real play at the Actors Studio—*Things That Go Bump in the Night*. We did it, and sitting in the audience was someone called Arthur Balliett, who was developing a new Rockefeller program which was going to pay for two new productions of American plays at the Guthrie Theater [in Minneapolis]. So my first play was done at the Guthrie Theater.

Interviewer: That's not bad.

McNally: This was in 1963 when everyone wanted to do new American plays, partially because *Virginia Woolf* was not only so successful on Broadway but was making so many people so much money. Everybody who was writing plays was getting done on Broadway, and my first play, the same play, was done on Broadway the following year, 1964, to probably the most disastrous reviews I've ever gotten. One review began, "The American theatre would be a better place today if Terrence McNally's parents had smothered him in his cradle." I don't think you can get worse than that! They haven't called for my actual death since the first play. I was kind of in shock, I must say. My family came up from Texas. They didn't understand that anyone could be so horrible to their beloved brother/son, and they left the next morning on a 6:00 a.m. flight. My brother said, "You have no place to go but up." That was true, so I went back and worked on a magazine; I had journalism as a thing to fall back on. The play did get one good review, to my memory, and that was in the *Village Voice*. I never quite understood the cruelty of those reviews. There's a lot wrong with the play: it's a first play; it's too long. It purports to tell you what's wrong with American society and with Western culture, and it foresees the end of the world. It's a very ambitious piece, as first plays are. I was going to combine *King Lear*, *Endgame*, and I think *The Oresteia* into one nice drawing room play.

I know why I went on writing plays: because we came in under budget, which is pretty unheard of, the producer, Ted Mann, said, "We have thirty thousand dollars left in the bank; instead of closing the play, I'm going to run it for two full weeks, and I'm going to charge two dollars for the orchestra seats and one dollar for the balcony, and at that price and with the thirty thousand dollars we have left we'll break even in two weeks." I still thought no one would come because the reviews were so derisive. Every performance was sold out, there were pickets in front of the theatre saying: "This is a wonderful new play; it should be seen." That, I think, is probably why I went on writing plays. Otherwise, the experience would have been so devastating I don't know if I ever would have had the courage to do it again.

At any rate, I went back to the magazine, and in that period, I don't know what inspired me—chutzpah, or blind faith. I applied for a Guggenheim. I won one and quit my job at the magazine and started writing plays. I wrote *Next* in that period, which was my second play to be performed. It was very successful. It ran about three years, and that's where I met Jimmy Coco and Elaine May. Elaine directed it, and everything I learned about playwriting I learned from Elaine. We were in previews for six months with that show, and when it finally opened, I couldn't get any friends to come. They said, "We've seen it six times already. Who's going to come?" The critics were going to come because this was in the days when the critics all came on opening night rather than to previews. The producer said, "The play is opening tonight," and I said, "It's not finished; I have work to do." She said, "I'm sorry. It's opening. I've had it with the previews." We opened, and it got very good reviews. Ever since then, I've earned a living as a playwright, though there were years when I've been very close to going under financially. But I haven't had to wait tables, drive a cab, or work for a magazine since the opening night of *Next*, which was in 1969.

Interviewer: In this country that's a pretty impressive record.

McNally: I'm very lucky; I count my blessings. I really do. I never decided to become a playwright. I sometimes still think: I could go to graduate school, I could become an architect. Seriously, what's the cutoff age of being accepted as a pre-med student? I think I've passed it, so I guess I have to do it now. I never really had that moment. I love being a playwright. One day I said I really like what I do for a living, or for my life, which is a wonderful feeling. I think the moment was when I saw Ethel Merman come out in that fringe outfit with a gun and I just didn't want to admit it for twenty years. That's where I wanted to be, in the theatre.

Interviewer: Could *Things That Go Bump in the Night* be produced now on Broadway?

McNally: I assume your question means if it was a brand-new play, not a revival. The odds would be very, very remote. Last season there was one new play done on Broadway. There were about five plays done on Broadway to begin with, I have to say. Most plays done on Broadway come from either regional theatre or the not-for-profit arena; they're transfers. Producers used to read a script and say, "Boy, if I put this on Broadway, I'll get some stars and a famous director and maybe it'll be a hit." That doesn't happen now; people go out to Seattle Rep, or the Alley Theatre, or come to Washington to the Arena [Stage] to see a play, or they bring plays over from London. They want that protection. Very few theatres in New York are willing to take a chance on a brand-new script, which I was very aware of when we did *Lips Together*. We did do a workshop production first, and we opened it cold. We did a workshop production of *Frankie and Johnny* first; with *Lisbon Traviata*, we did a workshop production first. Part of this is because the road has died out. It used to be, traditionally, plays went to three or four cities before they ever dared show their face in New York. Most plays take a real shakedown period. The production of *Lisbon Traviata* that we opened on the West Coast in San Francisco and L.A. was far superior to the New York one because it took me that long to get the text really where I wanted it to be. So, in answer to your question, for a young playwright now, who thinks his play is going to open on Broadway like mine did, the odds are one in a million.

Interviewer: It's opening night, the critics are all there, and you have to stop working on your play. When do you know it's the last brushstroke? When is the painting finished? And could you say something about how you work in the living theatre? Not necessarily what you do in your study in the morning, but what the process is like once you hit the rehearsal room, starting with actually casting.

McNally: When I write the play, it doesn't involve anyone; no one cares that you're off writing it. Once you've given it to the theatre and they say that they're going to put it on, then suddenly you're very connected with lots of people. Your whereabouts are really important; you can't disappear for five days, which is something I like to do, not when you have a play in rehearsal.

I'm very involved in casting. I write plays for specific actors, and I've been very lucky for the most part getting those actors to be in these plays. I wrote *Frankie and Johnnie* for Kathy Bates and F. Murray Abraham, who really did create the play. Murray then decided to do a movie, as opposed to going on with a commercial run, so the vast majority of people who saw that play saw it with a wonderful actor, Kenneth Welsh. With *Lips Together*, four actors were in my mind when I wrote. Three created the roles, and Swoosie Kurtz was an actress that I had known. She was like family, I had seen so much of her work and loved it so much; it was very easy to have her come in.

I don't shop my things around. I go to the theatre a lot, and when I see a good actor, I write their name down. I saw Nathan Lane ten years before anyone else did. I couldn't believe that, after his performance with George C. Scott in *Present Laughter*, he wasn't instantly given a leading role in a television series. With my good luck he stayed sort of a state secret until *Lisbon Traviata*. It was not my idea to cast him in *Lisbon Traviata* at all. I thought he was too young for the part; I didn't even think of him. Someone said, "What about Nathan Lane?" And I did say, "Oh, God, I think he's the best, but I think he's too young for this. But let him come in." He read three words, and he could have stopped right there. All he did was read the first sentences of the phone call when Mendy calls Discophile. Actors either hear you or they don't hear you, and if they don't hear you, the play is doomed.

Chekhov had an experience kind of like I did with my first play. He was devastated. Someone found the script of *The Seagull* and showed it to Stanislavski, who said, "This is wonderful; it was just not performed properly," and got him back into the theatre. I've been very lucky that way. Shakespeare must have had an extraordinary company of actors, and those Moscow Art Players must have been wonderful. I don't think a new play can survive a bad production. When you do *Three Sisters* now, Chekhov is really not being criticized, your production of it is; but on a new play, what we see in the theatre's pretty much what you absorb, and that first person who walks out and says, "My name is Hamlet, Prince of Denmark," is how you accept the role. If he had been a bad actor, I don't think Shakespeare would have wanted to stay in the theatre, and I think his plays would not have been successful, and they would have vanished.

Interviewer: Yet if only those original actors can play those roles, then the play has a limited life. What would you say about that, about the possibility of a playwright's work being reinterpreted by many actors?

McNally: Well, I think it has to be. In a good play there are many ways, as the film of *Frankie and Johnny* shows. Michelle Pfeiffer's is, I think, a really magnificent performance, but it is a very difference interpretation of Frankie, much darker actually than Kathy Bates, who was playing a very defensive hurt woman. Michelle's playing a woman with no self-worth, which I think in many ways is more painful. I think it's a more painful performance to experience.

Interviewer: Were the changes in the film *Frankie and Johnny* made for the actors, or were they for the form?

McNally: They were for the form. When I was writing the screenplay, I would have been thrilled if they had said Kathy was going to do the film. The change was made with that hope. I thought Kathy, and I always wanted Al Pacino to be in it. But it was the change of form. I thought, "They're paying me good money; here's a chance to write a screenplay."

Interviewer: Whose decision was it to cast Michelle Pfeiffer instead of Kathy Bates?

McNally: The decision to cast any film is never the screenwriter's. I have no rights. I do not have cast approval, nor does any screenwriter. It would be as if I bought your house and you came by a year later and were furious because I had painted it pink and put a lot of flamingos in the front yard. It's not your house anymore. Once you sell Hollywood your screenplay, they own it; they can put whoever they want in it. They certainly listened to me. Kathy was very much considered for the role, but finally Paramount, who was going to put up a lot of money to make the film, and Garry Marshall thought the combination of Al and Michelle was better box office, and that it would be a more interesting combination. The fact that Kathy had won an Oscar made her much more in the running than if she had never made *Misery*. Kathy, on the other hand, at the same time *Frankie and Johnny* was being made was doing the film version of *Road to Mecca*, in a role which was created in this country by Amy Irving. Hollywood is very much who's up, who's down this week, and that changes literally every Friday night. In theatre I take full responsibility for the cast; I have cast approval. In a movie, no screenwriter does. If I wanted to raise in excess of twenty-five million dollars to produce my own movie, then, yes, of course, I could hire anybody I wanted. You're dealing with megabucks here, and they have a lot to say about casting.

Interviewer: Had you ever written a screenplay before?

McNally: I wrote *The Ritz*, a play of mine, as a film. That play, though, is pretty much cinematic in its structure. It's as if we put the play on camera; we had very little to do.

Interviewer: But this was really major work. You changed the characters and the structure.

McNally: *Frankie and Johnny* is a two-character play in a tiny little room in real time. No one wants to see a movie like that. I don't want to see a movie like that; it would be boring. So I said, "Here's a chance; I'm going to put the play away. I'm not going to try to drag dialogue around." There's really very few lines from the play left in the screenplay. I wrote those lines for this small play which I thought would never be produced. It's the only play I ever wrote totally for myself; *Frankie and Johnny* is my little private chamber play. I thought no one would produce it, then Lynne Meadows said, "I'll put it on in the little theatre for three weeks," and then it moved to the bigger theatre, and then it moved to the commercial theatre. Actually, it's probably been the most accepted play of mine, the one done the most in other countries and all around the world.

Interviewer: Why do you think that is?

McNally: I have no idea. It's a good lesson to write what you really care about. If you start worrying about whether this will be a good scene for the people in Nebraska so if we do it at Nebraska Rep we'll have a reference, you can get in a lot of trouble. Then you'll start thinking the way Hollywood moguls think: it's all computers and "This is what our audiences want." Tell your story the way you see it. I think when writing is truthful, it tends to interest other people. We all have a way of knowing when the person we're talking to is bullshitting us. Good writers can bullshit as well as the next person, and when our writing gets a little generalized, people turn off. I think we should really say, "This I how I see it. I'm not trying to speak for you." I'm glad I'm a male writer, because a playwright like Wendy Wasserstein suddenly has to be this spokesman for the women of her generation. Thank God, I don't have that weight on me. There's too many middle-aged male playwrights.

Interviewer: Does anyone ever ask you if you feel that you need to be the spokesman for gay American writers?

McNally: People have wanted me to be. It's an interesting issue, and I think about it a lot. When we did *Lisbon Traviata* last year in San Francisco, the gay community there is much more political. They don't seem to do anything in San Francisco but have opinions. No one has a job in San Francisco; they just sit around having opinions. *Lisbon Traviata* is not a politically correct play, which I was aware of, but I just think all one has to do is look at the art of the Soviet Union. Whenever artists are trying to obey a party line, I think that art vanishes fast. The stuff that was happening last year at the [National Endowment for the Arts] I found terrifying. So many artists were quick to write letters to the Dramatists Guild, of which I'm vice-president, because I wrote this ringing editorial saying don't take the NEA grant if it has any strings. To say my new play examines life in Puritan America and it has nothing to do with these homoerotic issues so why should I care means they don't get it. We're all linked. All the arts are connected, and freedom of expression is terribly important.

I was speaking at a theatre convention about a week ago, and somebody told me that the president's new program to take education into the twenty-first century has four major study fields and the arts is not one of them. I didn't know this. As someone who works in the arts, I should know this and I should be doing something about it. That's appalling. We say, "Where are the new young audiences?" and the arts are not even going to be a priority in our educational system! *Lisbon Traviata* was enormously successful in New York City, and at the Mark Taper Forum you couldn't get a ticket for it. It was the biggest hit they ever had there. I think that's wonderful for what it says for an audience's willingness to sit and see a play about four gay men. I think that's a statement, frankly. I thought *The Ritz* said a lot fifteen years ago. It said it through farce; there wasn't a shrill voice in *The Ritz*.

Interviewer: Some people have said *Frankie and Johnny* is a play about the potential for commitment in the modern age or about one-night stands within the gay community.

McNally: No, *Frankie and Johnny* examines intimacy and what people who are over forty do about having a relationship. It's not *Romeo and Juliet*. It's not about people who meet and in one night say, "I'm going to love you forever." It's about love among the ashes, which was a subject that interested me as I got into my forties. I identify with that need, the feeling of loneliness, but also the feeling of wanting to be alone sometimes. When Frankie says, "I just want to be alone and eat ice cream," I understand that enormously. There are days when I don't want to talk to anybody. I just want to watch a really junky movie on HBO and eat lots of Häagen-Dazs; it doesn't make me a bad person. It makes me a human being, and certainly one of the impulses for writing *Frankie and Johnny* was being aware of the number of single men and single women on a Friday night in a video shop renting three or four movies. You know that's how they're going to spend the weekend. They're not going to a singles bar. You know they're not dating. They've got their four movies and the Sunday *Times* and that's how they're going to spend Saturday night. That kind of loneliness interested me in writing this play.

Interviewer: What usually gets you to start writing a play? Do you have to be bugged by something?

McNally: Deadlines. Looking at the bank account and saying, "I'd better go write something now." It's things like that, really, or sometimes an incident in real life. Sometimes a character interests me; sometimes a "what if" situation interests me. *Lips Together* I very much wanted to write for the four actors who agreed to show up April first of last year to rehearse it. Kathy Bates at the last minute got another movie, so Swoosie Kurtz came in; but very much part of the inspiration for that play was knowing I was going to have those four actors. Secretly I knew that if even one of them showed up I'd be very lucky, but to get three of them was great, and then to have Swoosie! Talk about a great replacement! She's someone I always wanted to write for, but when I wrote the play, I heard Kathy saying the lines for sure.

Interviewer: Could you say something about how you feel about the casting of your plays after the first production vis-à-vis multiculturalism? How true should subsequent productions be to the play as written?

McNally: *Frankie and Johnny* with my enthusiastic approval has been done with a cast where both were black. I've also seen a production where Frankie was black, and I've seen a production where Johnny was black. I'm all for it. Part of that is because I come to theatre out of opera, which has been integrated since I first came to New York. I wouldn't even have trouble with a new play of mine being done with an interracial cast. There are other issues that interest me. I saw a *Frankie and Johnny* with a black actress, and the language did not come easily for her. She said, "It's very hard for me as a black woman; this is not how I speak." I was torn. I didn't want her to change the words, but I felt that she was constricted by the language, not opened up. I saw an all-black production of the play in Philadelphia where a few words had been changed, which I didn't like, but I felt the actors were adding rhythms that were not mine because they very much wanted to make it their play. There are cultural differences, and I'm very ambivalent about it. Certain lines said one way didn't sound the same, or certain jokes were lost because the rhythm was different. These are real issues.

I'd like to feel more comfortable writing a black role. The few black roles I've written, I've had problems with the actors saying, "I wouldn't say this." There's a black role in *It's Only a Play*, and it's always very painful when somebody says, "A black man wouldn't say this." No one's ever said to me, "A woman wouldn't say this," or "A forty-year-old man wouldn't say this" or "An eight-year-old wouldn't say this." I would like to see our theatre reflect the multiculturalism of our society, but we've all got to be able to find a way to work together. It's tense. I think there are some wonderful black writers around. I wish more of their work was getting done in a larger arena. I think that every actor should feel that, if I'm up to it, I can play Hamlet, I can play Chekhov, and I can play Neil Simon—just as I should be able to write any character I want so long as it's truthful and my imagination allows me to go there. If we get bogged down in discussions about rhythms and speech and vocabulary, it's painful, but I can't really give you a tidy answer to this. It's something the theatre should be thinking about.

I was just at a seminar on color-blind casting which the Dramatists Guild sponsored. It was filled with actors, and there was only one other playwright there. I thought so many playwrights would be there. The audiences at my plays are mainly white, and I'm white, but that's not the world I live in, and I want to lose my inhibitions to write more black characters. I was very happy when I wrote my first black character, but it has not been easy whenever that play's been done. I'd like to find a way to get beyond that as a theatre artist, because, if our theatre doesn't start reflecting this country, what is called the theatre is going to drift more and more away from "the real world." That's one reason a lot of young audiences aren't interested in theatre. *Lips Together* takes place in sort of a ghetto, a white resort on an island, so no reality can intrude. They're three miles out in the Atlantic Ocean in that play. There's things I want to talk about in our culture, and I've got to find the courage and the freedom to do it with other theatre artists.

Interviewer: If the theatre does reflect what's going on in our society, then it's reasonable that that strain or tension would also be reflected in that theatre, isn't it?

McNally: I'd like it to be onstage in the play and not in the rehearsal room is what I'm saying. That's no fun. Three weeks of rehearsal go by so quickly; I don't know if anyone who has not written or directed or acted in a play realizes how hard it is to get a play even remotely approaching anything decent. Those three weeks go by so quickly, and a waste of time in a rehearsal is a luxury that you can't afford.

Interviewer: What about directors? You've talked a lot about actors.

McNally: Do I like them? I've no desire to direct, so I'm very grateful for them. I work with a small group of directors I trust, and we can work in shorthand, which is nice. When I say how involved I am in rehearsals, there is a point where I cut off. When the leading lady comes up to the director and says, "Should I wear the red shoes or the blue shoes?" I would say, "I don't care. I'm busy, don't ask me!" but you have to say, "Oh, darling, maybe the blue." To the actress it's very important that she feel comfortable in the red or blue shoes. Also, if you get bored at rehearsals, as a playwright you can leave. Directors are very patient people. I think they work very hard for their money, a good director does, I really do. I'm grateful to good directors.

I think, though, you find people you work well with. Geraldine Page did a play of mine, and she couldn't hear the way I write, nor could she inhabit the world I was trying to create. It was a disaster. I'd be one of the first to say she's one of the great actresses our country has ever produced, but she just didn't hear. She was reading the music from a different chart; she was singing somebody else's score. Someone like Nathan Lane, you know in three seconds; it's not a question of after three weeks of rehearsal. We knew in three words he was Mendy. More than that, I knew that this was an actor that I would want to work with the rest of my life, because the actors who hear you become an extension of you, and they also make you braver as a playwright. I think I took a lot of risks as a writer in *Lips Together*, but I had four actors I could trust not to make me look bad; they would know the transitions I meant.

I don't think I've written a stage direction other than "Enters," "Leaves," or "Dies." You have to write those three. Otherwise, it gets very confusing. I don't say, "Sitting stage right and crossing his legs on that line." Who cares? In *Frankie and Johnny*, in the script I said they're in bed naked, but I never indicated when they got dressed. I went to see the first production of it in Houston with my mother and brother, and my mother said, "They're naked!," and I said, "It'll be over in a second." One hour later they're both still stark naked, for the whole first act! I said to the director, "They're naked." And she said, "You said they're naked." I said, "Yes, but they get dressed." She said, "You didn't put it in the script." So the audience sat there and there wasn't a laugh, not a titter, for the entire first act. I was so embarrassed. My mother now waits; she doesn't to go to openings anymore. After the first play, she waited twenty-five years until I got a hit and went to see *Frankie and Johnny*, and I did it to her again!

Interviewer: In *Frankie and Johnny* you have Frankie spit out one four-letter word over and over again. Do we have to have that kind of language?

McNally: Do we have to? I think it implies that, when you come to see a play, I'm not going to do anything that upsets you, or my characters won't. That traditional notion of theatre I kind of reject. I go to the theatre to be appalled, to be stimulated, to be upset. I can't imagine four-letter words today being offensive to anyone. The theatre to me is not a sanctuary from the language, when people say the language you hear on the subway and in the streets. I don't think the theatre should be a sanctuary, but that's an aesthetic decision about what you want art to be. I want plays that try to deal with contemporary issues in a way that holds together. Otherwise, you're doing revue sketches of what's on everybody's mind this day.

The fact you say, "Do I have to?" implies that you expect something from the theatre that maybe I don't agree with. I was never bothered in the sixties and seventies when actors came out in the audience and confronted me. That was my generation, so I don't expect the theatre to be comfortable. In fact, one of the reasons that I rail so much against opera productions and the way Shakespeare is done is that it is so boring. Shakespeare is not a boring writer, but he's produced as a boring writer. Operas have been just stripped of any passion. I can't believe that someone like Puccini didn't want to rip your heart out with *La Bohème*. It was about young love, and dying at a time when a lot of people didn't live beyond twenty-five, and now we present *La Bohème* as an antiseptic experience.

I just saw a production of *Traviata* where Violetta had AIDS, and I thought it was a wonderful idea, if only for the last act where she was dying in a ward with other beds. That's what happens if you're poor, you know. In the libretto she says, "I have no money," but usually she's in a single room the size of the Metropolitan Opera House! If you have no money, you don't get a room like that. I thought this director made the experience of death and being broke very, very real, and I think a young audience would say, "Hey, *Traviata* is about something which can affect my life. It's not just this boring nineteenth-century thing for my parents to go to."

Interviewer: How did you develop your love for the opera?

McNally: I didn't. It just happened. I heard three bars of Puccini and I loved it. I was at a parochial school with a very strange nun, I guess, because she let us listen to Puccini love duets every Friday. It was a very tormented convent, obviously. I thought it was very beautiful. Everybody else had paper clips and airplanes and was napping, and I just thought it was beautiful. Last summer I was going to Seattle to speak at an opera seminar, and the woman next to me said, "I heard you're going to speak at our opera company. It's one of the great opera companies in America. I really want to get into opera. How do you get into opera?" I said, "I think it's like liver. You either like it or you don't. You're fine not liking opera. It doesn't make you a better person." You either think that it's wonderful that people sing about these things and get stabbed and sing about it for another ten minutes, or you think it's totally stupid and have no interest in it. I've never successfully gotten any of my friends to like opera. In fact, my parents now really hate opera, because ever since the sixth grade it was, "Shut that door!" I started then saving all my money to buy opera records. Probably one of the reasons I write plays is because opera to me is theatre.

Interviewer: Could you tell us how you go about writing a play? What is your writing process?

McNally: It's very simple, really. You have to go to the typewriter; that's all you have to do. I have a word processor now, and you turn it on and something happens after a while, and that's all writing is to me. If I don't go to the typewriter, I don't write. I'm not being facetious. I think it's a very practical thing, and deadlines help a lot. You realize that *Lips Together* opens April twelfth and it's December twelfth and you haven't written a word of the play. I carry them up in my head for a long time. That process is very hard to talk about. It's partially my unconscious. It's usually a year or two before I sit at the typewriter, but people say, "God, you write plays so quickly." Well, I think walking around with things in your head for two years is not exactly quickly. The typing part is pretty quick if you really know what you're doing in a play. Once I know what my characters are doing, the play just comes very, very easily. I learned from Elaine May that playwriting is about what characters are doing, not what they are saying. My first play, *Things That Go Bump in the Night*, is just too conversational, people sitting around talking—which people seldom do in real life. This is a totally artificial situation right now; we're sitting around talking, but this is not real life. Elaine taught me: what are your characters doing? That's how she directed the actors. She never said, "You're feeling this here, Jimmy. You should be sensing that." She'd say, "You've got to open the door. You've got to go over there and do this." Theatre is not all that different from real life, and I think I'm usually doing something; so when I write a play, I remember that it's not about two people sitting around having a conversation. It's about people doing something, and *Lips Together* is filled with the minutiae of daily life, but everybody's doing something. They're sweeping the deck or they're checking the chlorine in the pool, but they're not sitting around talking, even though it looks like they are. I'm glad I learned that at such an early age, because you can write ten plays before you learn anything about playwriting. I really give Elaine an enormous amount of credit, though if she had directed my second play we would still be in previews!

Interviewer: What is it like for you when you work on a musical?

McNally: Writing the book for a musical is very, very difficult. I find that it's not enough to love musicals to write a good book for one. I learned a lot working on the book of *The Rink*. It was a wonderful experience. I'd never worked with stars like Liza [Minnelli] and Chita [Rivera] before. It was very much our show when it opened; it was a wonderful collaboration. It got a standing ovation at every preview. Then Frank Rich came and reviewed it and said, "I hate this show," and the audience stopped standing. They'd go, "I like it," under their breath. It was also a rare thing, an original musical. There are not many. Usually we're seeing a musical of *Romeo and Juliet*. It was one of the happiest theatre experiences I've ever had until the morning of the reviews. His review was very, very condemning. It was the kind of review that made audiences not enjoy the show anymore, if you know what I mean. He really profoundly disliked what the show was about. In a funny way, he never reviewed the craft of the songs, the script, the choreography, or the acting. I'm doing another musical now, an adaptation of *Kiss of the Spider Woman*. I'm finding again that everything I've learned about playwriting is gone when I try to write a musical.

Interviewer: Have you ever learned anything from a critic?

McNally: That's very hard to answer. Not the way I can say what I learned from Elaine May, what I learned from working with Chita Rivera, what I learned from all sorts of people. Critics are observers who are outside the glass window looking in; they don't go through the joy and agony of the rehearsal period. That's where you learn about your play. All you have to do is sit in the middle of the audience, and if the audience is enjoying it, you don't really need Frank Rich to tell you that. I can't say I've learned a lot. Now that I've written enough, someone occasionally will write kind of an overview essay about my work and point out themes, and I can see similarities.

Interviewer: Would the New York theatre be better if the critics were eliminated?

McNally: Maybe. I think it's going in circles; because you have play-wrights saying the critics are the bane of our existence, yet if they like us then we spend fifty thousand dollars in the Sunday *New York Times* saying, "Wonderful! Fabulous! Brilliant!" One way to break the power of the *New York Times* is not to advertise in its pages. No one's willing to do that. In the meantime I don't think the standard of criticism is very high because people want a consumer tip—do I want to see this or not? The *New York Times* has started excerpting the news in a little box just this past week, like *USA Today*; so I'm pretty sure they'll do the same with criticism, as a service to their readers—so they don't have to read the review anymore. Frank Rich: yes, no. Good, got that dealt with. "Honey, we don't have to go see the new play, it's terrible." I don't envy the critics because they're not allowed to have intelligent considered opinions. They have to say, "This is Mr. McNally's deepest and richest play yet," or it will read like they didn't like it. Every play

I've ever seen I've liked things about and I've disliked things about, including *Hamlet*. I think *Hamlet* has some real bad stuff in it, but because it's *Hamlet* I can have a real opinion about it.

Interviewer: Why do you think the level of criticism has fallen?

McNally: I don't think the level of criticism has fallen. There are fewer papers. People are less willing to spend the money; they want some sort of guide. I found myself falling into it once. I was out of New York, and I came back and the paper said, "Martha Graham Ballet Performance Tonight, *Rite of Spring*," and she was ninety years old when she choreographed it. I called a friend and said, "What kind of reviews did Martha Graham's new ballet get?" As I said that, I realized that's what I'm objecting to. Martha Graham at age ninety with all of the masterpieces she's given the world hardly needs the approval of Anna Kisselgoff; but I was doing this because I felt I didn't know enough about modern dance and I needed a guide. Should I see it or not? Then I said, "Don't tell me, don't tell me!" I bought the tickets and I loved it.

Interviewer: Is there any way that one can make the audiences feel confident in their own judgment?

McNally: That's not the problem.

Interviewer: What about the price?

McNally: The price, of course, is very, very high. It's getting just people who love theatre. How many baseball games are interesting? Nine out of ten are incredibly boring, but you're a fan of baseball so you go for the game and it's exciting. That's why you go to the theatre, to say, "Hey, this is great." But unless you're developing a new audience the way I was hooked for life at age five, then you don't get a theatre audience. I think by the time we're teenagers we're so opinionated that it's almost too late. We've got to do something as a theatre community. I don't think that we as a community are doing enough. Where are the five-year-olds at our theatres, the ten-year-olds?

Interviewer: What can we do about that? What can anybody do? Most people who come to the theatre want to have a good time; they didn't pay their money to have a bad time.

McNally: What's their expectation of theatre? We live increasingly in a society of such hype. You've got to be a musical like *Phantom of the Opera* or a play like *Death of a Salesman*. There's no room for anything less. The Hollywood mentality has seeped into the theatre, and people are only interested in producing blockbusting shows. At this theatre convention, all these producers were saying, "Do you know what it costs to do a big Broadway musical? A minimum of six and a half million dollars." But who said that's the only kind of theatre you can produce? You can produce a small two-character play Off-Off-Broadway; that's theatre. People are confusing Broadway with theatre. Theatre is very healthy in this country. Six blocks of real estate is not where the theatre is.

Interviewer: But it's not only the people in New York who need the theatre, and not only the people in New York who see the theatre, and not only the largest theatre in every city that is producing art. We fall into those traps of thinking that our time is limited, our money is limited, our attention span is limited. Isn't it about people feeling confident themselves about art, instead of someone else having to tell them whether it's good or bad? Come and have some patience and see and be moved.

McNally: Something has happened to our audiences. The fact that Arthur Miller had to go to London to get his new play on, that Edward Albee has had a play now for six or seven years that is going to open in Houston: men who have created works like *Salesman* and *Virginia Woolf*! That they should have to go begging says something about the way the powers that be have rejected two of our most distinguished playwrights because they are not guaranteed money-making machines.

Interviewer: But New York is not America.

McNally: I can only talk about the New York theatre. Finally, all theatre is regional. New York is a region. Its premier theatre of years and years was Broadway. Now you take away Off-Broadway, and New York has one play running, by Neil Simon, and ten musicals, most of which have been running for over six years, which everybody's seen now six times.

Interviewer: Are there plays that you particularly like, now?

McNally: Of mine?

Interviewer: No, not of yours. Productions that you've seen lately that you can recommend.

McNally: There are so few plays that are running in New York right now. I think that *Dancing at Lughnasa*, which is an Irish play, is very beautiful. I think it's wonderful. That's the only play that's opened on Broadway so far this year. Off-Broadway, the play at Circle Rep called *Babylon Gardens* was very unsuccessful, but I think that Timothy Mason is going to write a wonderful play. The reason he's going to write a wonderful play is because Tanya Berezin, the artistic director there, is committed to him, and she's doing his first three plays until he gets it right.

No one even remembers Arthur Miller's first play; Tennessee Williams's first play closed in Boston. Edward Albee was Off-Broadway for ten years before he wrote *Virginia Woolf*. At the opening night of *Virginia Woolf*, I remember that Abe Burrows came over to Edward and said, "Welcome to

the theatre, young man." I just wanted to puke. But that was the attitude—
welcome to the real theatre. At this theatre convention, the head of the
Shubert [Theatre] said, "You should try to put that play of yours in a big theatre and try to sell a thousand seats a night. You're in a three-hundred-seat
theatre, and of course you can run for six months." Try to do a play in a real
big theatre, as if, we're the big boys, give us the real estate.

The big producers keep saying, "Where are the playwrights?" The playwrights are everywhere. They don't want to know about the playwrights
because it involves a risk and everyone is scared right now because of our
economy, which I understand the reality of. Don't say, where are the playwrights? The question is, where are the producers? A producer used to be
someone of vision and courage who said, "I'm going to put this playwright
with this actress and this director and let's see what happens." He didn't sit
around reading the papers and saying, "Oh, here's a play that got a good
review. Let's go see about doing that." He created on an empty bare stage.
They took chances, and you can still do that. You don't have to spend six
million dollars. That's the Shubert's idea of producing, to do another *Cats* or
another *Phantom of the Opera*. They don't want to produce anymore.

There aren't many young producers. All the young people who are going
into the theatre now out of the Yale Drama School program in theatre management are being absorbed by the not-for-profits, which are the healthy
arena of the American theatre. Suddenly, they're at Seattle Rep, the Old
Globe, the Mark Taper Forum. They're all working, and they're wonderful young minds, but they're working in the not-for-profit arena. We're not
getting the new David Merricks, Roger Stevenses, and Robert Whiteheads
on Broadway. Joe Papp really was the end of an era. His plays said, "Joe
Papp presents." They didn't say, "Joe Papp in association with Suntory, Mit-
subishi, and ten other conglomerates presents." When *Frankie and Johnny*
was moved commercially, it had twelve producers for a two-character play!
Nick and Nora has many, many producers. It used to say, "David Merrick
presents," and it meant that the taste of David Merrick presents this evening, or the taste of Joe Papp; Joe Papp thinks this is a good play for you to
see. No one is making those personal statements anymore. The producer
was always a very, very strong force in theatre, and without him now, we've
drifted. Broadway is now competing with rock video; it's competing with
restaurants. People say, "We've got to find a musical that the Japanese tourist will like. It's got to be very visual. With *Phantom of the Opera*, they know
the plot going in, so we can run." My plays don't play well if you don't speak
English. I'm sorry, I'll do my best next time.

Interviewer: Would you care to comment about whether playwriting is a craft or an art?

McNally: With questions like that you always wind up talking about semantics more than anything. Yes, it's a craft, and if it's good, it's an art; but it's not some mystical thing. Writing plays is very practical. Theatre is the most practical art form I can think of. One, you have to deal with a lot of people, and it takes place in real time. A novelist or a screenwriter can jump-cut from here to there. In the theatre, if I'm sitting here I have physically to get up and you have to watch me go through that curtain. That could be really boring to watch, but there's no other way for me to get back there. That's all craft. That's another reason I don't want to direct a play: actors say, "Should I come in stage left or right?" I don't know. I just wrote it, and I just say, "She enters"; I don't say, "stage left" or "stage right." It's not that I'm making fun of something I take very seriously, but I'm trying to convey that it's very, very practical. Yes, it's a craft; I think a good play, of course, is art; and other than that, I think we just get into semantics.

Interviewer: Do you write to discover what you feel about something?

McNally: That's not the motive to write something, but I do discover something and how I feel about things while I'm writing a play. But it's not the motive. I don't say, "Well, I'll write a play about suicide so I can see what it would be like to kill myself." Writing a play is not psychotherapy. But I do learn an awful lot about myself, and it makes me more aware of other people. I would like to think that my work is about equal parts autobiographical feeling, imagined feeling, and people I've observed. I've never created a character that I've had no empathy for, and I've never based a character one hundred percent on a person I've known in real life. It's a blend, and in the process you learn something about yourself.

Interviewer: Do you have a most and a least favorite piece of your own work, and why?

McNally: I definitely, quite objectively, think that *Lips Together, Teeth Apart* is my best play. I'm proudest of it. I think I'm more affectionate toward *Lisbon Traviata*. My least favorite? It's not the kind of thing I sit around making a list of. I have affection for the deluded immature person who wrote *Things That Go Bump in the Night*; he wasn't a bad person, he was just overambitious. I don't hate him for writing a play like that. I can't say I'd rush to see a revival of that play. *Where Has Tommy Flowers Gone?* I have enormous affection for; it's considered a sixties play, so it doesn't get done. Technically, in terms of the craft of playwriting, I thought a lot of *The Ritz*. It was very good writing. But because of AIDS, *The Ritz* will probably never be done again. I think the second act of that play has some really wonderful farce situations.

I'd love to write another farce, but I don't have another three years of my life to devote to a play. Farce is the hardest form of theatre for the writer, and it's hard for the actors. Farce has to be boring for the first hour to get all the plots going, for it all to pay off. I spent the loneliest month of my life in Washington at the National Theatre getting *The Ritz* right. Fortunately, the president was gone, Congress was gone; there was no one in town— about twelve people and I wandered in to see this play. So we were very free to make huge changes. Actors went around carrying pages, but we found that play at the National Theatre one very dark December and January. We were here for four weeks. Farce really needs the out-of-town experience. I'd love to do another one. Just to have a line like "I think I'll go in the next room" bring down the house is so nice. It's not funny, but you know what they're going to see when they go in the next room. I've written another farce, called *Up in Saratoga*, which we tried out at the Old Globe Theatre [in San Diego], and I hope one day it will be done in New York. It has eighteen characters, it's in five acts, and it's a period piece. Needless to say, producers are not looking for eighteen-character five-act period plays right now.

Interviewer: Do you have any suggestions of where young playwrights should go to get the nurturing you mentioned?

McNally: Well, I got my early nurturing from actors. I would just see actors whose work I liked or Off-Off-Broadway theatre groups. I've never been a particularly naturalistic writer, so if a theatre company was well known for doing very naturalistic productions, it was not a good company for me to try and hang out with and get interested in my work. With *Next*, Jimmy Coco was an actor I saw in a play and I thought he was fabulous, so I wrote the play for him. He said, "Oh, that's great. I'm this character actor nobody's ever heard of. Who's going to do a play for me?" I don't know if you know *Next*, but it's very much a vehicle. He had this play which I thought would maybe never get produced, and I had left the magazine and was on my Guggenheim. He was off at summer stock doing a play, but the fourth play was canceled. So the producer hysterically said, "We don't have a fourth slot. Oh God, what are we going to do?" And Jimmy Coco said, "I've got this play," and that's how things get done in the theatre. Not through agents. So many young writers think they need an agent. No, network through actors, other playwrights, and up-and-coming theatre groups.

Somebody's doing *Bad Habits* in New York and begged me to come. I said, "I don't know if my nerves could take it. Once I'm done with a play, then I feel I have no business being in the theatre because I'm not working that night. I love being in rehearsal. I hate watching the play once it opens. The other night I went to see *Lips* because an understudy was on, and I really had to make myself stay. Once during the first act I walked out, and I missed the first ten minutes of Act II; but I said, "No, you've got to watch the performance." On opening night I'm sitting there right in the middle of the audience, and people say, "How can you sit there?" I don't feel nervous because I feel I'm working. But to criticize the understudy is the stage manager's and the director's job. I very seldom say anything to actors other than, "Where do you want to eat after the play?" or "You were terrific." I can think an actor is doing a scene wrong, but if I tell them and the director tells them, then he's had two different versions of what he's supposed to do. I learned early on that you're sabotaging your own play if you start criticizing the actor.

Interviewer: When you saw that Geraldine Page was wrong for the part in your play, did you sit quietly or did you do something?

McNally: We had a lot of fights. We had made a mistake. She was the star of the play, so we weren't going to fire her. What can I say? I was in agony for the three weeks. It wasn't fun. I didn't look forward to being in rehearsal because there was no collaboration. She wasn't having joy speaking my lines, and I wasn't having joy listening to her speak them; so I have no impetus to go home and make it better or enrich it. It was just painful. It's a play called *It's Only a Play*, which closed out of town. It was a Broadway play that closed in Philadelphia. Manhattan Theatre Club redid the play a few years later with Christine Baranski (the first time I worked with her), and the play was quite successful then.

It's not just because of Geraldine Page that this production worked whereas the original production didn't; it was a series of things. I should have known from Geraldine Page's other work that she was not the kind of actress for my plays. They're too artificial for someone as naturalistic as Geraldine Page. Kathy Bates is not a naturalistic actress. People kept saying about *Frankie and Johnny*, "You've written your first naturalistic play." An audience can be fooled that if you eat meat loaf and make an omelet onstage that it's naturalism. *Frankie and Johnny* is a very artificial play. That's why so much of the dialogue had to go in the screen version because a movie is automatically naturalistic unless it's a total fantasy. With Geraldine Page, it was bad casting and we used bad judgment, but it was a star who wants to be in your play, and that means it's going to Broadway. I was thrilled the day she agreed to do it. It was only after the first day of rehearsal that I thought that this may not be the ideal combination of actress and role.

Interviewer: What terrifies you?

McNally: In theatre nothing terrifies me. I think it's very exciting. I think it's great fun. I did write a play called *It's Only a Play*, and I really try to keep reminding myself of that. The point is to write the next one. People in this country get so worried about topping themselves, about overcoming a failure. Just go on and write the next one. Shakespeare is the best inspiration in the world. From hits to flops he's all over the place; it's a roller coaster. He goes directly from *Hamlet* to *Timon of Athens*. Playwrights are only mortals. If you have actors who want to do your plays, consider yourself lucky and get on with it; so I'm not terrified. I think it's challenging; I think it's fun. I'm fifty-two years old as of last week, and I do this because it's fun. No one makes you write plays; the world could sort of get along without me turning out a play every year, so I do this because I enjoy it enormously. It gives me great pleasure, and working in the theatre is, I think, its own reward. I think people always want to know how much playwrights earn. Well, most years it's very, very, very little. If you have a success, you earn quite a bit.

You have to enjoy the collaborative process to work in the theatre. If you don't, you're going to be unhappy as an actor or director, or as a ticket taker. It's body contact in the theatre, and if you don't enjoy that, go off to your desert island and write your novel or your sheaf of poems. You have huge fights in rehearsals sometimes, but they're healthy fights because it's family fighting; it's trying to make it better. An actor whom I really trust and work well with (the four that were in this last play) can say, "This line doesn't work for me," and I don't take it as a personal statement like "I don't like you, Terrence." They're saying, "This line doesn't work for me," and we try to make it better. It's family; it's trying to find a continuity in your work. That's why I work with the same people over and over as much as I can, and I go to the theatre a lot. I'd never met Kathy Bates when I wrote *Frankie and Johnny* for her, but I'd seen her in three or four plays and I thought that she was one of the greatest actresses I'd ever seen. She was so present and physical for me; it was easy to write for her. Most of the actors I've written for I didn't know. Now they're friends. When I wrote the second part for Kathy, she was a friend. With Nathan Lane, I can't believe it's taken ten years for America to recognize what I thought was the finest comic actor since Jimmy Coco. I'm just lucky I've had Nathan all to myself the last couple of years. Now the worlds of Hollywood and Broadway revivals have discovered him, but I hope Nathan and I can work together again soon.

The Playwright's New Directions: Terrence McNally, Exploring Parts Unknown

Judith Weinraub / 1994

Originally published in *The Washington Post*, September 26, 1994, D1. © 1994 The Washington Post. All rights reserved. Used under license.

Corpus Christi, Texas. The early 1950s.

Young Terrence McNally is doing what he always does on Saturday afternoon: listening to a broadcast of the Metropolitan Opera. As the sounds of Verdi's *Rigoletto* issue forth from the family's only "good radio," his parents listen to a football game in the car. And Terrence—totally absorbed—moves makeshift figures across a miniature stage he has fashioned after illustrations in *Opera News*.

"It was a finite world you could control," he says now.

Fast-forward to New York City. 1956. Scholarship student McNally has just arrived at Columbia University, one of the first from his high school to go east to college. He unpacks his bags and heads straight down Broadway to see *Damn Yankees*. The next night: *Will Success Spoil Rock Hunter?* Then *Cat on a Hot Tin Roof*. Over the next four years—often studying at intermission—he will spend as many nights there as he can.

"The opera, the theatre—I had to make these things come true for me," says McNally today.

And he has. The author of so many plays he says he can't keep count of them (twenty-eight have been produced, in addition to several TV scripts and two screenplays), McNally, aged fifty-four, has become an enduring presence on the American stage. His two newest plays will be mounted in New York this season (one next month, the other in the spring), joining the long-running, Tony-winning *Kiss of the Spider Woman*, for which he wrote the book. The drama he wrote between those works, *A Perfect Ganesh*, is currently receiving its first production outside New York, at Arena Stage.

He treats his considerable achievement modestly. "You learn there's nothing precious about writing," he says. "It's a job like any other."

Artistic success, of course, is an elusive thing, not given to easy explanations—nor, for that matter, to a straight path. But beyond McNally's obvious talents, his career is a tribute to some early influences (a nun who played Puccini love duets for her sixth-graders, a high school English teacher whose influence so transformed him that he dedicated a play to her and still stays in touch); some good old American virtues—persistence, perseverance, discipline; and the power of love and friendship.

"You don't have to be tough," he says of a profession in which he insists he puts his self-esteem on the line with each new production. "But you need people who love you and whom you love back."

The fragile boundaries of both love and friendship are investigated in *A Perfect Ganesh*, a tale of two women who abandoned plans for their yearly island vacations to seek healing in India. (The story was triggered by a chance meeting with two American women on a train in Rajasthan almost a decade ago.)

The themes of homophobia and AIDS, which have found their way into several of McNally's recent plays, are part of *Ganesh* as well. And racism. Though an openly gay man, McNally is irritated when labels are applied to his or anybody else's plays. "It becomes a way of distancing to refer to a gay play or an AIDS play or a black play. I think it's belittling—but I think it's going to end, and I hope I'm a part of that."

Whatever critics call it (New York reviews were generally favorable and the play was extended beyond its scheduled run, but the *Washington Post's* Lloyd Rose termed it "lackluster"), *Ganesh* is praised by McNally's peers as a new direction for him.

"He's always challenging himself," says playwright Wendy Wasserstein, a close friend. "Just when he's written one kind of play, he goes on to another. . . . And knowing the body of his work, it's amazing that he did this. It culls from many sources, from the comedic in a very Terrence way to Tennessee Williams to a sort of mysticism. And there is an innate theatricality to it."

"I thought [*Ganesh*] was Terrence's most probing play," says Shakespeare Theatre artistic director Michael Kahn, who long ago directed the Varsity show McNally wrote at Columbia, where they were friends. "He's writing more and more about people's emotional condition. . . . He was getting to a part of the center of his characters with these two women in a way I'd never seen it—not just relying on his cleverness."

What Kahn calls clever, McNally sees as satire. But he agrees he's left it behind. "In my earlier work, I was very much the star of my plays. The author's voice is everywhere. My opinion of the characters and the world they lived in was my main concern—a kind of critique of the feel-good generation, people who wanted to be excused from human belittlement, let alone suffering. . . . Now I like to think I am less a character and less controlling of my characters' lives and destinies."

McNally has been writing plays since he was fourteen, when he penned an imagined—and totally inaccurate—story about George Gershwin. His enthusiasm was nurtured by trips with his parents to New York and musicals like *Annie Get Your Gun* and *The King and I*.

They expected him to be a journalist. But his passion for the theatre made him change course. After college—and a grunt job at the Actors Studio—his first produced play, *And Things That Go Bump in the Night*, was a Broadway flop. But eventually a Guggenheim writing fellowship freed him, and success came Off-Broadway not much later with *Next*, a one-act play about an overweight, overage man who has to report for an Army physical. He's been earning his living as a playwright ever since.

Not that it's been easy. "I've had about four careers," he says as he ticks off the successful and not-so-successful plays that he's written. After a particularly humiliating one—the failure of the comedy *Broadway, Broadway* before it even got to New York—he didn't write for three or four years. It was only after a stranger in a New York store recognized his voice from radio's "Metropolitan Opera Quiz" (he'd been a regular for years) that he realized he was waiting for the theatre to seek him out rather than continuing to write.

"I could just picture it," he says, tracing the imagined obit headline in the air. " 'Terrence McNally dead at forty-two. Earlier in his career, he wrote some plays.' "

"But nobody's going to produce your plays if you haven't written them."

He pulled himself together, rewrote the flop as *It's Only a Play*, and saw it successfully produced at the Manhattan Theatre Club, which has been his primary theatrical home ever since. It has staged seven of his plays, including *Lips Together, Teeth Apart*; *The Lisbon Traviata*; and *Frankie and Johnny in the Claire de Lune*.

For some time now, his plays, always stylishly written, have reflected the pains of contemporary life. Loneliness, AIDS, racism, homophobia are givens—all part of a larger interconnected picture. And it's that larger view he cares about. "I'm more interested in what links us as human beings rather than what separates us," he says.

For example, his new *Love! Valour! Compassion!*, which is set in a country home where eight gay men gather over the course of three summer holiday weekends, could be seen as a gay play, or even as an AIDS play (one of the characters is HIV-positive). But McNally sees it less symbolically and wants a broader audience to identify with it.

At a recent rehearsal of the play at the offices of the Manhattan Theatre Club, McNally watched and listened to the actors discuss their characters—in particular a line that one of the actors had difficulty with because of a racist reference. Conversation continued for nearly a half-hour before McNally finally volunteered that he had written the line to make a specific point and thought they should stick with it.

"I don't want to inhibit them," McNally said later, explaining why he hadn't weighed in earlier. "They're the ones doing it onstage, and I have to have a loving and supportive relationship with them. They're trying to find these characters.

"And they need to become a family. That's part of the process."

He understands the importance of family in the theatre and has virtually created his own, frequently writing for a small coterie of actors. *Ganesh*, for example, was written for actress Zoe Caldwell. His personal relationships have often come from this world too, including two of his long-term emotional commitments (to playwright Edward Albee, with whom he lived for eight [*sic*] years, and the late actor Robert Drivas).

McNally has not talked much about those experiences—at least not publicly. He says he's reluctant to betray confidences or talk about other people's personal lives. He's even close-mouthed about the year he spent after college tutoring John Steinbeck's children. "His widow is still alive," he says simply.

He's voluble, however, about his pre-opening-night jitters as he helps ready *Love! Valour! Compassion!* for its first performance on October 11. "It's hard for someone who wants to be perfect all the time," he says. "I don't think I'm unduly hysterical. But no one sees what's good in my plays—or the flaws—as much as I do."

He's turned out virtually a play a year recently, though last year he wrote two. Arena's associate artistic director, Laurence Maslon (who directed *Ganesh*), thinks his constant output may have made it easier for McNally to concentrate on his own writing rather than get too involved in the company's current production of *Ganesh*.

"Terrence has moved on, and wishes us all the luck in the world. He told us, 'You must think you understand the play or you wouldn't be producing it. Go ahead and do what you think works for your people and your space.' It shows he's embraced the message of the play—to let things happen as they happen—to allow, to accept, to be."

McNally takes that message—and its relevance to how we all spend our days—even further. "There's divinity in everybody," he says. "The play tries to deal with the presence of God in our lives—and the acceptance of life in all its horror and radiance."

It seems to work for him. After a lengthy stretch on his own, two years ago he began a new personal relationship—the fourth committed one of his life. "I've always felt confident that if you're a decent person, other decent people will show up," he says. "Sooner or later when you least expect it."

He's older now too. And almost relieved to be. "Maturity makes us less judgmental of others, more tolerant," he says. "My work is more compassionate. I don't make fun of people now."

Not that he's repudiating his earlier plays. "It's all just one writer's attempt to make sense of existence," he says. "And that's what I think art is—an interpretation of our world. If we're successful, more people will identify with our work than not."

On a Roll

Richard Alleman / 1995

Originally published in *Vogue*, May 1995, 152–54. Reprinted by permission.

"I still think that I win, hands down, the contest for worst first-play reviews—or any-play reviews," playwright Terrence McNally says of his Broadway debut, exactly thirty years ago last month. The play, *And Things That Go Bump in the Night*, an ambitious black comedy about a dysfunctional family living in a bomb shelter, was savaged by virtually every critic in town. Walter Kerr, writing in the *New York Herald Tribune*, called *Bump* "an infertile cross between Sartre's *No Exit*, Edward Albee's *Tiny Alice*, Wagner's *Götterdämmerung*, and the most portentous high school pageant you last saw." The *Daily News* critic wrote that 50 percent of the play was inaudible, and "this was the part I liked best." "Every other review was like, 'The worst play ever written,'" McNally recalls. "There was no 'This man is talented; it will be interesting to see what he does next.' They were 'This writer should be killed' kinds of reviews.'"

But there was no killing the twenty-five-year-old writer. "In a funny way the reviews were so bad that it almost didn't hurt me," McNally explains. "The experience was such a complete betrayal of the American/Hollywood dream of the young man—his first play is done on Broadway and it's a great triumph and he's carried on the shoulders of an adoring audience into and out of Sardi's—that it almost had a black humor side to it." Just as surprising, *Bump* continued—at least for sixteen performances. "We had come in under budget. So instead of closing in one night, as most producers would, the producer [Ted Mann] decided to keep it open for two weeks." The result was extraordinary: the show not only sold out; audiences went wild. "There were fistfights and arguments inside and outside the theatre at every performance . . . and I thought, At least my work is affecting people and there are people who like what I write. I think if the play had closed in one night . . . I don't know if I would have written another play."

Four years after that debacle, he saw one of his short comedies, *Next*, about an overweight, middle-aged man mistakenly drafted into the army, share an Off-Broadway theatre with Elaine May's *Adaptation*. The double bill ran for more than seven hundred performances. More important, McNally points out, "ever since, I've earned my living as a playwright."

Not that it was all smooth sailing. "I've had about five careers now," McNally says of his up-and-down life in the theatre. Among the ups were *Bad Habits*, a pair of one acts set in an insane asylum, that earned him an Obie in 1974, and *The Ritz*, his outrageously funny 1975 Feydeau-esque farce, set in a gay bathhouse. Among the downs were the movie version of *The Ritz*—a major bomb—and the 1978 play *Broadway, Broadway*, which closed in Philadelphia.

These days, however, McNally's on a roll. His book for the musical *Kiss of the Spider Woman* won him a Tony Award (his first) two years ago. His recent *Lips Together, Teeth Apart* had critics comparing him to Chekhov. And now there's *Lovel! Valour! Compassion!*, which is being hailed as McNally's most mature, complex, and satisfying work; it transferred to Broadway from the Manhattan Theatre Club, McNally's Off-Broadway base for the past decade. Focusing on the lives, loves, fears, and hopes of eight gay men who meet at a country house on three holiday weekends during one summer, *Love! Valour! Compassion!* is the playwright at the top of his game—and is expected to land McNally his second Tony next month, and perhaps even his first Pulitzer Prize.

"What I think is most extraordinary about him," says fellow playwright William Finn, "is the way he's made a career. His early things were really entertaining, but he's become an artist, and he's a real role model for playwrights. He's gotten better. Unlike most people, he saved his best for last."

Even now, McNally is not obsessing about prizes. Instead, he is at work on a new play, *Master Class*, a portrait of the late Maria Callas, starring Zoe Caldwell and currently at the Mark Taper Forum in Los Angeles, after which it will go to the Kennedy Center in Washington, DC, and then on to Broadway this fall. McNally's new play watches "la divina" come down to earth to teach aspiring opera singers a few tricks of the trade. In the early seventies, Callas did in fact teach master classes at Juilliard in New York—but McNally is quick to point out that his play is not a historically accurate documentary. Instead, it is the playwright's homage to "the romantic grandeur . . . the great theatrical presence and force" that an artist like Callas represents.

This is not the first time McNally has dealt with Callas. In *The Lisbon Traviata*, the two main characters are Callas-obsessed opera queens. But, as McNally puts it, "I go back with Callas a long way." All the way to Corpus Christi, Texas, in the early fifties, when the fifteen-year-old McNally discovered the diva on a radio broadcast from nearby Monterrey, Mexico. "There was this soprano, Maria Meneghini 'Cai-yas,' and I just thought she had the most wonderful voice." Indeed, it was quite some time before the young fan learned the correct English pronunciation of the name of "this disembodied voice coming from Mexico." He soon found himself sending away for Callas records, and eventually standing in line at the Met, Covent Garden, and La Scala.

Like his characters in *The Lisbon Traviata*, McNally can go on and on about Callas. But when he finally met her, it was a major disappointment. "She seemed very ordinary and very pedestrian and utterly without an artistic bone in her body, talking about the price of things, about where you get a good manicure," McNally remembers. "There's a Callas that really matters to me, and I could not equate the woman sitting opposite me with the woman I'd seen as Norma or Violetta."

Master Class is about the Callas that matters—which is not to say that McNally is easy on his idol. In the play, she is a tough, imperious, and uncompromising teacher. "But master classes *are* tough," says Zoe Caldwell, although while researching the role, she found a kinder, gentler Callas than the one McNally wrote for her. "Her caring was very strong," adds Caldwell. "Her involvement and her attention while you were singing was total. Totally on you. . . . Terrence hasn't followed that line exactly because he's trying to evoke the whole of her."

Caldwell, it turns out, was another of the playwright's idols. When he first met the Australian actress back in the sixties, he vowed to write a play for her one day. Whether he wrote his 1993 Off-Broadway hit, *A Perfect Ganesh*, with Caldwell in mind is not completely clear (he claims he did; she's not sure). Still it was with this play, about two American women looking for enlightenment while traveling in India, that McNally coaxed Caldwell out of semiretirement. "Zoe is not a TV actress; she's not a film actress; she's a great stage star and there's not many of them left," McNally explains. "I said to her, 'You know, you've worked with Olivier, Gielgud, Edith Evans—you owe it to the younger generation to get back out there.'"

McNally at times sounds as if he's trying to save the American theatre single-handedly. He loathes the fact that today many young actors and writers look on the theatre as "some horrible thing you do between TV and movie gigs." He is also concerned about the prevailing notion that Off-Broadway is the only place to produce a [new] play in New York. "The playhouses on Broadway are the finest real estate in America in which to see a new play," he says. "But they're not used [for new plays, as opposed to revivals or musicals] . . . and eventually they're going to be sold if we can't find a way to keep them alive."

Rather than whine, McNally is trying to do something about the situation. *Love! Valour! Compassion!* is being produced on Broadway under an arrangement called the Broadway Alliance, created to make Broadway more affordable for both audiences and producers. And when *Master Class* arrives in New York this fall, it, too, will be a Broadway Alliance production. "We're all in this together," says McNally, who also serves on the Dramatists Guild Council. "I just long for the day when enough good actors and writers and directors and designers will say, 'Here's where I want to be, and here's where I belong, and here's where I'm staying.'"

McNally also longs for the day when people will stop referring to him as a "gay" playwright. "When I get written up, the word *gay* usually appears in the lead sentence or paragraph. When that's just not important, that will be true liberation." McNally has never been in the closet. When *Bump* opened in New York, his main claim to fame was as the former boyfriend of Edward Albee. He remembers the wife of one critic commenting on entering the theatre, "Well, let's see what his boyfriend's written." McNally's writing has never been closeted either, with gay characters and storylines popping up frequently. Still, he says that he couldn't have written a play like *Love! Valour! Compassion!* twenty years ago.

Does McNally worry about a backlash? What about a Newt Gingrich who happens on *L!V!C!*, with its male nudity, same-sex love scenes, inside jokes, and unapologetic depiction of the "gay lifestyle"? McNally bristles as he points out that the play has no agenda—"because gay men aren't lifestyles, they're individuals. Any good play has to specifically be about people who are not you, and if it's a good play, you start finding the similarities you share with the characters—from Willy Loman to Blanche DuBois. And a play that promotes a lifestyle is going to be a very bad play."

Surprisingly, some of McNally's harshest criticism has come from the gay press, which has taken him to task for everything from dealing in stereotypes—such as Nathan Lane's opera queen in *The Lisbon Traviata*—to not having any gay characters onstage in his brilliant exploration of homophobia, *Lips Together, Teeth Apart.* "They said I reduced gay men to offstage characters who listened to Judy Garland. Well, number one, Judy Garland is never heard in the play. . . . the music that you do hear is Billie Holiday, Jussi Björling, and Gluck and Schubert, which I think says gay men have rather good taste in music!" While McNally can joke about this, he adds that "as a gay man I'm very aware of the vicissitudes of living in the era of AIDS, and to be perceived as someone who is a villain in the gay community, it's very hurtful."

At fifty-five and happy in his personal as well as his professional life (he's been involved with the same man, a writer and AIDS clinic office manager, for the past two years), McNally is very much aware of the younger generation and the need to pass something on to them. And what he'd like to convey most is his love of the theatre. "The theatre is something to give your life to," he states emphatically. "It gives your life value and joy. . . . Just stick it out like I did. It doesn't happen overnight, but when it does, the network of friends and extended family and the feeling of having an impact on other people's lives is so amazing. I don't think we in the theatre can change the world, but I think we can leave it a better and a different place than it was if we hadn't written our plays and acted in them. It's exciting, too—that you have to be there. It's like a good party. You can't hear about a party. You want to be at the party. And the theatre's the party I want to be at."

Terrence McNally:
The *Theater Week* Interview

Carol Rosen / 1995

Originally published in *Theater Week*, February 27-March 5, 1995, 12–24. Reprinted
by permission.

Over the past thirty years, the prolific Terrence McNally has become syn-
onymous with Off-Broadway theatre—both with its freedom and with its
testing of boundaries. Although he has had some success on Broadway (*The
Ritz* and *Kiss of the Spider Woman*, for which he won a Tony), McNally's
Broadway flops are legendary: his precocious first play, *Things That Go Bump
in the Night*, *Broadway, Broadway* (which later resurfaced as an Off-Broadway
pièce-à-clef, *It's Only a Play*), and the star-crossed *Rink*.

McNally's current Broadway play, *Love! Valour! Compassion!*, is his most
unflinchingly non-mainstream work to date. Set in a house in the country over the course of three summer holiday weekends, this *Big Chill* play
depicts gay lovers and friends who couple, work, eat, fall in love, fall ill,
skinny dip, reminisce philosophically, and speculate pessimistically about
the world outside their fragile cocoon. This fall it was a solid hit at the Manhattan Theatre Club, McNally's Off-Broadway haven since 1985; now *Love!
Valour! Compassion!* is attempting the leap to an old-fashioned Broadway
house (albeit the Walter Kerr, recently vacated by *Angels in America*), and
so far it looks like a success, one of the rare ones for the unlucky, but well-
intentioned Broadway Alliance, which subsidizes Broadway productions for
"risky" plays.

McNally's style is quicksilver, impossible to pin down. So, while snappy
urbane repartee, echoes of operas, campy pop-culture allusions, and cynical
world-weary wisdom are all recognizable elements in the McNally signature, there is always also the unpredictable flourish. His plays range from *The
Ritz*, a bathhouse farce in which straights and gays go bump in the night, to

Next, a political situation comedy about an unlikely middle-aged candidate for military duty mistakenly called in for a Selective Service physical exam, to *Frankie and Johnny in the Claire de Lune*, a tender love duet "among the ashes" for forlorn misfits, to *The Lisbon Traviata*, an affectionate mockery of the opera-obsessed, to *Lips Together, Teeth Apart*, a snapshot of couples claiming what's theirs at a dead man's beachhouse, and to *A Perfect Ganesh*, a log of a vacation gone awry. His voice remains fresh and inventive.

Experimenting in other genres, McNally wrote the heart-wrenching tele-play for *Andre's Mother*, a depiction of love and mourning in the absence of acceptance, and he contributed the books for two Broadway musicals, *The Rink*, the roller-palace predecessor of *'night, Mother*, and *Kiss of the Spider Woman*, an adaptation of Manuel Puig's book and screenplay in which sexual desire and political repression collide and a prisoner finds release and potential salvation in fantasy.

McNally's successes have ranged from outlandish farces to meditations on lost love. Always, his sympathy is with "defensive, hurt" characters who yearn for companionship along the journey. In recent plays, his tableaus recall Bruegel's *Fall of Icarus*, as he calls our attention to a speck in the far distance on the horizon, a figure in peril, peripheral to the action. As Sally says after seeing a stranger drown himself in *Lips Together, Teeth Apart*, "Even from a great distance we know so much about each other, but spend our lives pretending we don't."

Love! Valour! Compassion! is an ensemble piece that is languid in rhythm, desultory in action. Its tableaus have reminded more than one critic of Eakins's *The Swimming Hole*. Its episodes run the gamut from farce to melodrama. In a Chekhovian atmosphere of longing and vague betrayals, action boils down to an afternoon swim.

Arriving at the Manhattan Theatre Club rehearsal space downtown for an interview, McNally is unshaken at the prospect of a Broadway opening for this play. He is calm and gracious, accommodating and warm. Looking into his piercing blue eyes, I see no hint of his biting wit or the wicked cutting edge that he clearly saves for his characters' one-liners. Generous in his praise of actors, designers, producers—even critics—he seems almost too kind and even innocent for a life in the theatre. (During our interview he even demonstrates his famous endearing inability to get play titles straight. He mentioned *Love Story*, for example, meaning A. R. Gurney's widely produced two-hander, *Love Letters*.)

Yet McNally is nothing if not a man of the theatre. He devoted much of last year to co-teaching playwriting with John Guare at the Juilliard School.

And rehearsals start soon for his next play, *The Master Class*, in which Zoe Caldwell plays Maria Callas. Today, as ever, his eye is on the horizon, on the sea and sky and earth, as he envisions all the landscape plays to come.

TheaterWeek: *Love! Valour! Compassion!* has a highly unconventional structure. More than ever before, you take risks in your presentation of time, space, and point of view. How did this play take shape?

Terrence McNally: Maybe as I'm getting older, I'm more interested in plays that are more playful and just use the actors and the bare stage to create time, space, and travel. I think I couldn't have written this play if I hadn't written *A Perfect Ganesh*, which began with these kinds of fooling around with time and space. So I realized that this was coming. Also *Lips Together, Teeth Apart* had some inner monologues. They weren't to the audience; they were true soliloquies. I've seen them spoken to the audience but they shouldn't be. In my mind, they are inner. Here, in *Love! Valour! Compassion!* the monologues really break the [fourth] wall, which I did in *Tommy Flowers*. So this play seems to be a kind of a summation of a lot of places I've been trying to go.

What did it with me was *Lisbon Traviata*. You know what that play was like: phone calls and answering machines and stereos. And you really need all that. It's about how we clutter our lives up with ways of not dealing with people. As much as I loved that play, I said, "I don't really want to do another play with so many sound cues." And so, starting with *Ganesh*, I wanted to get away from my forte: telephone calls, the use of music.

There are these little code things you do to yourself as a playwright that are complex, but no one else notices. Almost the first thing that happens in *Ganesh* is at the airport her stereo with all her music is stolen. I was stealing it so I couldn't have lots of music in the play. And India's notorious for telephones that don't work so . . .

There is music, obviously, in *Love! Valour! Compassion!*, but it's people really singing or it's Tchaikovsky. It's almost all Tchaikovsky on piano.

TW: The songs in *Love! Valour! Compassion!* are all nostalgic of a golden age of innocence in America.

TM: Yes, a golden age. And they're very American. Stephen Foster is an American sound. I think he's a very profound composer. And there's something very beautiful about men singing which has nothing to do with sexuality, just a lovely sound. To me, a barbershop quartet is a great sound still. So that's sort of how I began the play. I didn't have real strong images of where I was going, but I saw all of them gathered together singing Stephen Foster.

TW: Like so many of your plays, the script has a minimum of stage directions. What are some of the ways in which the director and designers contributed to the creative process? For example, how did ideas evolve for the dollhouse model of the summer house, the black umbrellas at the top of Act Three, and all the wistful tableaus?

TM: Plays are truly a collaboration. I know what my contributions are, but I have no trouble acknowledging what the actors' and [director] Joe Mantello's and [set designer] Loy Arcena's are.

It was Joe Mantello's idea to have the [miniature] house there to ground the play. I did not have the cleverness to say the house should be there. Obviously, if Gregory just says that first speech, you don't know where you are. "Welcome." Welcome to what? You've got to see it. Joe quite rightly knew what my instinct was: that I didn't want to see the sofa, I didn't want to see the sled that Jerome Robbins had given Gregory. If the play gets real that way, then it would not be what I intended. My original stage direction for the stage was bare stage, and then, Rubik's cube, meaning primary colors: red, bright green. Now obviously, that would be a horrible set to look at, just one flat bright red, the floor bright blue, another flat bright yellow. But I was trying to say I know I don't want scenery in the conventional sense.

And so that's how Joe interpreted it, and that was so right. But I didn't know how to do that. And the mound was Loy's idea.

TW: Have there been any changes in staging the play as you've moved it from Manhattan Theatre Club to the Walter Kerr Theatre?

TM: No. Physically, it's the same set, slightly different proportions. It's actually narrower, but it's taller because Manhattan Theatre Club has that Cinerama stage but a very low opening.

TW: What was the trick, the "little code thing," as you put it, that you did to yourself to avoid familiar territory and to force yourself in a new direction with this play?

TM: I was going to try and make a bare stage work as much as possible. There's a cast of seven, and there's actually only six chairs, because John is not sitting at the table, and the table. There's not too much else. There's that chaise when he's watching TV. And the wing-backed chair. That's about it. That's what I wanted, but I didn't know how to do it. I knew I wanted to play without scenery, but a lot of designers and directors would have said, "How can you have guys going to bed, how can you have people in cars, how can you have a hand being stuck down a garbage disposal unit, without really doing it?"

One of my images for this play is it's eight characters telling their story about how we spent the summer. I intended for there to be overt theatricality;

it's meant to be stylized. We never pretend that they're diving into real water. That's the vision I had of the play without it being specific.

TW: Can you describe your process of envisioning this play?

TM: I never got stuck writing this play; it flowed. It was fun to write; is that the word? Fun sounds trivial, but it was fun. It was a joy to write.

I keep saying I'm going to write a play with a lot of plot, but I know my plays are getting more and more minimal in terms of plot. I think there is such enormous plot in "Let's go swimming. Yes or no." I'm interested in the little drama of why we go skinny dipping or don't, why we choose to eat Chinese food over Italian food. I think there's enormous drama in these little moments in our lives, and that just fascinates me. I'm really into these guys and what's going on in that house.

TW: In *Lips Together, Teeth Apart* and *A Perfect Ganesh*, your two recent companion plays to this one, you also reduce action to the basic issue of whether or not to go for a swim.

TM: Yes, in *Ganesh*, those women cannot bring themselves to go into the Ganges. If Indians see water as a symbolic cleansing place, to the women it's something of terror. The Ganges is filled with dead bodies and disease, and their fear. I don't think of water as a symbol when I write, but obviously it has meaning and resonance to me.

I'm working on a one-act play that we're going to do this summer out at Bay Street Theater in Sag Harbor that takes place on a beach [*Dusk*]. I said, "These are the three elements I care about, the earth, the sky, and the sea." It's like a Rothko painting to me, these three bands of color, and I like what that evokes. That's a kind of theatre that I see for myself. I can't imagine writing, "At rise, the TV is playing, mom's in the kitchen cooking." Really, I think *Frankie and Johnny* was my first step away from that. A lot of people thought that was a very naturalistic play because they were cooking and it seemed to be in real time. But I think actually that's one of the more poetic plays I've ever written.

TW: You have said that when you were a fledgling playwright at the Actors Studio, Mollie Kazan told you to learn stagecraft, not to write just dialogue. You've also said you learned the secret of playwriting from Elaine May when she directed *Next*. What is the secret? And how do you teach it?

TM: It's such a simple secret: what is the character doing? If you know what the character is doing, the dialogue will flow. So when I write, I have very clear images of what people are doing. That doesn't mean it's going to get directed that way, but there's an impetus.

I think anyone who wants to be a playwright should probably take some acting [classes], but I'm much too inhibited and I'm too old now anyway, but when I was at Actors Studio I did do one play and I learned nothing because I was so terrified. But if you had the opportunity to play some bit parts in a young company, you could get a sense of how an actor must think, "What am I doing?" It's not about reciting words.

A lot of playwrights come to playwriting as I did, through the English department, as if you're going to be a writer. So you think playwriting is sitting in your room alone writing dialogue. And then you see it done in the theatre and it doesn't work. I think that's why so many novelists come to grief in the theatre—because it's just people talking back and forth and not doing anything.

TW: What is your method of teaching playwriting?

TM: I don't believe in assignments. I think the only thing you can do as a good teacher is free somebody to be who they are. Two things, I think: Get them to write characters and not their opinions of the characters; and get them to understand that theatre is action, character is action.

John Guare and I taught at Juilliard last year, and one of the things we did "for fun" was to go back and read Aristotle. And it's all there. It's kind of terrifying to think that this man, B.C., came up with the real nuts and bolts of playwriting. The best playwriting is always the action, the characters revealed through action, not through monologues or people talking about them while they're off stage.

Another thing I try to teach playwrights is to find their own voice and not write like Sam Shepard, or Neil Simon, or Tennessee Williams, or Edward Albee or whomever they may admire at the moment. I think I was lucky in that I found my voice by my second play. My first play [*And Things That Go Bump in the Night*] has traces of me in it, but there's a lot of Albee in it. I was very influenced at that time by *The Zoo Story*. I thought it was the most amazing explosion of fresh style, that it was so different from the way any other characters had talked. But by *Next* I think I started sounding like myself.

The other thing I say to young playwrights, young actors, young anybody, is start your own theatres. They all think, "Well, I want to be a playwright and I'll send my first play to Manhattan Theatre Club before I go on to Broadway." You want to say, "Twenty years ago we did *Bad Habits* up at the old Manhattan Theatre Club space on folding chairs with overhead lights, you know, and this is now a theatre with I don't know how many million dollars a year budget. Start your own companies. Get your work out there."

Finally, you've got to get out of the classroom. I had a student last year. I said, "What are you going to do?" He said, "I've applied for graduate school." And I said, "You just spent a year at Juilliard doing nothing but writing plays. Now you're going to go do a three-year playwriting program? Get a life. Get out there. Get your plays done. Get out of the sanctuary of the schoolroom."

TW: Your most recent plays—*A Perfect Ganesh, Lips Together, Teeth Apart,* and *Love! Valour! Compassion!*—all take place on vacation. They could also be characterized as landscape plays. Do you see these three plays as interrelated in these or other ways?

TM: I guess I love vacations. I love summertime. A lot of my plays take place in summer. And I find myself moving outdoors more and more. The first scene I ever wrote outdoors was *Tommy Flowers* at the Tour at Lincoln Center. And then the scene outside the Women's House of Detention (which has been torn down) on Sixth Avenue and Greenwich. I was like, "God, these scenes are outdoors!" Because when I first started going to theatre, plays took pace indoors, sort of. There was supposed to be a living room with doors; when actors went over there, they were going to the bedroom; when they went over there, they were going to the kitchen.

There's one point in *Love! Valour! Compassion!* where the blind guy is coming back to the house and Ramon is looking at him. Perry and Arthur are unpacking and saying they don't like the towels so they've brought their own. People are crisscrossing. It's like there's no set, but you're in eight different places. And that's the kind of theatre I want to work for more and more.

TW: The offstage death of a sibling triggers the action of *Lips Together, Teeth Apart.* The tourists in *A Perfect Ganesh* have both lost sons. And in *Love! Valour! Compassion!,* Bobby gets a phone call about his sister's fate. What is the function of these off-stage losses in plays ostensibly about, as you have put it, the dilemma of "shall we swim or not"?

TM: There are these things that we have that are private. In a way, we are helpless. What can you do when someone says something awful is happening, other than try to console him? And I do feel that there is a randomness to life. One minute you're sitting here and the next minute the phone rings and they say something awful happened. We are finally powerless and "As flies to wanton boys are we to the gods." I think I feel that. My favorite thing man has made is *King Lear.* I think it's the most perfect expression of who we are. Personally, I would put it ahead of a symphony of Mozart, the fortieth, or a painting, or the Taj Mahal, or the dome of St. Peter's.

TW: In *The Ritz,* you created a farce out of collisions between gay and straight characters in a bathhouse. But more recently, your Fourth of July play, *Lips Together, Teeth Apart,* is set in the Pines of Fire Island, a predominantly gay community, yet its only characters are two heterosexual couples. *Love! Valour! Compassion!* also depicts isolationist characters, this time gay ones, over a series of summer holidays. In fact, Buzz gets one of the biggest laughs in *Love! Valour! Compassion!* when he complains, "I'm sick of straight people. They're taking over." Do you see these two plays as companion pieces about two separate Americas, two parallel, self-contained worlds?

TM: I'm trying to think about this as a companion piece . . . two Americas aware of each other, but . . . maybe it is. I don't think that way when I write. Some people said, "In *Lips Together,* he kept the gays off stage." Well, the play wasn't about them, so why have them on? To have them drop in periodically to borrow a cup of sugar seemed rather silly. I've written gay characters; certainly if I want to write a gay character, I'll write a gay character. So with this play, it would have been too easy to have Buzz on Fire Island watching people go by on the beach. That comes too easily. I wanted to make it a little harder for myself and isolate them in the country in an ideal setting. You feel they're on three hundred acres, that it's a big ground. I wanted them to be away from the city, and I love that image of these two Wall Street guys driving in the car with their suspenders. You know what their life is like. You can get to the country; you can take your clothes off and run around in old shorts or naked. I love that.

At the house in the country, it very much is an extended family with relatives you like more than others. Buzz is everybody's favorite uncle—or aunt. And John is the cranky one, the eccentric. And Perry and Arthur are the reliable ones. And Gregory is the provider.

I want to write about family. To me a very important line is when Gregory says, "Are you going home to Texas?" Bobby says, "No, home is here. Texas is where my parents are." Gay people do create a society for themselves, an extended family. And when he says, "Will you be there, will you promise me?," that's a very strong reality for a gay person. It may not be to someone who has a wife or a husband and six children. I think it's the way we all deal with these human needs.

TW: Was John a difficult character to include? He seems the odd man out.

TM: At the end he's come somewhere, and it's very painful. I care about him. But he's not a likable character. Last night, at the end of the first act, someone said to me, "I love all the characters. But I don't like the character of John." And I thought, since this is somehow going to be seen as some kind of portrait of gay men today, I think it's great that there's people who have a little problem in it; they're a little prickly. I think Perry's a little prickly, too.

I'm very glad we began this play at Manhattan Theatre Club, which is hardly a gay theatre or gay audience. In fact, I think some people were a little nervous about how the play would go with such a middle-class, middle-aged audience. And they embrace the play. We're reaching a large audience.

TW: Many characters in *Love! Valour! Compassion!* are disillusioned, self-absorbed, and cynical. Buzz even yearns for a "musical in which everybody dies" to reflect his hopelessness. Yet at the center of this play is a real shocker. Bobby speaks directly about "unconditional love" and answered prayers. Where does that vision of redemptive love come from?

TM: I'm in a very nice period of my life. I feel it's so important to convey that, without unconditional love, we don't blossom as human beings. As a kid I was always told, "We will do this for you if you do that for us." That's conditional love.

I feel unconditional love for the Manhattan Theatre Club. I could not have written this play if I didn't have Lynne Meadow and Barry Grove and Michael Bush, those three particularly, saying, ever since a preview of *It's Only a Play*, "We will do your next play." I think I'm the only playwright that I know of that has such a deep commitment and such unconditional love from a company. Usually play productions are very conditional: "I will do your next play if it looks like it will be a hit, if, if, if . . ." Sometimes I feel I'm just beginning as a playwright; I have so much I can do because they ain't putting any brakes on me or conditions.

TW: But that speech about unconditional love and the later reference to answered prayers are astonishing. They open up the action, offer a universalizing vision, and transform the whole atmosphere of the play. What is the impetus for that shift in tone?

TM: I've learned as I get older, without unconditional love, we never reach our potential. I've had it in my life personally in the past couple of years, and I'm like, "Wake up and smell the coffee. You are so lucky, celebrate this and go, man. The sky is the limit. Why are you holding yourself back?" And this play is just the beginning. I'm starting to really appreciate where I am, who I am, and what's been given me. I've been given a most precious gift. I think it's being aware of my own mortality, too, and learning to be in the moment. I'm getting a little bit of wisdom maybe. I'm fifty-six, so you hope you get a little wiser about all this? I don't think I could have written this play in my twenties, thirties, or forties. A lot has happened to me in the past couple of years. I mean, the loss of friends. You're not supposed to be prepared to lose your best friends when you're forty years old. Life had not prepared me for that.

I used to drink quite a bit and I stopped drinking and that's an enormous difference. If I am sad about something now, I'm really sad; or if I'm angry, I'm really angry. I don't say, "Oh, fuck it," and go out and have four martinis. Sobriety is a huge change. I don't do drugs or alcohol anymore, and that's a wonderful change. I couldn't have done any of that alone. My friends and strangers that I've met have helped me to stay sober. And I have a wonderful man in my life. God put this angel, this magnificent person in my life [Gary Bonasorte]. Zoe Caldwell said, "I think one day God said, 'Enough is enough, I'm giving Terrence Gary,' and popped him into your life." Just out of the blue. And he lives down the street. It was amazing. Our song is "Liza"—you know—"Ring them bells." You go all around the world, and love is three doors away. Anyhow . . .

TW: "Well, anyhow" is a recurring phrase in "Colored Lights," the opening song in *The Rink*. It's also used in *Love! Valour! Compassion!* as a gracious way to change the subject.

TM: [The character] says, "I don't say it when I'm cornered, I say it when I'm overwhelmed." Sometimes life—the feelings—overwhelm us.

TW: Do you expect any negative response to the use of male frontal nudity on Broadway?

TM: There was nudity on Broadway as long ago as [David Storey's] *The Changing Room*, but it was fast and it wasn't sexual. Here, people are admiring other people. It's sexy. But it's very much integral to this play. And I don't think it's an issue on Broadway. I think by now if people don't want to see a naked male body, they aren't going to come see this play. Every review mentions it, and they feel amply warned. And the poster is eight men, some with their arms around each other in bathing suits, on a raft looking up at the moon. It's pretty clear that it's not a boy meets girl comedy.

TW: It's an old Broadway joke that an exclamation point in the title sells tickets. But why are there three exclamation points in the title of this play?

TM: The title of the play is simply an entry in John Cheever's journals. He just wrote "Love! Valor! Compassion!" I guess it's like a sigh.

The cast has started calling it *Love! Valour!* or *LVC*. People get tired of going *Love! Valour! Compassion!* because the exclamation points make you say each word. But that's what I wanted. I thought the title is something to write up to. It promises something of substance.

TW: You've said that you don't envy Wendy Wasserstein's having been lassoed into being the spokesperson for every woman of her generation. You'll have to be wary now, with *Love! Valour! Compassion!* opening on Broadway, that an analogous fate doesn't befall you.

TM: I will just fight it. Listen, this play, for example, has gotten very good reviews from the gay press. The gay press was horrible to *Lisbon Traviata*, so . . . I've always had reasonable expectations.

Zoe Caldwell said, "What are you going to do after *Love! Valour! Compassion!*? It's really hard to follow a hit." I said, "I've already written a play." I wrote *Master Class* before this ever went into rehearsal. And now, thirty years after I saw Zoe Caldwell's debut in *All's Well That Ends Well*, she will be in this new play of mine [which premieres in Philadelphia and then plays engagements at the Kennedy Center and the Mark Taper Forum before opening on Broadway in the fall].

Master Class is the play that probably comes closest to how I really feel about theatre and art. Even though I use opera as a metaphor, clearly opera is theatre to me. And Callas is an artist who took her own personal passions and fears, and channeled them into art. And she tried to teach, to pass it on to younger singers.

Love! Valour! Compassion!

Melissa Burdick Harmon / 1997

Originally published in *Biography* 1, no. 2 (February 1997): 58–62. Copyright and licensed by A&E Television Networks.

Picture a six-year-old boy growing up in Texas in the years just after World War II. Picture him walking around the house belting out "La Vie en Rose" in French with all the world-weariness of Edith Piaf. Probably not the behavior of your typical Texan first-grader. Now, imagine a slightly older boy, hungry for the cultural knowledge he gets from the liner notes on record albums, who develops a special liking for what he imagines as the happily married, husband-and-wife songwriting team of George and Ira Gershwin.

It's obvious that Terrence McNally, today one of New York's most prolific playwrights, came by his exposure to the arts the hard way, grabbing at any opportunities to be found in Corpus Christi, the smallish Texas city where he grew up a good deal more than "forty-five minutes from Broadway." And when speaking with him, [I found it] equally clear that he holds a lifelong appreciation for those who helped him on his journey into the larger world.

For example, there was the Ursuline nun who brought in opera records to play to her fifth-grade class. "They were 78s, that's how long ago it was," McNally recalls. "She brought in Puccini love duets, and I was just instantly drawn into another world, the same way as when I first heard Edith Piaf. It's like when you have the first bite of a food you just love. You sink your teeth into it and say, Wow, where has this always been?"

McNally's parents also played a role in showing him a world beyond Corpus Christi. His father, after all, was the one who bought the Edith Piaf records. Even better, the elder McNallys, a wholesale-beverage distributor and a bookkeeper, twice took young Terrence to New York, where he had the golden chance to see Ethel Merman in *Annie Get Your Gun* and, later, Gertrude Lawrence as Anna in *The King and I*, just weeks before her death.

"They bowled me over," McNally says. "I guess my nervous system is just more receptive to the impact of a live performer because none of the movies I saw as a child affected me as strongly. I just like that excitement before a play begins, when the house lights go down." Now, he typically attends the theatre three or four nights a week when he is in New York—it is, he says, one of his primary reasons for living there.

But one of the most important influences on his life was a high school English teacher named Maurine McElroy. "She was truly blessed with that gift of inspiration and of helping young people to realize their potential," he says, adding that she introduced him to the then-foreign concept that it was possible to attend a college other than the University of Texas.

Ever grateful, McNally, who is a Phi Beta Kappa graduate of Columbia University, dedicated his 1987 play *Frankie and Johnny in the Clair de Lune* to her. And just recently, some forty years after he sat in in her classroom, McNally took Mrs. McElroy along "as my date" when he spoke at the Lyndon Baines Johnson Library in Austin, Texas, followed by a dinner with Lady Bird Johnson and her two daughters.

Pleasure, Ecstasy, and a Certain Solace

If there is one theme that runs through McNally's childhood recollections and through his plays, it is his profound love for opera. As a child he built his own "Metropolitan Opera" and constructed sets for it, which he would change on cue while listening to the Met's Saturday broadcast. However, it was through a radio station across the border, in Monterey, Mexico, that he discovered what was to become one of the grand passions of his life, the voice of Maria Callas. (Or, as he then heard and believed it to be, Maria "Ca-yas.")

Later, as a freshman at Columbia, McNally camped by the Met box office for three days to buy a standing room ticket for Callas's debut in Bellini's *Norma*. "She gave only twenty performances in New York, and was cheered—and booed—at nearly every one," he recalls.

Maria Callas is, of course, the subject of McNally's Broadway hit *Master Class*, written for actress Zoe Caldwell. And Callas is also the voice heard on the elusive, pirated recording of the opera *La Traviata* that forms the comic core of his hilarious and terribly sad play *The Lisbon Traviata*.

McNally's character Mendy, the fanatical record collector in that play, expresses his rapture over Callas when he says, "She's given me so much. Pleasure, ecstasy, a certain solace, I suppose. Memories that don't stop. This doesn't seem to be such a terrible existence with people like her to illuminate it. We'll never see her like again. How do you describe a miracle to someone who wasn't there?"

Let's Go See What He's Written

McNally, now fifty-seven, always intended to be a writer, but assumed that would mean a journalist. While at Columbia, however, he began some serious theatregoing and found a new inspiration. "I sort of drifted into playwriting," he claims with characteristic modesty.

In fact, he got an early start in the playwriting business. Still in his twenties, having recently ended a relationship with playwright Edward Albee, he saw his first [play], *And Things That Go Bump in the Night*, produced at Minnesota's prestigious Guthrie Theater. The play then moved to New York—where critics absolutely and unequivocally destroyed it.

That negative reaction may have resulted from the Albee connection. As McNally grimly recalls, when critic Walter Kerr and his wife, Jean, entered the theatre, he heard Jean mutter, "Well, let's go see what the boyfriend has written."

Reviews ranged from "the worst play ever written" to the *Daily News* critic's comment that half the dialogue was inaudible—"and this was the part I liked best." Remarkably, McNally found strength to pick up a pen and try again.

His next play, *Next*, directed by Elaine May and starring James Coco, was the comic story of a middle-aged man mistakenly drafted into the Army. It fared much better, and McNally began to build a solid reputation. And his work began to evolve, developing greater complexity and tackling tougher issues as the years passed and his expertise grew

Of course, he explains, "I really began to develop a sense of what makes a play work. I think you have to separate playwriting from literature," he adds. "There's a very practical side to writing for the theatre, and it's pretty hard to learn that all by yourself working in your room. Being a good playwright is learning how to collaborate with directors, designers, actors . . . and finally, with the audience."

Unconditional Love

For McNally, part of that education has come from collaboration with the small, not-for-profit Manhattan Theatre Club, a relationship he describes as "unconditional love." McNally firmly believes that the security it provides has given him the room to grow.

Of course, it would be perfectly possible for a playwright of McNally's current reputation to skip the Manhattan Theatre Club phase and head right for the bright lights of Broadway. After all, he has had three works—*The Kiss of the Spider Woman*, for which he wrote the libretto, *Love! Valour! Compassion!*, and *Master Class*—staged on Broadway within the past couple of years, and all won Tony Awards for either Best Play or Best Libretto. Yet he remains faithful.

His abiding loyalty to his theatrical home is eclipsed perhaps only by his loyalty to the theatre in general, at a time when more and more talented writers are heading west, chasing the big dollars to be made writing screenplays. For McNally, that is simply not an option, although he has adapted several of his own plays for film, including the movies *Frankie and Johnny*, starring Al Pacino and Michelle Pfeiffer, *The Ritz*, and the upcoming *Love! Valour! Compassion!*

"I don't dream in movies," he states matter-of-factly. "I dream in theatre. I like the physical reality of theatre. Movies are like looking through a very pretty window at Saks Fifth Avenue, but it's one step removed from the moment. At the theatre, you have to be there that night. You feel like an active participant."

McNally is also one of a tiny handful of playwrights who has always supported himself solely through his craft. He admits, however, that one year that meant living on something like $3000.

That low-income period doubtless occurred during the great writing slump after his theatrical tell-all comedy, *Broadway, Broadway*, was savaged by critics during its Philadelphia tryout. This time the barbs really did wound, to the point where he quit writing for about three years. The turning point came when someone in a store stepped up and asked if he was Terrence McNally. McNally expected to hear something about one of his successful plays, but the stranger said, "I thought so. I recognized your voice from the Texaco Opera Quiz," for which he is a regular panelist. Immediately, he envisioned his obituary—"Terrence McNally, the former Texaco Opera panelist, died yesterday"—and realized it was time to stop feeling sorry for himself and get on with it. And he did just that, proceeding to write some of the most densely textured and critically successful plays of his career.

What Do You Think as a Member of the Human Race?

While McNally has never made a secret of his homosexuality, one can hear the weariness in his voice when the subject of his stature as "gay playwright" comes up. While he recognizes that such designations are inevitable ("if people want gay liberation, this is part of the price"), he also anticipates a day when "such designations will just drop away, as people realize that gay men and women are everywhere in the fabric of our society." Or as one character says in *Love! Valour! Compassion!*, "No one cares what you think as a gay man, doc. That wasn't the question. What do you think as a member of the human race?"

McNally, as a member of that race, is thinking more than he once did about far more serious subjects. If his early plays, such as the door-slamming, Feydeau-style farce *The Ritz*, made audiences laugh till they cried, later McNally works make theatregoers laugh as they cry. His recent plays have dealt, in ferociously touching ways, with issues ranging from AIDS to aging to infidelity to the simple struggle to connect in a world where human bonds seem ever more fragile. Comparisons to Chekhov are now making their way into reviews of his work, and everything he writes these days seems to win some kind of award. He's riding high. And, as he completes the libretto for the new musical *Ragtime*, pens a new play for Manhattan Theatre Club, and awaits the premiere of the film *Love! Valour! Compassion!*, he says he's in one of the happiest periods of his life.

But then he seems to be fundamentally a happy person. In his work, as in his conversation, McNally's good humor and native optimism assert themselves. To see a Terrence McNally play is to know that, whatever the subject of the day, there will be ample opportunity for laughter.

Yet make no mistake. These very funny plays are very serious indeed. Or as Johnny says to Frankie in *Frankie and Johnny in the Clair de Lune*, "This isn't small talk. This is enormous talk."

Love! Valour! McNally!

Alan Frutkin / 1997

Originally published in *The Advocate*, April 15, 1997, 31–34. Reprinted by permission.

With the screen version of his play *Love! Valour! Compassion!* arriving in movie theatres next month, Terrence McNally does something he rarely does: speak to the gay press.

"I'm always accused of saying that I'm not a gay playwright," Terrence McNally insists. "I'm not saying that at all. I'm a gay man who is a playwright. It's not just about my sexuality."

To McNally, the distinction is obvious. But his critics haven't always agreed. At a time when gays and lesbians want their heroes loud and proud, McNally's tough stance on his own gay identity has often put him at odds with gay activists. As a result, he's become increasingly reticent to talk on the record about gay issues. In fact, after years of requests, this is the first time he has agreed to speak with *The Advocate* since 1988.

"I really hate talking about this because it always comes out wrong," he says, explaining why he's hesitant to discuss gay topics. "It doesn't come out wrong in my life. It comes out wrong when I read about what I allegedly said, and I feel very misinterpreted."

However, in his work McNally never holds back. It's no small irony that this playwright—who shies away from gay issues off the stage—has addressed the gay experience more than any other playwright of his generation. And in addressing the gay experience, he's helped to define it.

Since his Broadway debut in 1965, McNally has consistently introduced audiences to gay themes and gay characters. Among his most famous works are 1975's gay bathhouse farce *The Ritz*; 1985's gay breakup drama *The Lisbon Traviata*; 1991's gay-themed comedy *Lips Together, Teeth Apart*; and 1992's hit musical *Kiss of the Spider Woman* (for which McNally wrote the book, winning a Tony Award for his efforts). Add to that list 1994's Tony Award-winning *Love! Valour! Compassion!*—now adapted as a film to be released nationwide May 16. It follows a tight-knit group of eight gay men and the changes that one summer brings to them.

Along with these gay landmarks are several works by McNally that don't always address the gay experience—at least directly—including 1987's two-person drama *Frankie and Johnny in the Claire de Lune* (later given the big-screen Hollywood treatment in 1991 as *Frankie and Johnny*) and 1993's spiritual fantasy *A Perfect Ganesh*. The diversity of his work is yet another issue that has put McNally at odds with some gays and lesbians. The playwright cites 1995's *Master Class*—for which he won his second Tony Award for Best Play—as a prime example. Although the play treats audiences to a fictional evening with gay icon Maria Callas, McNally says the gay press ignored it. "It's like I was a gay playwright three years ago because I wrote a play about eight gay men," he says. "But there's as much in *Master Class* that I want to say to my gay brothers and sisters as there was in *Love! Valour! Compassion!*"

The rigidity that McNally sees within gay circles is a source of frustration for him. "Sometimes you want to say to the people who criticize you, 'What more can I do?' " he says. "I'm out. I hope I've made a contribution to our society."

Yet he's all too aware that some gays don't think he contributes enough. "Why am I being attacked?" he snaps. "Because I say I hate the expressions 'gay theatre,' 'gay plays,' 'gay playwrights'? Those expressions are so limiting. It's a way to say to the rest of the world, 'You don't have to deal with me. I'm a harmless fairy.' "

In other words, McNally is determined to compete on a level playing field—not discriminated against but not indulged either. He illustrates his point by talking about his latest project, *Ragtime*. McNally wrote the book for the highly acclaimed production, a musical version of E. L. Doctorow's novel that opens in Los Angeles on June 15 and moves to New York in December. The rest of the show's creative team is straight, but McNally adds that's a moot point. "They all know I'm gay," he says. "We don't talk about my sexuality. We talk about the script of *Ragtime*."

McNally is already steeling himself for a chilly reception from the gay press, simply because *Ragtime* contains no gay characters. "Which doesn't mean I don't do my bit for the 'cause' today," he says. "I do my bit for the cause if *Ragtime* is a fucking good show and people say, 'You know, the book writer is a big queen.' "

For McNally, fifty-seven, visibility is the ultimate political act. "I think the most important thing we do in our lives is to be out," he says. "But I think being out is all we can do. Then just live a life that's of use to other people."

McNally never had to come out. The first time he hit the public eye, the New York press outed *him*. In those days the only big news about McNally was his lover—Pulitzer Prize-winning playwright Edward Albee. "No one had ever heard of me other than gossip that Edward and I had lived together for about six years," says McNally. "So when my first play came out, it was reviewed as a play by a gay playwright."

The play was 1965's *And Things That Go Bump in the Night*. It concerned an eccentric family living in self-imposed exile in their basement. It featured two gay characters. The critics savaged it.

McNally now sees the play's failure partly as the result of homophobia— not to mention what was perceived as his riding on the coattails of Albee's fame. "The press didn't know we had been broken up for about a year," says McNally. "So they were reviewing Edward Albee's boyfriend—and they were going to get me."

After the show closed, McNally swore off playwriting and spent the next year and a half as the assistant editor of his alma mater's alumni magazine, *Columbia College Today*. With the encouragement of friends and colleagues, he finally ventured back into the theatre. And by the mid-1970s he had begun to work at the astonishing pace that he's been known for ever since.

"I read the reviews of *And Things That Go Bump in the Night*," says *Boys in the Band* playwright Mart Crowley. "It was an enormous failure. How Terrence ever got the stamina, the guts, the courage, the moxie, the sheer will to go on, I'll never know."

It's not only his staying power that sets McNally apart from his peers, but the sense of adventure he brings to his work. "Terrence doesn't write the same play over and over again," says playwright Tony Kushner, author of *Angels in America*. "You might see that it's all by the same author, but you also see that there are real experiments with form and content."

Especially gay content. Although McNally incorporated gay themes into his work from the beginning of his career, it wasn't until *The Ritz* that he pulled out all the stops. "To me, *The Ritz* was the most subversive play that has ever been on Broadway," he says. "Here was a sex farce about gay men back in the early '70s, and the villain in that play is the heterosexual who's humiliated at the end. People were laughing hilariously at what they're supposed to be terrified and appalled by."

With *The Lisbon Traviata*, however, McNally learned a harsh lesson about gay story lines in his work: much of the straight audience wasn't ready to watch gay love onstage. The play was roundly criticized in the press for what McNally describes as its frank sexual talk. "There were times that the straight men in the audience would look at their watches or put their arms around the woman they were with. It was when there was affection between the gay characters," he says. "But I was so tired of gay plays where everybody was just an opera queen. Queens, people can deal with. Gay men having real emotions and feelings and dicks is much more threatening to people."

McNally kept those criticisms firmly in mind as he wrote *Love! Valour! Compassion!* "Almost the first image you see is of two men—who are practically naked—kissing," he says. "I wanted to get that over with." Admonishing an invisible audience, he adds, "If you're not going to be able to deal with men kissing, then leave now." This time most audience members stayed.

McNally adds that *Love! Valour! Compassion!* was just as much of a political statement for him as was *The Ritz*. "People came to the play because it won a Tony Award, but there was a point when you could feel the audience embrace the characters," he says. "When they do, the most obvious response is, 'I identified with these people.' And I consider that important."

McNally believes it's just as important that his gay messages are realistic, not melodramatic. "I don't feel as disenfranchised as some plays or movies try to make me feel," he says. "We're not Jews in Elizabethan England forced to live outside London, with Shakespeare writing *The Merchant of Venice*. You couldn't write the gay equivalent of a Shylock today," he says, referring to Shakespeare's Jewish villain. "That's how much we've been accepted. That's how much we're in the mainstream."

And mainstream acceptance of lesbians and gays is the basis of McNally's political views. "Being gay isn't enough anymore," he says. "The stakes are high now. We asked for acceptance, and we got it. What are we going to do with it?" The playwright quickly answers his own question: "Take it and be judged by the same standards that everybody else is."

Terrence McNally

David Savran / 1998

Originally published in David Savran, ed., *The Playwright's Voice: American Dramatists on Memory, Writing, and the Politics of Culture* (New York: Theatre Communications Group, 1999), 119–38. © David Savran. Used by permission of Theatre Communications Group.

Growing up in Corpus Christi, Texas, Terrence McNally spent his youth hanging out at the drive-in and the beach, skipping Sunday Mass to play poker and listening every Saturday to the Metropolitan Opera radio broadcasts. He also became fascinated with the theatre. "My first play was made up from the background notes on a George Gershwin record album, and I had George marrying a pretty girl named Ira. Doesn't it strike you as odd that not one of my teachers knew enough to say, 'Nice play, Terry, but Ira was George's *brother*'?" Moving to New York to attend college, McNally was able to nurture his passion for opera, camping out at the old Met for three days in October 1956 to buy a standing room ticket for the Met debut of Maria Callas, a figure who would reverberate through several plays. He made his Broadway debut with *And Things That Go Bump in the Night* (1965), a dark comedy about a young man who brings home his transvestite boyfriend, which was savaged by the critics. This was followed by a string of much more successful comedies that led up to *The Ritz* (1975), a farce of mistaken identities about a garbage man who seeks refuge from gangsters in a gay bathhouse. Following the disappointment of his second flop, *Broadway, Broadway* (1978), McNally went through a fallow period during which he wrote for television but was unable to finish any plays. Finally returning to the theatre, he not only turned *Broadway, Broadway* into the hit *It's Only a Play* (1985), but also inaugurated a series of more serious and ambitious plays that have made him probably the most successful dramatist to have come of age during the 1960s.

McNally is also the great chameleon among contemporary American playwrights. Over the past thirty-five years he has written an extraordinary range of plays, from the sinister farce of *Next* (1967) to the operatic tragedy of *The Lisbon Traviata* (1989), from the edgily romantic *Frankie and Johnny in the Clair de Lune* (1987) to the mystical *A Perfect Ganesh* (1993). Despite its diversity, all of his writing is characterized by a quizzical, comic touch (in even the most serious situations), by a frankly presentational style that delights in all the possibilities that the theatre offers, and by a tendency to construct a play by piling up what seem at first to be almost innocuous events. As a builder of artfully artless dramatic structures, he brings to mind playwrights like Chekhov or Tennessee Williams, who manage to turn the minutiae of everyday life into a richly dramatic and moving spectacle. For McNally's plays have a way of creeping up on you, as patterns begin to emerge out of the interplay of conflicting voices and the incidental details of characters' lives. Eschewing the big dramatic events that punctuate the work of many writers, he focuses instead on the almost random, almost insignificant, personal choices that produce momentous consequences.

Since the mid-1980s, McNally's plays have become increasingly preoccupied with questions of meaning and mortality, his characters more reflective, and his use of theatrical conventions more subtle, elastic, and bold. Thus, for example, his Tony Award-winning *Master Class* (1995) calls up the ghost of Maria Callas in order to explore and speculate on the function of theatre, the nature of an artist's calling, and the impact of one's life on one's art. Coaching three students on three different arias, Maria painfully and obsessively revisits her great roles and relives her relationship with Aristotle Onassis. For Maria is a woman truly possessed by both her art and her own ghosts, and she takes her students' arias as a cue to recall a past filled with fury, erotic passion, and loss. The play uses opera, moreover, as a way of proving the antiquity and immortality of great art: "When I sang Medea I could feel the stones of Epidaurus beneath the wooden floorboards at La Scala." At the same time, Maria's total dedication to her art—and to her past—is the sign that the artist must be prepared to sacrifice everything. Trying to explain Verdi's Lady Macbeth to a complacent student, she asks, "Is there anything you would kill for?" The student's inability to answer proves that the great artist must be prepared both to kill and die for her art. For *Master Class*, written during the ongoing controversy over the NEA's funding of allegedly indecent art, demonstrates that real art is always excessive, brazen, and dangerous, and that to shackle or censor the artist is to destroy her.

Despite the always ingratiating quality of McNally's plays, there remains something slightly dangerous and even confrontational about his work.

Many of his recent plays focus on the proximity of sex and death, comedy and tragedy, the terrible and sublime. Thus *Prelude & Liebestod* (1989) exposes the dark and menacing subtext of Wagner's far-too-readily desexualized opera [*Tristan und Isolde*] by using it as a key to unlock a conductor's memories of wild sex and an inspiration for his bloody (and comically scandalous) suicide. Or *Love! Valour! Compassion!* (1994), in which the joys, desires, and disappointments of eight gay men are set against a knowledge of mortality and the inexorability of loss. Or *A Perfect Ganesh*, which brings two American women, who have both lost sons, to India to confront their losses. Moving from the terrible beauty of the river of death, the Ganges in Varanasi, to the blazing radiance of the Taj Mahal, they finally recognize that Ganesha, the elephant-headed deity for which they had been searching, has in fact been traveling with them all the time; that he is simultaneously man, beast, and god; leper and prince; the Lord of Obstacles and the deliverer. For so many of McNally's characters, like the immortal Maria, are possessed. They are haunted by their memories and by stories (and rationalizations) from the past that they use to structure their lives. And the plays in which they appear, despite their sometime improvisatory feel, are similarly haunted by opera, musical comedy, and classical dramatic forms; for McNally's is a theatre in which characters grope toward transfiguration just as the darkened stage itself seems to await a blinding flash of light, like the one that illuminates the end of *A Perfect Ganesh*, in which characters and spectators alike are given an intimation of the divine. In an almost perverse way, it is a holy stage. And even in the face of death threats that greeted that tabloid press's misrepresentations of *Corpus Christi* (1998), McNally remains committed to a dangerous theatre: "Write plays that matter. Raise the stakes. Shout, yell, holler, but make yourself heard. It's time for playwrights to reclaim the theatre. We do that by speaking from the heart about the things that matter most to us. If a play isn't worth dying for, maybe it isn't worth writing."

June 23, 1998—Terrence McNally's apartment, New York City

David Savran: You could start by telling me how you got interested in theatre.

Terrence McNally: Got interested in theatre as opposed to just enjoying it—I've always enjoyed theatre. My very early memories as a child involve theatre. Right after the war we lived for a while in Port Chester, New York, and I remember watching *Kukla, Fran, and Ollie* and *Howdy Doody* on television. And I didn't care for *Howdy Doody* because I thought he was too real and with the strings and mouth moving. But I loved *Kukla, Fran, and Ollie,* which took place on a little stage within a stage—the interactions between Fran Allison and these archetypes. That stage was very real to me, and I made my own theatre down in the basement. I had copies of Kukla and Ollie. Once I read an interview in which Edward Albee talked about no one ever detecting the great influence of Kukla and Ollie in his work, especially the early plays like *American Dream.* And then when I was really young, my parents took me to see *Annie Get Your Gun,* which was the first play I guess I saw. This would have been about 1944 or '45 when I was six or seven years old, and that had an enormous impact on me. When we moved to Texas, Corpus Christi had no television station. Even all through high school, it only had kinescope television, so I didn't get to see those very popular shows that most of my generation loved—we were still watching the old kinescopes of *Kukla, Fran, and Ollie.*

So even through high school I still listened to radio, *Masterpiece Theatre,* the *Shadow,* the *Phantom,* and comic book versions of *Treasure Island, The Prince and the Pauper,* those kinds of things. That was a great appeal to my imagination, and also by that age I had fallen madly in love with opera. When I was in the sixth grade, a nun played some recordings for us, and I just liked it instantly. I didn't have to learn to like it. I listened to the Metropolitan [Opera] broadcasts, and I made a stage, and I would stage *Aida* and *Rigoletto* while they were broadcasting. Most of my stages weren't very original; I would just copy the pictures in *Opera News* magazine. These were also places my mind wandered.

I started buying a lot of show albums. My parents were native New Yorkers and came up to New York at least once a year and would always come back with programs. My father liked shows like *South Pacific* and *Kiss Me, Kate,* and Edith Piaf, whom he played a lot, which I think developed my taste for rather eccentric, rather identifiable voices like Callas rather than a generic soprano sound like Tebaldi or Sutherland. There was no theatre in my high school. The only play I remember seeing was *Picnic,* because this sad spinster teacher was playing Rosemary, and we just wanted to see her go to pieces and rip the guy's shirt off just like in the movie. And for all the wrong reasons, that's about the only play I remember seeing in Corpus Christi. Opera was as much an influence on me as theatre. For a period, we moved to Dallas, and they had this huge theatre for operettas: Starlight Operettas, they were called. They had a reputation for getting stars to do shows they never would have done on Broadway or developing shows that went on to Broadway. They had to compete with June bugs, big beetles that fly around and are particularly attracted to light. And there was a famous night when one flew down the front of June Havoc's dress, and she literally went berserk on stage. She was on the floor; she had little convulsions. She was so upset at the idea of some beetle crawling around in her cleavage and brassiere, whereas most of us were used to these flying bugs and batted them away. This was before we had air-conditioning, so the only bearable theatre would have been outdoors.

When we moved to Corpus Christi, opera was more accessible than theatre: the San Antonio Opera, the Metropolitan Opera toured to Dallas. A bunch of us who liked opera conned one of our mothers into driving us up to Dallas on the weekend to see three operas in two days. Opera was a form of theatre, but theatre was *Annie Get Your Gun*. When we lived in Dallas, stage shows would come through periodically. I remember Mary Martin in *Annie Get Your Gun* and Carol Channing in *Gentlemen Prefer Blondes* and other Broadway shows, but also *Red Mill, Naughty Marietta, Rose Marie*. This was long before I thought of becoming a playwright. I remember once I said something terrible to my brother, and my punishment was not going to see *Paint Your Wagon*, and I was really, really upset. I remember I couldn't believe it when my parents took off to see it without me—that was like capital punishment.

So, obviously the theatre spoke to me on some deep emotional level, and I still don't know what it is. It's like Boy Scouts sitting around the campfire, and the scoutmaster tells you a story and you get open-mouthed, wide-eyed. I don't think I considered writing for theatre until sometime after college. When I was at Columbia, I wrote the varsity show my senior year, but that was more of a lark. I still thought I was going to be a journalist, and that seemed more appropriate for a pre-journalism major because it was a spoof. It was about a lot of the celebrities of the day. There was a film company that went to Africa where they were making this film and exploiting the natives, but what they didn't know was that the natives were cannibals. And one by one they were eating the crew until only the ingenue and juvenile were alive at the curtain call. Evil people from Western capitalism had been destroyed, and Ed Kleban, who wrote the lyrics for *A Chorus Line*, wrote the music and lyrics, and Michael Kahn directed it. I was always involved with writing. In grade school I was writing puns and stories, and in high school I was the editor of my school newspaper and founded a literary magazine.

The summer of my junior year in high school I went to Northwestern. There's a famous program where they choose twenty-five outstanding students from around the country, and you go there free and pretend you're a real journalist for six weeks, and it's the first time I'd really been away from home, and it was very exciting. My roommate was Jerry Rubin. It was fun when he became [counterculture icon] Jerry Rubin. I have one friend, a poet, to whom I've stayed close all these years. I had wonderful influences and opportunities as a young man to explore the feelings I had for the arts. My parents were probably as supportive as they could be, even though their idea of becoming a writer was probably writing for *Time* magazine. They thought anyone who wrote independently was asking for poverty. It was certainly not the nineteenth century, "You will become a doctor," or something like that. And there were always playbills on the table. I remember them talking about *Death of a Salesman* and [A] *Streetcar [Named Desire]*. They saw shows I think all of America saw when Broadway was still where you went for intelligent writing. Movies were kind of a stepchild.

There were always people to point the way: a teacher in high school in Texas who cared about the English language and taught us the glories of Shakespeare. I'm one person who was not traumatized by her introduction of Shakespeare. Quite the opposite, she had such a humane and simple approach to him, she taught him as a playwright and not a poet. I'm just so grateful. I read Shakespeare a lot and he's such a profound force in my life, and so many bright friends of mine can't stand Shakespeare—and these are very good playwrights who read *Hamlet* or *Macbeth* in high school. I spent a lot of time at Columbia with him, the whole works, and then a seminar just in *King Lear* for a year.

Coming to New York was very fortuitous. I applied to Harvard, Yale, and Columbia, and I needed a scholarship. Harvard didn't give me a scholarship, and Yale and Columbia gave me the same scholarship. My best friend and I flipped a coin because we thought it was silly to go to the same school. He got Yale and I got Columbia, and as it turned out, part of my education became being in New York. I got here in the fall of '56, the tail end of the "golden age" of Broadway: plays by Tennessee Williams and Arthur Miller, and musicals by Rodgers and Hammerstein and Frank Loesser were still happening with some regularity. You couldn't see all the shows in a season unless you were a critic. It's like Off-Off-Broadway now; there's so much product. I saw a lot of shows. I also went to the opera and the ballet a lot. It was a great day for Balanchine at the City Ballet, and at City Opera, Beverly Sills was fabulous and no one knew who she was yet. And the debut of Callas—all those things I would have been denied had I been stuck up in New Haven.

I've never studied playwriting, but I've seen a lot of plays and I took some courses in theatre at Columbia. Eric Bentley had a course in modern drama, which was pretty much his paperback volumes in modern Italian, French, and German theatre. Other than Shakespeare, I think that was the only theatre course I took. Besides New York, Columbia didn't have a lot. Theatre was totally extracurricular. Michael [Kahn], with all of his work, was extracurricular. The only time I've ever acted was at Columbia when Michael directed a production of *The Little Prince*. I was taking a lot of French courses, and he encouraged me to be in it, saying it would help me lose my inhibition of speaking French in public. Everyone else in the cast was a native Frenchman, and coming backstage, I only understood enough to hear them say, "It was wonderful except for that American with that horrible accent playing the fox." Skipping ahead, the only other time I did act was in a little workshop at Actors Studio, and I was physically ill on the day we did it. I knew everyone in the audience. It was like I was hurled out onto a Broadway stage. My knees literally shook, and I had uncontrollable twitches in my face, and I think I threw up a few times before the play began. It was so horrible. That cliché that you could see his knees trembling through his slacks—you literally could.

DS: How did you get involved in Off-Off-Broadway?

TM: I wrote a one-act after college called *This Side of the Door* [1961], which I sent to Actors Studio. And because of that, I got a job as stage manager at the Playwrights Unit despite the fact that I had no practical knowledge of theatre. I had no idea how a director worked with actors or anything like that. But Molly Kazan, Elia Kazan's wife, said, "There's a job here as stage manager and I think you'll learn a lot about how a play's put together, how actors work, how directors work." So I did that for two years and learned a lot. And then Barr-Wilder-Albee did *This Side of the Door*. That was the first time I ever heard my lines spoken by professional actors. Estelle Parsons—she was magnificent—played the lead. It was done at the Cherry Lane for two weekends. And that was not even considered Off-Off-Broadway in those days; it was considered a workshop because Off-Broadway was very healthy. There were many more theatres, and it was when Beckett, Albee, Ionesco, and a whole generation of American writers like Jack Richardson, Arthur Kopit, Jack Gelber were all being done Off-Broadway. You could be at the Cherry Lane or the Actor's Playhouse or the Provincetown because these theatres were so small.

So Off-Off-Broadway came out of Off-Broadway's facing the same economic problems that Broadway was to face in the seventies and eighties. But in the sixties, Off-Broadway was very fertile—hundreds of theatres and lots of activity. This was the height of Circle in the Square reestablishing O'Neill as a writer, the Brecht-Weill evenings, *Brecht on Brecht* and *Threepenny Opera*. It was seen as an alternative to Broadway, and the difference in ticket prices was enormous. Everyone forgets. Right now, to go to the Manhattan Theatre Club costs five to ten dollars less than to see *Art* or whatever play happens to be on Broadway. It used to be, if a Broadway play was twenty dollars, Off-Broadway was five. Now, no one goes to Off-Broadway because it's cheaper. It was the only way to see all this great surrogate European drama: the Theatre of the Absurd, Genet, and people like that. Those plays were not being done on Broadway. So the question is really how did I get involved with Off-Broadway, because my first play was on Broadway. In many ways, everything's changed and nothing's changed.

My first play that I put in the credits, *Things That Go Bump in the Night*, was a very long one-act, an hour and a half, three scenes, and it was too on-the-nose autobiographically and emotionally. Too much airing of family business. I didn't enjoy watching it. I thought, That's not the purpose of theatre. I should be able to watch the play with the normal discomfort of seeing my work up there as opposed to, Would this upset my mother and father and brother if they saw this? It just seems an inappropriate use of theatre. While I was at Actors Studio, I wrote *Things That Go Bump in the Night*, which we did there with minimal sets and props and a very good cast. Then in Minneapolis we had a full production and a new cast. So in a way, I did a workshop, an out-of-town tryout, and then New York. Which is what happened with *Ragtime* [1996] or *Master Class*, which we did originally in the town of Big Fork, Montana, then at a little theatre in Philadelphia, and then at the Taper, then the Kennedy Center. So things are the same but they're wildly, wildly different, too.

DS: Reading your work and hearing you talk about opera and theatre, I've noticed that your plays are so self-consciously about the theatre and dramatic literature. I'm thinking about the highly theatricalized relationship between Steven and Michael in *The Lisbon Traviata*; or *Lips Together, Teeth Apart* [1991], a comedy of infidelity with its references to *Cosi fan tutte*, another comedy of infidelity; and of course *Master Class*, with Maria looking back at her different roles. How conscious are you of that in your writing?

TM: Maybe not as conscious as you think. For example, I never thought of *Cosi* as a comedy about infidelity until you just said it. But *Lips Together* is a play very much about fidelity and infidelity. I chose that music because that trio to me is a prayer for safe passage. In the context of that play, life is very fragile and it's a moment of prayer. Going back to *Kukla, Fran, and Ollie*, I'm not interested in naturalism. My plays are always plays, and the actors I work with most successfully are not internal, Actors Studio method actors. They enjoy being in a play, and you know they are acting for you, and it gives them great pleasure. That doesn't mean they are any less honest than the method actor who loses himself, and it's all about truth, truth, truth: "This is exactly how I felt when my mother died." I would rather see that theatricalized, made into a little larger gesture. Almost every actor I've worked with I've learned from enormously. If you look at people like Zoe Caldwell, Nathan Lane, Christine Baranski, actors I really admire, they're aware the audience is there. I like that dialogue. I like being welcomed to the theatre. Lately I've started using narrative more, but always think, We know you, the audience, are here, let's find out what connects us. When I write a play, I don't write the truth, a documentary, a proto-real experience. I write a play by Terrence McNally. I like the devices of Shakespeare. I have asides, monologues, soliloquies in my plays. I like the devices of opera: arias, trios, cabalettas.

Usually actors say it's very easy to learn my dialogue. The only play where they had trouble was *Lips Together*, because there are a lot of trios, quartets, four people with different conversations, under the house talking to people on the deck, talking to people in the bedroom, behind the screen. I was trying consciously to work like music there. In the last act, after John goes into the pool, it becomes a verbal quartet. I don't know if it really works, but I wanted a canon, overlapped dialogue, four people doing interior monologues. In real life, people do not verbalize four monologues in a situation and then freeze—so I would say my theatre is theatrical. My art is painterly realism, and my theatre is very real to me, but it's theatre and a different reality from you and me sitting here. That seems who I am. I never wanted to write a fourth-wall play. Or totally didactic theatre—I'm not terribly drawn to the works of Brecht. I feel I'm being lectured, and things are being demonstrated to me. You see three or four plays as a child, you listen to two operas, you have this high school English teacher, you go to Columbia, and that all adds up and you write this sort of play.

If I have any sort of artistic credo, I would say it's almost entirely *Master Class*. That's in many ways the most autobiographical play I've written, and I just put all these outrageous thoughts about art into Maria Callas's mouth. I honestly believe she probably wouldn't have said them but would have agreed with them. She wasn't known for her articulation about the world of art. But it's a very autobiographical play of my feelings. I went through a terrible period after I wrote it, after seeing it. I thought I would never write another play. It seemed very valedictory to me. But that passed, and I moved on to other projects. I like writing. I like being in rehearsal.

Almost everything else about the theatre has gotten very unpleasant. The commerce of it, the business, the fact that a show has to become an institutional hit, run for twenty years, to be considered successful. That's not a new story. People don't want to see a new play by a good writer; it has to become a media frenzy. *Corpus Christi* has become a "story," and that's totally the doing of an irresponsible journalist at the *Post*. It's not something we welcome or love.

DS: I'm interested to hear you talk about the importance of a theatre that acknowledges its theatricality because you sometimes seem intent on bringing up things that are difficult to articulate in other ways. And I've noticed a change in your writing. Your plays of the past few years strike me as more risky, both in terms of form and subject matter, than most of your earlier work.

TM: I'm not sure I would agree with that. I think they're less judgmental of the characters. I'm less conspicuous than I was in my early work. You could divide my work into that which promotes my opinion of the characters and that which tries to let the characters be themselves. There's a big difference. Friends even say, "Your work used to be so much riskier." They always point to *Tommy Flowers* [*Where Has Tommy Flowers Gone?*, 1971] as being so risky and experimental. Those are exactly the kinds of things, one, I don't think about and, two, it's bad to think about, because you get writer's block. "Is this play risky enough?" That's for critics, people like you. *Master Class* is really not a play. The program said, "A Master Class with Maria Callas in the Singer's Program at Juilliard." The play's taking place in real time. Certainly, *Corpus Christi* is very theatrical, [as is] *Ragtime*. The first line is to the audience, and in the first number they all sing about who they are in the third person. These are all techniques. Maybe I'll discard them. The next couple plays I have in mind are plays where there is actually a fourth wall. So maybe I'm going back to something.

There are only two plays I wrote overnight: *Next*, the play that got me out of journalism and earning a living as a playwright, and *Master Class*, where I just had a vision. I knew the first line, "No applause," and the last line, "Well, that's that." I was at a benefit dinner writing on a program. I think about most of my plays, like *Corpus Christi*, for two or three years minimum, and then I wait and turn on the computer when I feel like I'm not just going to sit there and think, Now wait, how am I going to write a play called *Corpus Christi*? How do I write this play about Christ? I don't think, This should be more theatrical. This play's not going to have monologues, but address the audience instead. This play's going to have audience participation. Every so often I do. In *Master Class* she talked to the audience quite a bit, and in the original draft of *Love! Valour!* there's so much more of that. I think they were self-conscious. I like the *idea* of talking to the audience, but in reality I hate it. I hate it when an actor addresses me, especially when he wants a response from me, so it's especially sadistic of me to put it in my own plays. There's four or five passages from *Love! Valour!* that didn't make it to the first preview.

So there's writing that comes easily emotionally to you, that's maybe just a technical thing. And there's making the play work. Basically, you want to keep the audience in their chairs for two to three hours. That's the primary goal, and everything else is just talk. There's nothing worse than seeing a play and sensing that massive indifference, that absolute void of nonenergy between stage and performance. I think that's the most horrible sound of silence in the world. There's also the very painful thing of seeing audiences leave at intermission. Lately, I've done two three-act plays where you have two chances to lose them. So much of rehearsal is about how do we keep this alive and interesting, not intellectual conversations about meaning. You never discuss meaning with a director and an actor; you discuss why a line doesn't work, why an audience is restless at a certain point. Theatre is incredibly tactical, and it's the only art form where you are so involved with other people. It is a collaboration.

I don't know exactly what percentage of the draft that goes into rehearsal becomes the final product. I sometimes think it's not much more than 50 percent. When you go to *Master Class*, you experience the set, the lighting, the contributions of Zoe Caldwell, Michael McGarty, Lenny Foglia. It's not all me. If *Master Class* had been done with a different director, designer, and actress, it would have been a very different experience. I've been very good lately about getting what I want on a stage; that's why I write for specific actors. I know the directors I want to work with and the designers. John Guare and I were teaching playwriting for a year at Juilliard, and our theme was: be responsible for who does your sets and costumes. I don't design the sets and costumes, but I have a stake in it. It's difficult working with really good people that share a vision. So many playwrights get passive when it comes to production. "They're giving my play to Peter Brook. They're letting Martha Graham do the choreography." Well, maybe Peter Brook and Martha Graham are not the right people to do *Pal Joey*. You've got to say, "No, I don't think this work is in their vocabulary."

People talk about the theatre as if the text were everything. I think it's just a part. I don't think you can talk about a play without talking about the production. When you talk about *Streetcar*, you're talking about Marlon

Brando and Vivien Leigh and that movie. How can you erase these memories? It's not this flat, two-dimensional thing that we read. That's what's special about theatre. *Moby-Dick* is in two dimensions, but when you experience *Hamlet*, you experience him in three dimensions, and it seems to me you cannot separate notions of what Hamlet looks like or is about from Gielgud, Burton, Olivier, Kevin Kline. It makes it a very special art form. I think you can interview Ernest Hemingway and get the essence of anything by Ernest Hemingway. I don't think you can talk to me about theatre without talking to a thousand other people that contributed to what I consider to be theatre.

DS: I'm thinking of *A Perfect Ganesh*, for example, and how crucial the lighting is in producing a sense of the sublime.

TM: Lighting is very, very important to me. Only recently have I started to get the lighting I want. That was an example of being disappointed in the lighting but not speaking up, thinking, That's technical. Now I feel that a lighting designer is a collaborator. and I'm much more eager to hear his impressions of the text, how lighting could enhance it, but also to give him my ideas for it. Brian MacDevitt did my last play, and Jules Fisher and Peggy Eisenhauer did *Ragtime*. It's extraordinary work. I used to work with a lot of different people who said, "Here are your lights. Goodbye." Now these designers are there through previews, when the critics come in. I want to work with people who care 101 percent, and I know that's obvious, but a lot of people don't. I've gotten in trouble when my own aims are 101 percent. It takes enormous effort on everyone's part. Nothing is good enough in the theatre unless it's right. You can't be almost right.

Sound is very important to me. I sometimes have to say, "There should be a dog barking here." "Was that important to you?" "Yes, or I wouldn't have put it in." I have no stage directions, I never write, "Crying through her tears sardonically." I never write those kinds of descriptions. When I write, "A dog barks," and it's the only sound effect in the entire act, I want to hear it. I think Lee Strasberg did a terrible disservice. I hope his influence is starting to fade because I remember him saying to actors and directors, "The first thing to do is to cross out all the playwright's directions, including set descriptions and indications to the actor." And maybe that's where the barking dog gets overlooked or the lights rise to a blinding intensity. Lee Strasberg was always contemptuous towards playwrights' punctuation. To me, it's the same as reading a Mozart score: that's a quarter note, that's an eighth note. If you make them both eighth notes, it's not the same melody. Zoe Caldwell said to me, "You're very easy to act. I just follow your punctuation." Nathan Lane, another actor with whom I've worked very well, just says every word as I wrote it. The actor needs to just show up and say it. You don't need to embellish it with "oh," "ah," "I mean," mucking about it. In the cast of *Ragtime*, no one adds a comma to the script. When actors add all this other music, suddenly it's not me anymore. I get so crazy about that. I think it's sloppy. The music of a play is there. You try to find people who say, "You've given me all I have, the script, the words, the music. Let me sing it to you." As opposed to actors who say, "This is your script; let me make it mine." That's the kind of actor I don't work very happily with.

A lot of actors and directors don't look at the basic stage directions. It's really unimportant whether a character is standing or sitting. Playwrights who still write "crossing downstage right" are wasting time. Who cares? That's not what makes a scene work. The actors will find a place to be if the scene is well written. These other details are part of what I consider the score of the music and the lighting. I'm not very good at describing things, which is maybe why I'm a playwright, not a novelist. I couldn't look around and describe this apartment, but I could have a drunken divorcee in her early fifties who's thinking about having a facelift describe it, or a teenage boy describe his apartment. I write dialogue as opposed to a more objective observation, so I try to give an indication in my first stage direction of the style of the play. I remember the beginning of *Love! Valour! Compassion!* was nothing like what Joe [Mantello] and Loy [Arcenas] came up with. But they could tell I did not want a realistic set. Before Joe was going to direct it, I'd spoken to directors who said, "We're going to need two turntables." I said, "The first stage direction makes it so clear that I don't want realistic scenery. A chair becomes a car." They just didn't get what I wanted. So a stage direction is a description of the kind of set, which is a way of saying, "This is the kind of designer I think is right for this show." The first thing an audience sees is the set. The psychology of scenery and colors and light— there's no getting around that. A stunning example of that would be *The Ritz*. We did it in Washington, and it got very, very few laughs. We thought it was hysterical. Someone came to see it and said, "The set is three stories tall and battleship gray; it looks so foreboding." The producer ordered a paint call and stayed up all night and painted the whole thing red. The next night, with no other changes at all, the laughs started right away. I thought, You can write five hundred plays and never know that the battleship gray set will not be conducive to a sex farce.

DS: So much of this is about taking the audience on a ride, and your job is to engineer that in every way, including working with designers.

TM: It's our job, yes. Every play has different rules. Writing *Love! Valour! Compassion!* only helps you write *Love! Valour! Compassion! II*, not *Master Class* or *Corpus Christi*. Actors can create a persona and do it for ten movies and get away with it, but playwrights can't. Everyone talks differently. If you read Shakespeare, you may not know a passage is specifically from *Othello*, but you know it's not *Hamlet*. They're all different sound worlds. You make that a goal: how do I create this world through my words? It's got to be in the text. If everyone talks the same from play to play, it won't work.

DS: And there are other elements that also produce the unique character of a play. I was thinking about how the nudity in *Love! Valour! Compassion!* is so important in producing an almost transcendent, sublime vision of sexuality.

TM: The design helped. Randy [Becker]'s nice ass to look at up there. The lights just go, and the crickets chirp louder. Joe and Brian really worked to give me what I wanted. I didn't even write the stage direction, and I've seen other productions where the lights just stay the same through act two. There's not that moment where they're struck dumb by nature. It also comes during that speech about Alaska and the glacier, and there's this incredible silence. In other productions, that moment doesn't exist. It's supposed to be nonverbal for a moment or two. Silence is very important in my work. It's there, [but] I can't make a director do it. They did a production of *Lips Together* up in Providence, and at the end of the play, the actors saw the shooting stars and then Mozart comes on and then the lights come up in the audience just as they do on stage. It was a very good production, the music plays, and they're frozen, and the lights start coming up in the auditorium, and three and a half, four minutes later, we're all in the same room, in the same light, and then everything went out. It was thrilling. They didn't do that in New York. I said to the director, "Why did you do that?" He said, "It's in your script." It was in the published version, and I'd forgotten I'd left it in. It's so interesting to see someone do what I actually wanted, and I thought it worked. It's pretty scary to stand there for three and a half, four minutes, but it worked. You've just got to take risks. I think a gesture like that says, "This play's about you, these are human beings groping through marriage, fidelity, infidelity, mortality, homophobia, all the things that trouble these people. They're not actors; they've just been tap-dancing out here all night. Let's all listen to this sublime piece of Mozart together. We're all in this thing called life together."

The theme of *Lisbon Traviata* is people trying to connect and failing. I think there's some real connection between people in *Love! Valour!* There's virtually none in *Master Class*—she's trapped in a world of art, as much as Mendy is in *Lisbon Traviata*. There's a world of beauty and wholeness when she sings, but when she's Maria Callas, she's as fucked-up as anybody who ever lived. She's a terrible teacher in trying to communicate what she has that made her great. It's her secret, and she can't give it away because she doesn't know what it is. So she gets very angry, "I want some of your genius, your fire. I'm not here to give tips." It's like when I'm teaching playwrighting. "How do you get an agent? How do you get your play produced?" No, let's talk about why your scene doesn't work. Frustrating. I don't think it's impossible to communicate with another person, but I think it's very difficult. That's really important to me. I find theatre very visceral and very central. I want theatre that has the immediacy of a good lasagna or an exquisite wine. To me, you can feel it and taste it. The theatre is not a place to exercise your mind. I want the theatre to introduce me to people I would not meet in my own life, shock me, startle me, but I don't want it to tell me what I should be thinking.

DS: It should seduce.

TM: Yes, theatre is very sensual. And ballet is a form of theatre I'm very drawn to. I go to ballet quite a bit. My favorite painters have a very strong dramatic sense, like Giotto, who is an incredibly dramatic painter. And the relationships between people: how do you get to that moment of the Judas kiss? Writing *Corpus Christi*, I'm very aware of that moment in the Giotto fresco of the life of Christ. The paintings are well staged; he is a masterful director. The angle he chooses, his point of view towards the material is dramatic and useful to me as a playwright. Every playwright has to go his own road, and maybe there are very good playwrights who don't go to the museum or the ballet. I have a lot of friends who are excellent playwrights who don't go to the theatre much. I happen to enjoy going to the theatre, and also that's where you find the Lenny Foglias and Joe Mantellos of tomorrow, by going to workshop productions. If you wait until they're on Broadway and being nominated and winning Tony Awards, then everybody wants them and they're not going to go to Big Fork, Montana, to work on *Master Class* with you.

DS: It seems to me that in the years you've been writing, the American theatre has really become much more explicitly gay. It's almost as if it's coming round to you rather than the other way around.

TM: I don't know if I agree. People happen to be out, and there are a lot of damned good playwrights who happen to be gay. I don't think that American theatre is becoming gayer. Even ten or fifteen years ago, Paula Vogel's play [*How I Learned to Drive*] would have been done, and she would probably have been out. I just think that there's a lot of really good playwrights now who happen to be gay. I don't see theatre getting gayer. There's always been a very significant number of great actors, writers, directors who have been gay.

DS: I agree that there've always been a lot of gay men and lesbians active in theatre. But it seems to me that people are more out now than they were a decade ago, and also there's a certain sexual frankness that's more permissible.

TM: Unquestionably.

DS: You couldn't have written some of the characters and events in your recent plays twenty years ago.

TM: My very first play, *And Things That Go Bump in the Night*, was considered really shocking because there were two gay men in it. In a way, I feel I've even been punished for it. That certainly wasn't a masterpiece, but people were really shocked by the relationship between the two men. I think people have stopped being shocked by gay characters. Now it has to be a good play. Additionally, they've stopped saying, "Mr. McNally's a homosexual and the women characters are inauthentic." I think a gay playwright can write gay or heterosexual characters without that kind of comment. I'd like to believe that. Anne Heche has opened in a romantic comedy without anyone going hysterical about it. I really think the climate I grew up in has changed. You remember about Tennessee Williams and Edward Albee, and the horrible, horrible homophobic critics [of them]. I'm so glad [critics] can't get away with that anymore. They either like *Tiny Alice* or they don't. I just think that's terrific. I'm all for everything that's happened in terms of frankness in writing about sex. I'm surprised heterosexuals haven't been quite as frank in writing about sexual relationships. Sex is very important in my work. And then there are other writers for whom sex never seems to be of interest. It's the difference between apples and oranges.

The only criticism of, say, *Love! Valour!* that offended me was that the nudity was gratuitous or it was an attempt to please a gay audience. That really angered me; it just wasn't true. The nudity is an incredible part of *Love! Valour!* I'm saying these people have dicks—just like you—some of them have flabby asses and some don't—just like you. When a theatre says, "We'd love to do *Love! Valour!* but we can't have nudity," I say, "Don't do the play then, if it can't be a spontaneous, 'Hey, let's go swimming!'" Now if someone comes out nude or in a jockstrap and starts erotic dancing to turn the audience on, that is a very different use of the naked body than skinny-dipping, which is the most innocent pastime. That's when we all become children; we rip our clothes off and jump in the lake. I've had theatres say, "We'd love to do your play, but there's too many four-letter words, can we take them out?" I say, "Don't do my play." That's like saying, "We're gonna show the *David* here, but we're gonna put pants on him," then you're not showing the *David*. I have no problem if you don't want to do *Love! Valour! Compassion!* because of the nudity and the four-letter words and the physical contact between men. I'm sorry you have that problem in your community. You should aspire to resolve these problems, but don't do the play with bathing suits and the men never kissing or touching each other and someone not saying, "Fuck you." Then it's not my play. Do my play or don't do it—don't do a bowdlerized version.

So I don't think there's gay theatre anymore. I think there's less now than there was fifteen years or so ago. We begin with *Boys in the Band*. I think people say whether plays are good or bad. People say, "Is yours a good play? It's about three lesbians. It's about eight gay men." Not, "Let's go see it, there's naked men, these cute guys take their clothes off." The whole gay community has changed. In the sixties, we used to go to restaurants because they were gay and the food was horrible, but we thought it was so important that two openly gay men could sit in the middle of the restaurant on X Street. Now, we're too integrated. A gay restaurant has to be as good as a straight restaurant. A gay play has to be not as good as a "straight play" but as good as a play should be. There's no more special favors. I can't say I feel there's a backlash, like, "We're so sick of gays in theatre." Someone told me about the night *Kiss of the Spiderwoman* and *Angels [in America]* both won Tony Awards: the parents of a playwright that didn't win said, "What have they got against normal people?" I think that kind of thinking is gone, too. I think we're very fortunate to have so many good writers around. And so what if some of them are gay? To say that gay works are not of interest to anybody but gay men and gay women is absurd. *Love! Valour!* would not have had the life it did if it interested just gay men. If *Master Class* were only of interest to opera queens, it would have run three weeks.

It's very healthy and it's great that so many gay people have taken that big step out of the closet. We still have a way to go in that department. In theatre it's gotten pretty good. There's one or two people who, even if they don't speak openly about their sexualities in public, don't deny it in interviews anymore. We're so over it at the Tonys. Everyone who's gay is there with a partner of their sex. You don't have to invite girls or guys, so that when the CBS cameras are on you, you look okay. There are a lot of gay people kissing their partners on the Tony Awards now, too. Why gay people have found a life in the theatre is another issue. That's for psychologists. I like to write plays; I don't like to psychoanalyze myself. I have a few patterns I'm not terribly proud of. I'm in therapy. But the crucial thing is not "Why am I drawn to the world of theatre?" Because it's fun. I always learn from it.

When theatre works, I find it deeply moving. It can be very funny, very bold, very dramatic, touching; you feel connected to people around you in a way. Whether there are ninety-nine seats or fifteen hundred, when a play works well, there's a sense of community and you feel connected to your fellow humans. That's how it should be. You don't have that experience when you're home alone reading a novel. You can be moved, but you don't say, "I'm in this with all these people around me." If a play's really good, people talk going up the aisle, "Didn't you enjoy that?" "Wasn't that moving?" "God, that was funny, wasn't it?" "I really got a lot out of this, didn't you?" When a play doesn't work, we don't talk to each other. Some connection has failed. I think we go to the theatre out of a very basic need to be instructed, enthralled, to learn something. There's a reason the scout master tells little boys these stories. There's a little learning in all of that. That's why we go to see something live at night. Even a very unsophisticated person knows it's not just like a movie—that unlike *Gone with the Wind*, they can't reopen it on Friday with a restored print. There's more theatre in New York now than when I came in the sixties. Broadway has shrunk, but Off-Off-Broadway didn't exist. Off-Broadway really meant the Theatre de Lys, twelve theatres in the West Village, one or two in the East Village, one or two on the Upper East Side, Circle in the Square, and that was the extent of it. About twenty Broadway theatres have been taken down since I came to New York, but a lot of those theatres that were considered Off-Broadway in the sixties and seventies are gone because they're considered impractical. So you have the really small, letter-of-agreement, Equity, ninety-nine-seat venues that didn't even exist ten years ago, a lot of them happening in Chelsea right now. But they can only run so long.

DS: So it's important to you that the theatre be free, uncensored. And it will be supported, one way or the other, because the kind of communication they facilitate is so essential.

TM: I thought you meant free—no ticket price—that would be nice, too. The cost of production in New York is truly frightening and also, as you get older, it's less possible to work for no money. A twenty-year-old out of NYU or Juilliard is more inclined to do a workshop production for no pay than someone who's got a family. As you get older, you have more responsibilities financially, and it's very hard. But I think the cost of putting on shows now is so out of hand. It's so disproportionate. I know that prices have increased incredibly, but not like it has in the theatre. When I came to New York, the best seats for *My Fair Lady* were $7 or $8.95. That's not comparable to the $85 for musicals now. I saw a lot of plays on Broadway, and $2.90 was the going price for the balcony. Now the cheapest balcony seat for a play is $45, and it's $50–$75 for the orchestra. That does not reflect the inflation in the rest of our society.

With the NEA slowly fading away, theatres get very conservative. "Let's keep our subscribers happy," [they think]. People didn't make enough of a protest about losing Circle Rep. It was terrible to lose that theatre. We just can't afford any loss. We should be welcoming the Vineyard at the same time we're celebrating Circle Rep's twenty-fifth anniversary, not its closing. The Manhattan Theatre Club has certainly gotten more conservative. Any subscription theatre is conservative because young people don't say, "I want to see a play September 12th and May 11th, and here's the hundred dollars to do that." They make their plans that week. You get the old crowd there. It's sad. These are middle-aged audiences. I certainly don't want Lincoln Center, Manhattan Theatre Club, or the City Ballet to go under. But if you took away the subscriber base, all those companies would really be out of business, including the Met and the Philharmonic. The person who knows they're going to see *Tosca* on January 1st is always less excited than the one who says, "Cool, they're doing *Tosca* with Pavarotti. I've always wanted to see it," and stands in a line for ten minutes or two hours. At the Manhattan Theatre Club, audiences just aren't as thrilled to be there. But I couldn't have been allowed to produce *A Perfect Ganesh* or *Love! Valour!* at the level to which I've grown accustomed, with that quality of actors, designers, and directors, if we didn't have that subscriber base. You don't get Joe Mantello and Brian MacDevitt to work at a little loft in Chelsea for fifty dollars. You just have to accept that. So that's the biggest change: subscription didn't exist then. Good plays used to open on Broadway. All of Arthur Miller, all of Tennessee Williams, most of Edward Albee after the sixties opened on Broadway.

Love! Valour! Musicals!

Nelson Pressley / 2002

At sixty-three, playwright Terrence McNally has become the musicals man. He doesn't write the songs; he writes the books. And he's good at it—"a master," according to the venerable lyricist Fred Ebb.

Two of McNally's four Tony Awards in the 1990s were for the musicals *Kiss of the Spider Woman* (score by Ebb and John Kander) and *Ragtime* (score by Stephen Flaherty and Lynn Ahrens). McNally is currently represented on Broadway, in London, and, starting Tuesday, at the National Theatre, by *The Full Monty*, the spirited and Americanized musical adaptation of the little British film about unemployed blue-collar workers who rally together as they create an unlikely strip act.

He seems omnipresent. Next month Stanley Tucci and Edie Falco will star in a Broadway revival of McNally's play *Frankie and Johnny in the Clair de Lune*. Two musical projects are scheduled for New York this fall, and a third may be in the works. *A Man of No Importance*, adapted from another small English film, will open at Lincoln Center in October. And New York's City Opera will present *Dead Man Walking*, best known as the film starring Sean Penn as a death row inmate and Susan Sarandon as the nun who agitates on his behalf. McNally adapted it with composer Jake Heggie; the San Francisco Opera staged the premiere last year.

The third possibility is *The Visit*, based on Friedrich Dürrenmatt's 1956 drama. That musical, written with old pals Kander and Ebb (the three wrote *The Rink* together nearly twenty years ago), was well received last year at Chicago's Goodman Theatre. Chita Rivera starred as the fabulously wealthy woman who returns to her small hometown bent on revenge.

Yet McNally, sitting in the sun-filled, high-ceilinged living room of his 1920s-era apartment in lower Manhattan, says he now has a sign over his desk, and this is what it reads: "No More Musicals." The famously prolific writer who reeled off eight notable plays in a little more than a decade, and who was, with August Wilson, the most dominant American playwright of the 1990s, hasn't written a straight play in four years—not since *Corpus Christi*, a ritualistic yet modern retelling of the life of Jesus from a gay point of view, was greeted with bomb threats from religious extremists.

"I think maybe I'm still licking my wounds a little bit," McNally says.

Fatwas and street protests will do that. Only it wasn't the fanatics who scarred Terrence McNally most deeply. It was the critics.

The question is about creative rhythm, and whether there is a source to particular floods of productivity—the rush of plays a decade ago, the rush of musicals now. Unbidden, McNally finds himself talking about the *Corpus Christi* experience.

"It certainly made me think twice about what I want to do as a playwright," he says in a soft-spoken but swift tide of thought that, for the only time during an hour-long interview, sometimes has the easily conversational playwright fumbling for words. "I mean, to have that kind of critical savaging certainly gave me pause. I did not see it coming. I felt very ambushed."

McNally had been on a winning streak for years, anchored by a rich association with the Manhattan Theatre Club. Lynne Meadow, the MTC's artistic director since 1972, says, "It's one of the most profound artistic relationships I've ever had, both in terms of the work he's done and in terms of the actors we gathered for his plays, and who in some cases became his muses."

One of those muses, Nathan Lane, says: "He likes writing for actors that he knows. . . . That's highly unusual. Playwrights don't like to depend on actors in that sense. But I think it helps him sometimes to have people to write for."

The McNally-MTC partnership began with the satirical *It's Only a Play*, a rewrite of McNally's 1978 *Broadway, Broadway*, which had closed in Philadelphia and sent McNally into a multiyear funk. "Only a writer who loves the theatre and has survived its bloodiest wars could have written a comedy like this one," went Frank Rich's glowing review in the *New York Times* when the show resurfaced at MTC in 1986. In the cast, playing a rookie producer, was Christine Baranski.

Looking happily at the new version on the MTC's stage, Meadow told McNally she'd produce whatever he wrote next. It turned out to be *Frankie and Johnny*, an off-Broadway hit that was ultimately turned into a movie starring Al Pacino and Michelle Pfeiffer. (The gold-plated casting of the blue-collar lovers—Pfeiffer particularly—drew howls from some quarters.)

Next came Lane in a revival of *The Lisbon Traviata*, about opera queens and the breakup of a relationship. That was followed by *Lips Together, Teeth Apart*, with roles tailored for Lane and Baranski. *Lips Together* had a heavy undertow of mourning and fear as two straight couples endure a Fourth of July vacation at a Fire Island beach house that one of the women has inherited from her deceased brother. Cancer, adultery and a pool onstage that no one swims in for fear of AIDS are among the dreads and disappointments shuddering through the work. Yet without false sentimentality, hope pokes its head through the door in the end, with a shooting star a fitting emblem of McNally's optimistic spirit.

McNally continued to work in this seam of mortality and benevolence in *A Perfect Ganesh*, in which two grieving women, played by Zoe Caldwell and Frances Sternhagen, trekked to India in search of spiritual solace. Their guardian angel: Ganesha, the whimsical elephant-headed Hindu god who is the remover of obstacles.

(McNally keeps a small sculpture of Ganesha among the few items decorating his neat living-dining area. Another object that catches the eye, placed squarely across the room from McNally's Tony Awards: a bust of Shakespeare on a pedestal three feet tall, displayed as pridefully as if it were in a museum.)

Lane returned for *Love! Valour! Compassion!*, a nuanced ensemble piece that explored the relationships among eight gay friends over three holiday weekends. The play was a further refinement of the exquisitely mournful/funny sensibility that McNally was honing. *Love! Valour!* won him his first Tony for playwriting and was soon made into a movie.

The urgency rippling through *Lips Together, A Perfect Ganesh*, and *Love! Valour! Compassion!*—attractive and often funny dramas that were widely produced across the country—came from complicated, often unhappy characters yearning to make sense of life before it's too late. They were angry pieces that stopped short of being strident; McNally's magic was in his ability to wend through all the loss and anxiety with elements of whimsy and humor, finding ways to land ultimately on a luscious transcendent note. Thirty years into an up-and-down career that had begun with the poorly reviewed Broadway drama *And Things That Go Bump in the Night*, McNally had developed a rich artistic voice that was theatrically confident and abundantly compassionate. His plays left audiences glowing.

In its way, the musical adaptation of E. L. Doctorow's *Ragtime*—which onstage was essentially about the unstoppable multiculturalism of America—followed suit. His hugely successful Maria Callas play *Master Class* (starring Caldwell again) did not. But McNally's hot streak continued; both shows were big hits and won Tonys.

And then, at the peak of his success, McNally offered a provocation in *Corpus Christi*. Not an indirect one, like Edward Albee's current Broadway attraction, *The Goat*, which uses the extremity of bestiality to ask where the limits of tolerance are. *Corpus Christi* was a frank slap at the homophobia that kept emanating from the fundamentalist Christian right, which had steadily bashed gay artists for years.

At least that was how it was generally received by the time critics and audiences saw it. The general view was inevitably affected by the warping heat of threats, protests, and headlines that preceded the show's actual appearance. Half a year before the play opened in October 1998, the MTC had announced it would cancel the show due to security concerns, then reversed course after an outcry from the artistic community and consultations with New York police. Lynn Ahrens recalls going to a demonstration and seeing people "screaming and very, very upset."

"It was very scary to be in the street there," she says.

McNally thinks key elements of *Corpus Christi*—set in the Texas city where he was raised—were obscured by the fracas.

"It's based on a medieval morality play format, all men playing all the roles, how they used to do these plays in front of cathedrals," he frets. "And no one seemed to get that."

And as for his intentions?

"It's saying gay men have as much right to participate and say 'Christ is us' as any other men," he says. "If I'd made Christ a woman or black, I don't think there would have been a peep. It's something that gay men have been made to feel not a part of—you know, *you cannot truly say you love Christ and be a good Christian if you are a practicing homosexual.* So that's not so much *against* [fundamentalist Christians] as I wanted to present a Mass that gay men felt they could attend with pride and dignity. Because I believe that there is divinity in all of us. That's what I thought *Ganesh* was about."

Once the reviews were in, it was clear that McNally's hot streak was over.

"Maybe it's not perfect," McNally says, "but the derision with which it was dealt was hard for me to encompass because I had been writing plays, I thought, successfully." He pauses, and starts again. "I thought I deserved better than those reviews. I don't mean raves. But not just, 'Oh, this is a piece of junk.' Which is the reviews it got."

The Next Act

Writing musicals: it's nice work if you can get it, and that's what was next on McNally's docket anyway.

"It was almost a relief," he says, "that I had *A Man of No Importance* or *The Visit*, you know?"

"Terrence loves to write, and is happiest when he's writing," Fred Ebb says. "I think he just loves to be kept busy and creative."

Music has long been a major ingredient in McNally's life and work. Seeing *Annie Get Your Gun* at a tender age helped nudge him into the theatre. He's written two Maria Callas plays, structured *Frankie and Johnny in the Clair de Lune* with Bach's "Goldberg Variations" in mind (notwithstanding the Debussy in the title), framed *Lips Together* with Mozart. He's been a frequent panelist on the "Opera Quiz" segments of Metropolitan Opera radio broadcasts.

He loved the idea of a musical version of *The Full Monty* so much that he says he would have been disappointed if he hadn't been asked to write the book. *Monty* turned into what he describes as a "very happy production": written quickly, staged soon after completion, no major creative complications.

Adapting *A Man of No Importance* was his own idea. McNally came across the obscure 1994 movie in a video store, and wondered what so many good actors (Albert Finney, Brenda Fricker, Michael Gambon) were doing in something he'd never heard of.

"It must be *really* bad," he remembers thinking.

But the story of a closeted Dublin bus conductor involved with an amateur theatrical group appealed to him, so he called Stephen Flaherty (the composer) and Ahrens (the lyricist). They didn't see quite how McNally envisioned a musical out of it. Later, "Terrence wrote some exploratory monologues," Ahrens recalls, "and we said, '*Oh. We get it.*'" Roger Rees and Faith Prince will star in the show this October.

What draws Flaherty and Ahrens and Kander and Ebb to McNally the librettist is his intuitive knack for musicals, structure, story, leaving the best bits for the songwriters: he gets all of that.

"He leaves room for us to be at our best," Ebb says.

"When he writes a scene," says Ahrens, "there is always a lyrical idea in there."

"God knows that's the hardest job in a musical, really," says Lane. "It's always the most troublesome part."

McNally doesn't seem to bring much ego to the job. "If the music ain't good, no one cares how good your book is," he says. "It's about the music."

Though his passion for his most recent work is evident, he also describes this spate of adaptations as "jobs," making the word sound about as blah as it can.

"I'm being creative, but doing a job," the playwright says. "I try to honor the spirit of *The Full Monty*, the spirit of Dürrenmatt, the spirit of Doctorow when I do these things. But it's not the same as a totally original piece like *Master Class* or *Love! Valour!*"

He's not precisely sure why he hasn't written a play since *Corpus Christi*.

"I was younger, and there were actors—you could write a play for Nathan Lane, for Christine Baranski. And now these people, their careers are in different places. Not everyone wants to do long runs for $750 a week, you know what I mean?"

Energy has been a factor, too. McNally has undergone two major surgeries for cancer this year, and though he has been told he is now cancer-free—he seems pretty chipper as he blows in from Long Island and prepares to zip out to the theatre on this warm New York evening—his health has been a major concern. And in 2001 he lost his partner, playwright and activist Gary Bonasorte, to AIDS.

On top of all that, McNally echoes what a lot of artists assert after a certain amount of success: "I don't want to repeat myself."

"What are the stakes?" he asks. "Why bother to write a play? It's very hard work, and it's got to be pretty special for me to say, I believe in this, and I want you to put up hundreds of thousands of dollars, or millions, in some cases."

Lane offers this: "He's reaching a point in his life where we don't have to have a new play every season. He's living his life."

Still, the writer who says he's never failed to complete any project he's started intends to head for a warmer climate after tending to this fall's projects and maybe start a play. "I've got a couple ideas," he says—which, according to Ahrens, is as much as McNally ever discloses when he's working on something.

"I love musicals, and musicals are probably why I'm in the theatre," McNally says. "But I just don't want to collaborate with anyone for a while. I want what you see next to be *my* sensibility."

Writers and Their Work: Terrence McNally

Gregory Bossler / 2002

Originally published in *The Dramatist* 5, no. 2 (November/December 2002): 4–15.
© 2002 The Dramatists Guild of America, Inc. Reprinted with permission from
The Dramatists Guild of America, Inc. www.dramatistsguild.com

Terrence McNally's first play, *And Things That Go Bump in the Night*, was produced on Broadway in 1964, when he was twenty-five. Since then his plays have included *Bad Habits* (Obie, Hull-Warriner), *Frankie and Johnny in the Claire de Lune* (Hull-Warriner), *The Lisbon Traviata* (Hull-Warriner), *Love! Valour! Compassion!* (Obie, Tony), *Master Class* (Tony), and *A Perfect Ganesh* (Pulitzer finalist), among some two dozen others. His musicals have included *Kiss of the Spider Woman* (Tony), *Ragtime* (Tony), and *The Full Monty* (Tony nomination). In addition to four Tonys, three Hull-Warriners, and two Obies, McNally has also received the Lortel Award for Outstanding Body of Work and the Emmy for *Andre's Mother*. He has been a member of the Dramatists Guild Council since 1970, serving as vice president for nearly two decades. *The Dramatist* sat down with him in his Greenwich Village apartment, just as the play *Frankie and Johnny* was being revived on Broadway, the opera *Dead Man Walking* was about to open at New York City Opera, and the musical *A Man of No Importance* was in rehearsal at Lincoln Center Theater.

Gregory Bossler: Recently, it seems you've had shows appear in tandem. The revival of *Frankie and Johnny* just opened on Broadway while you're going into rehearsal for *A Man of No Importance*. During your last show, *The Full Monty*, you were also working on *Dead Man Walking*. I don't know how you keep up with all that work at one time, or is your work pretty much done before you go into rehearsal?

Terrence McNally: If it's a revival, my work is pretty much done. If it's a new work, I'm up to my eyeballs in revisions. There was very little to do with *Frankie and Johnny*. I cut about four lines that made the play seem very much of the year it was written. I changed *The Carson Show* to *The Tonight Show*, things like that. With *Dead Man Walking*, that too is a revival—it premiered two years ago at San Francisco Opera. Besides, they don't make many changes in opera during the rehearsal period. And they don't have previews, just opening night and that's it. It's like being shot out of a cannon. It's just too hard to revise with an eighty-piece orchestra, though a lot of famous operas were revised after their first productions. Puccini famously revised *Madame Butterfly* a year after its disastrous premiere. Verdi made revisions in *Traviata*.

The opera house is the exact opposite of the theatre, where we have previews and can make changes. Although I've learned over the years to try to have the script as tight as I think it can possibly be, you still find things that are wrong during rehearsal and previews. But that feeling of "We'll work it out in the rehearsal room" I abhor now. I used to go into rehearsal with plays that were way too long, that I knew weren't quite right, and the whole idea was to "fix it in rehearsal." I try to fix it in my office now. I still find a lot to fix even when I think it's "perfect" and just by putting it on its feet you find little things that aren't right, but I don't knowingly go into the rehearsal room thinking, "The play needs a lot of work."

GB: You only made minor changes to *Frankie and Johnny*, but have you ever revised a play? For example, wasn't *Tubs* revised?

TM: *Tubs* was a play in progress, so I wouldn't call it revised. What happened with the play at Yale that was called *The Tubs* and became known as *The Ritz* in New York was that another play had opened with a similar title while we were in New Haven. That's the only reason we changed our title. I was very upset when we had to stop calling it *The Tubs*, but a play opened Off-Broadway called *Tub Strip*. Now, of course, I love the title *The Ritz*, but I hated it originally. I thought, "I named it, and it has to be called *The Tubs*," but the producers thought it just would have been too confusing for the audience. . . . No, that wasn't revision. That was really an out-of-town tryout at the Yale Repertory Theatre, just as the out-of-town tryout for *Kiss of the Spider Woman* was at Purchase, in the project there for new American musicals.

GB: That project at Purchase started with such high hopes, but it didn't last.

TM: That story's very simple. It was going to be a program to try out new American musicals, because the road is virtually dead. Very, very few shows go out of town anymore, and one of the big problems with a musical is that you can't workshop it as successfully as you can a play. Much of the music depends on production values: i.e., sets, orchestrations, choreography. So, everyone said, "If we could only have a place where we could work on our shows near New York, drawing on the incredible talent pool there, and do it with an audience without critics, wouldn't that be close to Shangri-La?" Then the *New York Times* insisted on reviewing us, and, of course, every other paper did too, and the whole point of going to Purchase was finished. We thought, "We might as well do it on Broadway. If we're going to have the *New York Times* coming to review us, why go to Purchase?" The *New York Times* has a lot to answer for come Judgment Day, but their callous disregard of what was in the best interest of the theatre community in this case is very high on the list of their more dastardly deeds.

GB: You can't even go to Chicago or Seattle nowadays either without someone in New York coming to find you.

TM: Yes, the internet has changed the rules. It used to be that you did not hear a word about a new show. Now, there are spies at rehearsals, and you go into chat rooms and read, "Such and such song was cut today. This lead stormed out because a scene was cut." It used to be that you didn't really know much about a show until opening night in New York City, and now everybody knows. There have been postings on *A Man of No Importance* already on the internet, and we've only been in rehearsal two weeks. I guess the *Times* and other critics feel really threatened by this. "If everybody else is getting to comment on these shows, why can't we?"

It's very infuriating, because theatre needs time to develop and artists should be allowed to work. We're all doing this for people to eventually see our work. It's not like we want to keep what we do a big secret. If we did, we wouldn't go into the theatre. I can't think of a more public place to do creative work or try to earn a living, but critics and carpers should wait till it's ready. It's like going into the kitchen and taking the food out of the oven. Your mom says, "Wait, it's not baked yet," and you say, "I'm hungry," so you eat this soggy cake. It just doesn't make sense to come and review a show before people want it reviewed.

A painter and a novelist can stay in their studios alone polishing and refining, and then open the door and say, "Come into my studio." It's a fallacy to say, "These shows are being performed in public, therefore we have a right to review them," because the theatre needs that public response and feedback. The audience is the final character you add to the cast list of a play.

GB: Right out of college, you went on the road, so to speak, as a tutor for John Steinbeck's children. How did you get that job?

TM: Well, it wasn't right after college, but a year later. My first year, I worked at Actors Studio as a stage manager, and Molly Kazan, who ran their Playwrights Unit, asked me if I'd be interested in going around the world for a year tutoring John Steinbeck's sons, and I said, "Yes." I'd never been anywhere. So the five of us went off. We didn't quite make it around the world, but we had an amazing year. It was on that trip I started writing *And Things That Go Bump in the Night*.

GB: You also did some writing at Columbia.

TM: I wrote the Columbia varsity show as a lark. I did not think, "I'm going to be a playwright." I was still interested in being a journalist, and the varsity show was just this fun tradition—Rodgers and Hart had written two varsity shows at Columbia. I read in the student newspaper that no one had written a varsity show that year, so they were thinking of reviving an old one. I thought that was terrible, and since I'd never, quote, given anything back to Columbia for being a full scholarship student, I thought, "I'll write the varsity show." So I wrote the script, and a young composer-lyricist called Ed Kleban said, "I'll write the score." That was the first time I heard my words performed in public.

GB: You didn't have any thought of pursuing theatre at that point?

TM: No, it was just fun. You're really asking for the gods to strike you down if you harbor such thoughts. It's called hubris, the stuff of Greek tragedy. But I always liked theatre. My very first night in New York, I tried to get a standing room [ticket] for *My Fair Lady*, but the only way to get [it] was to sleep on the sidewalk in front of the Mark Hellinger Theatre overnight, so I went and got a ticket for *Damn Yankees* that night and, the next night, I slept on the sidewalk in front of the Hellinger. People came out of that evening's performance and saw us waiting in line and said, "You're going to stay here all night to get a ticket?" I remember thinking if they didn't care enough to do the same, they didn't deserve to see *My Fair Lady* in the first place!

How I got through Columbia cum laude I don't know, because I went to the theatre or the opera every night. For Maria Callas's debut in *Norma*, we had to sleep outside the theatre for about three nights. Michael Kahn—who four years later directed the varsity show and now runs the Shakespeare Festival in Washington—was with me. Her debut was the season opening night, which was also my birthday and the first time I'd ever been to the Met. I'd become a huge fan of hers through her recordings but had never seen her.

I guess it's not surprising I'm a playwright, but it was hard to admit that's what I wanted to do. In my world, if you were going to be a writer, your parents wanted you to at least work for *Time* magazine. My best friend in high school went to work for *Life* when he got out of Northwestern. They kept telling me, "Jimmy Hicks is writing for *Life*, a very secure job."

GB: How did you get to the Actors Studio?

TM: While I was a senior at Columbia, I wrote a one-act play and sent it to the Actors Studio Playwrights Unit. They met once a week and performed new American plays. Molly Kazan, Elia Kazan's wife, headed the panel that critiqued the plays. The play was called *The Rollercoaster*, which Molly said, "shows promise but not much knowledge of theatre." I had stage directions that were impossible, like a car driving across the stage. She said, "You ought to hang around a theatre more, and I have this job as stage manager available," so I took it.

For a year, I moved furniture around and got sandwiches and coffee for the likes of Elia Kazan and Geraldine Page and Kim Stanley and Ben Gazzara. It was heady times. The Studio was at its height. Marilyn Monroe would show up twice a week, and everyone would treat her very badly by ignoring her. At least I thought so. I found her a place to sit once. It was the epicenter of the theatre world, it seemed. Actually, I didn't particularly care for a lot of the work they were doing there. I don't think I was ever a great fan of that extremely naturalistic kind of acting. I had a lot of opinions, even then.

The first show I ever saw was Ethel Merman in *Annie Get Your Gun*. I like actors who know there's a fourth wall and are trying to reach me way up in the second balcony—as opposed to actors who go inward. I like actors who are not withholding. I didn't think I was in the right place stylistically, but it was fun being there, I learned a lot of practical things about working in the theatre, and I made friends that I've had the rest of my life, like Doris Roberts, who just came in from L.A. for the opening of *Frankie and Johnny*. I wrote *Bad Habits* for her.

GB: I've heard you like to have actors in mind when you're writing. Is it easier when you have a voice as a springboard for the writing?

TM: It just inspires me a little bit more to imagine Nathan Lane in this role or Zoe Caldwell in that role, but that doesn't mean they end up doing it though. I wrote the role of Buzz in *Love! Valour!* for Charles Busch, but his play *You Should Be So Lucky* was accepted for production at Primary Stages and there was a conflict. He said, "What should I do? I've committed to your play." I said, "I know how hard it is to get a play produced in this day and age. You should not turn down a chance to have a play produced." Then some other actors read the part as the play developed, but Nathan wasn't available. When we were about to go into rehearsal, he became available and did it.

No, when I wrote that play, I did not imagine Nathan doing it. Whereas, I did write *Master Class* and *A Perfect Ganesh* for Zoe, praying she'd want to do them. Having Zoe or Nathan in my head is also company. Writing's very lonely, so I can use all the company I can get.

GB: What about the company of musical collaborators? Does that make the writing harder or easier?

TM: It's just totally different. You don't have a collaborator when you write a play. With a musical, you have to enjoy collaborating. There are days I enjoy it enormously, and there are days when I say, "I'll never do this again!" I'm sure my collaborators feel the same way: "We're going to write our own libretto next time, so that we don't have to put up with him." The secret to working in the musical theatre is choosing your collaborators well.

The American Musical is close to the Hollywood Big Deal: you've got Marlon Brando, Brad Pitt, and Julia Roberts with Martin Scorsese directing—it's on the front page of *Variety* as the biggest pre-production deal in the history of Hollywood: everybody is going to make millions of dollars—but none of them have even met and they haven't read the script because there isn't one yet. In musicals, the same thing too often happens. "Let's get this hot playwright and put him or her with that hot songwriting team and that hot director"—and they don't always speak the same language.

To collaborate is like a marriage: you're in for the long haul. You're going to see these people almost every day for months, and then in rehearsals, if a change is needed, you have to agree on it. You can't get into, "The scene's fine, but the song sucks," or "The song's great, but the scene sucks." You just can't get into that kind of blaming. It takes work and sacrifice to collaborate. Good personal relationships take work and collaboration too. People are not automatically happy together for the rest of their lives, and to be good collaborators you have to choose each other carefully in advance. I'd be very leery of working with someone I didn't know really well, because collaboration is too personal.

GB: How did you begin collaborating with John Kander and Fred Ebb?

TM: They called me to work on a show they had written the score for but weren't happy with the book. That was *The Rink*, and I learned a lesson there: if even one song has been written before they call you, it's too late. The book writer should be there from the very first moment. Even though the score for *The Rink* was terrific, I was writing to connect dots, and that's not a good way to ever write a book—ever. I learned from that, and on *Kiss of the Spider Woman* and *The Visit*, we started fresh.

GB: I understand that, for *Ragtime*, you wrote a play for Lynn Ahrens and Stephen Flaherty to work from. Is that the way you usually like to work on musicals?

TM: It's the only way. Most people think a book writer leaves big blanks saying, "She sings a song here saying how much she loves him." That's not how I work, and the teams I work with would not want that from me. They want me to write a play. It's a play I know is going to be musicalized, so maybe I write a little more generously and use some images I might not use in day-to-day speech. Usually an idea for a song comes directly from a scene I've written. Sometimes a line I wrote becomes the title of a song or the first line of one.

I think I know intuitively scenes that lend themselves to music. So far, I've never written a scene where the composer or lyricist said, "There's no way we can come up with any inspiration for a song in this scene." I would consider it a real failure if I wrote a scene and the composer and lyricist said, "We can't find any music in this scene as written." My job is to inspire them—not to write dialogue to connect songs. I'm writing it as a play for John and Fred or for Lynn and Stephen to read, not as a play for you to read, not as a work I expect to see performed as a play. It's an idea without the actual music is the best way I can put it. The librettist's other big job is to structure the show.

GB: Once the composer and lyricist musicalize a scene, what then?

TM: I'll do some tweaking in the dialogue before and after. Very often, the song accomplishes what the scene did, so a lot of the dialogue can go.

GB: Have you ever tried writing lyrics?

TM: No. They're extremely difficult, and I wouldn't presume to. Playwriting, lyric writing, and libretto writing are three very distinct disciplines. They're not interchangeable, though some people think they are. The demands of a play are very different than the demands of a libretto. Don't ask me to enumerate them. They're just different. Whoever won the Tony Award for best play of the year is not necessarily going to write a good book for a musical or write good lyrics.

GB: When you sit down to write a libretto as opposed to a play, do you begin with a different mindset?

TM: The musicals I've done—with the exception of *The Rink*—were adaptations, so that's a different mindset already. You're trying to honor the tone of [E. L.] Doctorow, for example. With *The Visit*, you try to honor the tone of [Friedrich] Dürrenmatt. When I'm writing *Master Class*, I'm writing a play. When I'm writing *Corpus Christi*, I'm writing a play.

I cared enormously about the characters in *The Full Monty*, and I treated them with as much respect as I would characters in a play. I didn't feel I was writing a musical comedy, though it's a story that has innately humorous moments in it. I felt deeply for those men, and I wanted to honor the spirit of that film, which is modest and unassuming. To do *The Full Monty* in the style of a big, splashy Broadway musical would have been absolutely wrong for it, and getting David Yazbek to do the score was absolutely right.

GB: I'm surprised that, given all the opera you've seen, *Dead Man Walking* was the first time you attempted to write one.

TM: First, no one had asked me. Second, I don't know many opera composers. I didn't know Jake Heggie when San Francisco Opera said, "We believe in this young composer and would like you to meet with him." He wanted to make an opera of a Jean Renoir film, but I said, "If I ever did an opera, I would want it to be contemporary and American." The project seemed to be over, until one day I thought, "*Dead Man Walking* would make a great opera." So I called him—this was a year or two after our initial meeting—and said, "Are you still looking for a libretto and want to do an opera?" He said, "Yes."

However, this was a commission from San Francisco Opera. We didn't sit down and write an opera hoping someone would want to do it. It was thrilling that San Francisco Opera commissioned this young guy, who wasn't even forty, and took that leap of faith in him. I wish more theatre producers would do the same: find a young playwright and, instead of workshopping him to death, give him a production. We're not going to have new plays, new operas, unless people take a chance on new people, not the same old faces, including mine.

That's a big difference between when I started working in the theatre in the early sixties and today. It was a lot easier to get your show on. Off-Broadway and Broadway had many more theatres, more shows. I think what's wrong with the theatre today is expenses. You shouldn't have to put up eight to ten million dollars to put on a musical or one-and-a-half minimum to put on a play. That's what's killing the theatre. Everyone got very greedy, and prices got totally out of hand.

People ask, "Where are the playwrights? Where are the plays?" Instead, I ask, "Where are the producers?" That was the theme of a speech I gave at the League of Producers annual meeting in Toronto about eight or nine years ago. I kicked ass that day. When it was over, all the commercial producers stopped speaking to me. I was a persona non grata at the convention. However, I learned this year that both the Araca Group guys—who produced

Urinetown and *Frankie and Johnny*—and Kevin McCollum and his partner Jeffrey Seller—who did *Rent*—were at that convention and that my speech had inspired them to become producers, which really made me feel good. It made me so proud that something I said had affected someone in our business. It's not about art twenty-four hours a day. We need producers; they need us.

It's also nice to see a new breed of producer out there. With the death of Robert Whitehead, the days of the hands-on, one-on-one producer seemed to be over. It's imperative to have *individuals* back in the theatre putting their tastes onstage and on the line. Theatre is a mom-and-pop operation. It always was, and we've seen too much corporate theatre, where it's about product. I don't like this merchandising of a show as a brand name. It's not what theatre is finally about, and it makes it harder for an individually written show to have a chance.

You used to come to New York to see a specific show, handcrafted and quirky. It was about seeing *this* play with *these* two actors written by *that* guy, so you had to go to New York City to see it. It wasn't anonymous or interchangeable.

Urinetown and *Wit* and *Proof*: those are the exception now, and they shouldn't be. That saddens me. In the sixties there were so many plays in New York every year. Most of them were not very good, of course. But when you're dealing with original works of art, maybe only one in a hundred is going to be a really solid piece, a contribution to the literature, but so what? That's the price you have to pay.

GB: Have you had difficulty getting produced or are you at a point in your career when it's easier?

TM: Sure, I have difficulties. Arthur Miller has difficulties. Edward Albee has difficulties. There's no playwright that doesn't—not even Neil Simon. Thirty years ago, Neil Simon could say, "I've written a play called *The Odd Couple*," and Mike Nichols said, "I can direct it in January" and they took an ad out. Now, it's "Let's do a reading. Let's do a workshop production. Let's try it out at a regional theatre."

Master Class had its debut in Big Fork, Montana. Zoe Caldwell played Maria Callas in a community auditorium there because everybody thought, "This play has no commercial potential. It will only interest people who care about opera or know who Maria Callas is." Instead, it's become the most commercial, the most performed play I've ever written. After Big Fork, we did it at a tiny theatre in Philadelphia. Then we did it at the Mark Taper Forum. It was a long road to Broadway. I'm the first to admit the play is probably better because it had this long, slow journey, but if it had gotten bad reviews in Philly, it would have died there. If it had gotten bad reviews in L.A., it would have died there. There was always that anxiety of wondering if the critics would knock us off.

GB: Do you read the critics for yourself or because the producers will be reading the critics?

TM: I haven't read them for the past few shows because you can tell. If the reviews aren't good, your phone doesn't ring. If the review is good, it's never good enough, and if it's bad, it's seared in your brain forever. But if I went out of town with a show, I'd read the reviews. I certainly read the reviews of *The Visit* because I didn't spend a year of my life writing the show for it to be done for just six weeks in Chicago. It's a show I expect to have a future, so I read the reviews.

Critics who write for newspapers actually have very little effect on how a play turns out. Their reviews are not going to inform the play the way a rejection from an actor or a theatre will. The quality of actor attracted to your piece is a criticism. If you get the director you wanted, I take that as a criticism that matters. Why doesn't Joe Mantello want to direct this play? Why doesn't Zoe Caldwell or Nathan Lane want to be in it? Why did André Bishop or Lynne Meadow turn it down? That's the real criticism that matters to me.

There are playwrights who have been stopped by hostile criticism. I guess my skin is thicker or my will to prevail is stronger than their will to squelch me. I'm more concerned about the repercussions of criticism of a play like *Corpus Christi*. I mean getting timid, editing myself with "I'd better not do that" or "This will get me in trouble." You hope criticism doesn't get to your courage or your nerve. You have to have real self-confidence to write a play, and if the experience of *Corpus Christi* has made me in any sense fearful of what I want to write about, then the bastards will have won.

GB: In one interview, you said that certain actors could make you braver as a writer.

TM: When you're writing for the A-plus team, you write up to them. Perhaps it's not braver but more imaginative or more ambitious. If you have Zoe Caldwell there, you know you can write big stuff because she can do it.

Theatre is a total collaboration. People think, "She was so great in that play"—but she couldn't have been so great in that play without a good script. "The play is so wonderful"—but the play would not have been *as* wonderful if it did not have *that* cast and *that* director. Any success in the theatre is a total collaboration. Even wrong design can kill a show, but people sometimes lose sight of that and it becomes this "great play" and the actors and director are forgotten or this "great production" and the actors and playwright are forgotten. It's truly collaboration, and I can't make that point enough. Plays are created in the rehearsal room, not on the page.

Just make sure you're working with the A-plus team. If you start going to the B and C level, the play is not going to ever be an A-plus experience. So you have to write plays that the A-plus actors and directors and designers want to work on—and hold out for them. I can't think of a play that doesn't go through an enormous amount of work during the rehearsal process, and no one knows really what a play is until it's performed. You write the characters, but you don't really know who they are until the good actors play them and an audience experiences them.

I don't think the playwright knows his characters any better than anyone else. You'd think we'd know them better than but we don't. By opening night, the actors probably know my characters better than I do. They inhabit them in a different way. They live them moment to moment. It all goes back to choosing the right people to work with, and if you don't like collaborating, you have no business being in the theatre. You'll be miserable or impossible to work with. You know the kind: "Here's my script. Don't change a line. I'll be back opening night." Playwrights who don't go to rehearsal and roll up their sleeves to work are writing "literature." I'm not writing literature. I'm writing plays.

GB: Has seeing Edie Falco and Stanley Tucci as Frankie and Johnny increased your understanding of your play?

TM: Yes. They found things not in the original production, different things than Kathy [Bates] and Kenneth Welsh and F. Murray Abraham. In *Master Class*, I saw moments that Patti [LuPone] made unforgettable and did differently than Zoe. The last thing I want to see is an actress imitating Zoe Caldwell. When I went to Paris, Roman Polanski directed it with Fanny Ardant. It was totally different, everything about it, and I thought it was thrilling. Instead of making the big diva entrance like every Maria in America had done, which is what I wrote, Fanny Ardant just walked out holding a bottle of Evian, said, "No applause. We're here to work," and started going through music on the piano.

I love to see different productions. I've seen some very good productions of my plays in Europe and South America. I'm like [the] audience then. It's not the same experience as I'm having now with *A Man of No Importance*, being there for the writing process, the casting process—which was very long on this show, because *A Man of No Importance* is a cast of twelve or thirteen. It's also harder to cast a show than it was [in the past] because more and more actors have moved to the West Coast.

I'm so thrilled that Chita Rivera got her Kennedy Center honor this year because they're honoring a life in the theatre. It's not because she also has a very popular TV series or made ten movies. She's been rewarded for her unstinting service to the theatre. I wish some of the playwrights who are not quite so up there in name recognition would be honored too. It's very nice for the theatre for one of our own to be honored like Chita is—and very well deserved. She's a role model for life. I've learned a lot working with Chita about generosity and giving all of yourself, about showing up on time and well prepared. I was pretty sloppy when I was beginning in the theatre, thinking "We'll fix it in rehearsal."

GB: Wasn't part of the sixties and seventies about feeling your way through the process?

TM: Yes, there was that. There was the idea "Let's improvise this." It was probably not the best time to be writing well-made plays, and certain writers were made to feel obsolete, but we've seen a big return to narrative—which scares me, since my plays are almost plotless. Audiences today seem to enjoy narrative, and I think they respect the craftsmanship of a well-structured show.

GB: If you don't start with plot, do you start with an idea about a trip to India, for example?

TM: No, that's too general. Where the idea for *A Perfect Ganesh* came from I have no idea. It certainly wasn't a trip to India. The creative process is very mysterious to me. I just have an inner bell that goes off and says, "It's time to start writing the play," and I find out that more of it is written in my head than I thought. Then I start thinking about characters and the general situation. Sometimes I don't start writing it for a year or two. I don't sit at a blank screen and go, "What am I going to write today?" I turn the computer on when it's time to.

The main thing a playwright must know is what happens next, and so many people don't get that. They think playwriting is about writing dialogue. No, playwriting is recording what people do. What they say is just the tip of the iceberg, the part above water. Our job is to know the 90 percent that's beneath. That's why I think so many great novelists write unproducible plays: they just have people exchanging dialogue, and that is not theatre.

You have to have a sense of drama, of timing. Theatre is about writing in space and time. It's like music. You need a sense of when to go slow or fast.

You can't just write an hour symphony that's all allegro. You have to make key changes in music, contrast allegro with andante.

Some people innately, intuitively can write plays, and some can't. We all know very bright, wonderful people who are very boring when they try to tell a story at the dinner table. If you don't have a feeling for it, I don't think you can learn it. I've taught enough playwriting classes to see that the gifted students are gifted, and the ungifted—you hope you can guide them to another form of literature. The best response I had in college to my writing was for the one-act play *The Rollercoaster*. So what did I do? I went to Mexico to write the Great American Novel instead. Fortunately, I had sent the play to Actors Studio before I left. Soon in Puerto Vallarta, I began thinking, "I don't really like doing this, and I don't seem to do it very well." Then I got the letter from Molly Kazan inviting me to be a stage manager at the Studio, so I came back to New York and started doing theatre.

Gay for Play: Prolific Dramatist Terrence McNally Riffs on Queer Theater

Eddie Shapiro / 2005

Originally published in *Out*, October 2005, 64. Reprinted by permission.

Despite the fact that the majority of Terrence McNally's theatrical works—ranging from *Love! Valour! Compassion!* and *Master Class* to the musical versions of *Kiss of the Spider Woman* and *The Full Monty*—have significant gay themes, his plays have found more widespread, mainstream acceptance and acclaim than those of virtually any other contemporary playwright, gay or straight. As he prepares for the opening of his newest work, *Crucifixion*, about a TV producer's murder by a Jesuit priest, presented by San Francisco's New Conservatory Theatre Center (his next show, *Chita Rivera: The Dancer's Life*, opens soon in San Diego, and *Dedication or The Stuff of Dreams* has just finished a run Off-Broadway), McNally seemed the perfect candidate to offer a perspective on the state of today's gay theatre:

"The whole definition of gay theatre is one question I just wish people would stop talking about. I think there are so many wonderful gay artists in the theatre who are out and proud, and their plays aren't always about gay subjects but they are still wonderful plays. I'm really surprised that this question is still being asked after all these years.

"We're artists before we're gay artists. We're gay as individuals first, but as artists [the art] cuts across all boundaries. [Gay content] is no longer covered up or written about in code, as it was in Tennessee Williams's day. I think the battle of gay theatre has been won! The days when it was enough to have some pretty people take their clothes off are over. I don't feel very self-conscious anymore when I'm writing about gay men. I don't feel *O-o-oh, I'm writing a gay play.*

"Theatre is a place to change hearts, and you change minds by changing hearts first. A homophobic person's heart has to be spoken to before his mind. Change the heart, and then people change their minds when they go to the voting booth. I think that theatre is still a forum for that. At any rate, ten years from now maybe we won't have this discussion at all. It's all changing, and I think that's great."

Terrence McNally '60 Prepares for Another Broadway Opening

Laura Butchy / 2007

Originally published in *Columbia College Today*, March/April 2007, 14–19. Reprinted by permission.

Terrence McNally '60 is one playwright who is never out of work. A stalwart in a profession known for erratic employment, McNally has sustained himself for more than forty years while enjoying one of the most successful careers in American theatre. With numerous plays, musicals, and even an opera to his credit, the prolific writer shows no signs of stopping.

"I count my blessings on a daily, hourly basis. I'm a very fortunate man, and I know that," says McNally. One of America's most important playwrights, McNally's modesty and genuine contentment seem understated for a man who has been described by the *New York Times* as "one of the theatre's most acclaimed, and durable, playwrights."

This spring's double helping of McNally's plays in New York is a perfect example. Following its world premiere in Philadelphia last year, *Some Men* runs Off-Broadway at Second Stage Theater March 2-April 15. On May 6, his newest play, *Deuce*, will premiere on Broadway.

Deuce will star Marian Seldes, lauded for her performance in McNally's *Dedication or The Stuff of Dreams* at Primary Stages in 2005, and Angela Lansbury. Lansbury's appearance has garnered considerable buzz as it will be her first appearance on Broadway in more than twenty years after earning four Tony Awards for her work in the musicals *Sweeney Todd*, *Dear World*, *Gypsy*, and *Mame*. "We all are floating around in the ether," Lansbury told the *New York Post* when the cast was announced in October. "It's a wonderful gig we're embarking on here."

"Listen, darling," added Seldes, "Angela and I are playing two women our own age. But we are not in a nursing home, we are not being pushed around in wheelchairs, we do not have Alzheimer's. Most times, you open a new script, that is where you are. But it isn't what I want to go to the theatre to see."

The veteran actors will co-star as retired tennis players who were once a championship doubles team. As they prepare to be honored for lifetime achievement, they look back on their relationship and the sport that gave them their livelihood and how it has changed. Directed by Michael Blakemore, the show will open at the Music Box Theatre just in time to be eligible for the 2007 Tony Awards.

McNally's Off-Broadway offering, *Some Men*, revolves around a subject close to his heart: gay marriage. Set at the wedding of two men, the play observes guests at the ceremony reflecting on their own lives and loves, mingled with scenes covering the evolution of gay life during the last century. The play premiered last summer at Philadelphia Theatre Company, which also produced the world premiere of *Master Class*, McNally's examination of legendary opera soprano Maria Callas that earned the 1996 Tony Award for Best Play.

"We are obviously enormous fans of Terrence's work," says Sara Garonzik, producing artistic director of Philadelphia Theatre Company. "When I read online that he was developing a new play called *Some Men* at White Oak as part of the Sundance Theater Institute, I began making inquiries as to whether it was possible for Philadelphia Theatre Company to jump into its development process and ultimately give it its world premiere."

A *CurtainUp* review of Philadelphia Theatre Company's production last summer read, "This is a lush, mixed bouquet of sex, pain, and laughs, and sometimes big laughs happen in the painful parts. Not quick montage, situations are presented with depth and poignancy. Time is taken to get to the heart of each little story. . . . This is a big, generous, multifaceted, ultimately joyful smorgasbord with an implicit plea for acceptance."

McNally believes acceptance of gay marriage is only a matter of time. In 2003, he and public interest lawyer Thomas Kirdahy traveled to Vermont to get married, initially meant as a political gesture. "We were standing in the hotel, and people started gathering as the ceremony went on," McNally recalls with feeling. "By the final 'I dos,' there were about thirty people, and it was very emotional saying those things: in sickness and health, until death do us part. It has really raised the quality of our relationship. Since then, I've convinced two of our heterosexual couple friends to get married, and they're very glad they did!"

Second Stage artistic director Carole Rothman found *Some Men* intriguing from an early reading of the show, and she is enthusiastic about the play's development. "It's very different than it was in Philadelphia," she says. "For example, there were two women in the play before, and those parts are gone. And they sang, and those songs are gone. Terrence has made a lot of changes; many scenes have been cut, new ones have been written. It's going to be very interesting."

Even with adjustments, the topic remains clear. "I really think gay marriage is a civil right that eventually will go to the Supreme Court," McNally says, "and no matter how conservative they are, with the right lawyers, it's going to make it. I hope that this play will make people feel a little more sympathetic to it."

Fighting for gay marriage is nothing the wide-eyed young McNally would have expected for his future while growing up in Corpus Christi, Texas. He doesn't recall living in Florida, where he was born when his parents were running a bar and grill on the beach. After a few years, the family moved to Texas, where his father became a soft drink distributor and then a beer distributor.

McNally's mother, however, set the course for his future. When he was seven, she took him to New York City to see Ethel Merman in *Annie Get Your Gun*, and he was hooked. Six years later, they returned to see Gertrude Lawrence in *The King and I*. Both experiences are burned in his memory. "Those were two very significant theatre experiences for a child. They were very real for me," McNally remembers. Though he would see Merman again, Lawrence died shortly after that, and the young McNally "just wept copiously. She was so beautiful and just the essence of the stage actress. I don't remember where we were sitting but it felt that she was right there. We were probably in the balcony, but she had a presence."

Meanwhile, McNally was excelling at the W. B. Ray High School in Corpus Christi, inspired by English teacher Maurine McElroy (whom McNally still respectfully refers to as Mrs. McElroy).

Though few students from the town went out of state for school at the time, McElroy suggested McNally consider the Ivy League, "which sounded very exotic," McNally says with a laugh. When he and his best friend were accepted into Yale and Columbia with identical scholarships, they thought it would be silly for the first two students from their area to go east to the same school. "We literally flipped a coin," McNally says. "He was very, very happy at Yale, and I ended up being very, very happy at Columbia."

The chance to attend theatre and opera in New York City was a major attraction for McNally. His first night at Columbia in 1956, he wanted to see *My Fair Lady*, but the line formed overnight to get tickets. So he went a few blocks away and saw Gwen Verdon in *Damn Yankees*, and after the show waited in line all night to see *My Fair Lady* the next day "One night when I saw it—I saw it twelve times—President Eisenhower was there, one time Frank Sinatra, Dean Martin . . . every celebrity in the world was going to see it," he recalls.

Those two shows only whetted McNally's appetite for the theatre. He spent most of his evenings as a college student seeing as much theatre and opera as he could, paying $2.90 for back row seats on Broadway or $1 for standing room at the Metropolitan Opera. In between classes and shows, he waited tables at a graduate dorm across Amsterdam as part of his work scholarship to pay tuition and invest in a winter wardrobe.

Though he may have had "nothing to wear," he was fortunate to arrive in New York in a mild September. McNally vividly remembers his first trip to campus via White Plains, where he visited family friends who drove him into Manhattan. "They knew how to get into New York without using toll bridges," McNally relates. "So we went right through Harlem, and suddenly they stopped the car. I was shocked because we went from a pretty gamey neighborhood to suddenly Morningside Heights, and it was like, 'Get out of the car, this is where you're going to school!'"

McNally soon adjusted to an urban campus and New Yorkers, whom he initially found "very brash and loud and aggressive. But by the time I went home at Christmas, I knew this was where I wanted to stay. And I think I began to realize while I was there that Columbia was really going through a golden age. My freshman history was with Stephen Marcus. I studied with [Lionel] Trilling, [Eric] Bentley, [Jacques] Barzun, [Mark] Van Doren. . . . I had an incredible education at Columbia."

The college also provided McNally his first opportunity to write for the stage. His parents had grown up in the New York area and become fans of the *Varsity Show*, seeing works by Richard Rodgers '23, Lorenz Hart '18, and Oscar Hammerstein II '16. When McNally read in *Spectator* his senior year that there would be no Varsity Show because there was no one to write it, he volunteered. Titled "A Little Bit Different," the show had music by Edward Kleban '59, who later earned fame as the lyricist for *A Chorus Line*, and was directed by notable director Michael Kahn '61. "I had a great time in doing it. I was even in it," McNally adds. "It's the only time I've ever acted. Someone got sick, and I ended up playing a bullfighter, with shoe polish in my hair."

After graduation, McNally moved to Puerto Vallarta, Mexico, on a traveling fellowship to write a novel. When he realized he didn't know how, he wrote the beginning of a play instead. He sent it to the Actors Studio in New York, and they invited him to work as a stage manager there to learn about the practical elements of theatre. After a year, the head of the Playwrights Unit recommended McNally for a job as a private tutor. McNally spent the next ten months traveling around Europe with author John Steinbeck and his family.

During that time, McNally finished his first full-length play *And Things That Go Bump in the Night*. The play opened on Broadway on April 26, 1965. Unfortunately for the budding writer, the play closed on May 6. "The play was a flop," McNally says, "so I took a job at *Columbia College Today!*"

While the show was a legendary bomb in terms of the press, McNally earned some fans and was awarded a Guggenheim Fellowship the following year. He continued to try his hand at playwriting, and in 1969, his one-act comedy starring James Coco, *Next*, became his first hit. "I've earned a living as a writer ever since," McNally adds. "Sometimes a very meager one, but I haven't had to have any other jobs."

Living in a $45-a-month apartment in Greenwich Village furnished almost exclusively by a bed and a typewriter, the young playwright continued to write. Following *Next*, he completed a series of well-received comedies, including *Where Has Tommy Flowers Gone?*, *Bad Habits*, and *The Ritz*.

It was *Bad Habits* that introduced McNally to Manhattan Theatre Club and its artistic director, Lynne Meadow. In 1973, the show debuted as part of a festival of twenty-three plays. Composed of two one-acts, *Bad Habits* went on to a Broadway run featuring F. Murray Abraham, Cynthia Harris, and Doris Roberts. McNally returned to MTC in 1986 after his play *It's Only a Play* found its way into Meadow's hands. "I thought it was really fun—vintage Terrence," says Meadow. "The night before it opened, I said, 'It doesn't matter what the press says to me about the play. I think it is great, and I'd like to do your next play.' It was the beginning of an amazing time and an amazing collaboration for Terrence and MTC."

MTC and McNally went on to collaborate on a series of outstanding productions that garnered critical and popular praise. "It was wonderful doing plays there—every artist should have something like that," McNally says. "It was kind of a family. I basically view theatre in New York like any other town—regional theatre—and MTC was my regional theatre, whereas the Alley Theatre in Houston or Seattle Rep might have been somebody else's."

The not-for-profit MTC turned out to be a life-changing artistic home for McNally, offering him the unique opportunity to write freely, knowing he would be produced and leading him to write some of his most heralded plays. *The Lisbon Traviata* (1989), *Lips Together, Teeth Apart* (1991), *A Perfect Ganesh* (1993), and *Love! Valour! Compassion!* (1994) all earned praise, with the last moving to Broadway and earning McNally the 1995 Tony Award for Best Play. Each of these dealt in some way with the AIDS epidemic and homosexuality, topics that McNally has never had difficulty addressing. In fact, *And Things That Go Bump in the Night* caused a stir in part because in 1964 Broadway was not ready for such a frank portrayal of a gay character.

"One of the proudest things during my time as artistic director at MTC is my collaboration with Terrence and the plays we worked on together," Meadow says of her thirty-five years with the company. "This was a very special commitment to a very special person who turned out to be one of the great American playwrights and a great human being."

The genuine human qualities of McNally's characters provide his writing with a universal quality. His characters often are people looking for relationships and commitments, trying to connect and achieve intimacy with others. In its embodiment of these underlying themes of loneliness and wanting to connect, *Some Men* hearkens back to another McNally MTC premiere, *Frankie and Johnny in the Claire de Lune*. One of his most popular plays, the story of two lonely New Yorkers trying to start a relationship was later made into a movie starring Al Pacino and Michele Pfeiffer and was revived on Broadway in 2002 with Stanley Tucci and Edie Falco.

For the revival, McNally flew McElroy in from Texas to attend opening night. The play is, after all, dedicated to his beloved high school English teacher. "I'm very, very lucky I had this woman as a teacher at a public high school. She's influenced me as much as anyone," McNally says. "I remember writing a short story in my writing class in high school that began 'Mrs. Johnson toyed with the maraschino cherry in her martini and thought about whether she should tell her husband she wanted a divorce.' And Mrs. McElroy said, 'Have you ever had a martini? Because the thought of a maraschino cherry in a martini is revolting. Write about what you know.'"

In a sense, that is what McNally has been doing ever since. Many of his plays include elements of the gay experience through the years, reflecting changes in homosexual life during his lifetime. He recalls being impressed when he lived in New York in his twenties that he could visit gay bars without them being raided.

"Gay life has changed enormously." McNally says. "When I went to Columbia, there was no gay student union. There were gay bars, but with no windows, just a door. Forty years later, the issue is gay marriage." While *Some Men* embraces themes he has dealt with before, the play reflects his passionate support of gay marriage and is more outwardly political than some of his other work.

Though his writing is far from "agitprop," McNally has met with his share of controversy. In 1997, his play *Corpus Christi*—a modern-day retelling of the story of Jesus's life in which he and his disciples are homosexuals—caused a furor in New York and London. After misinformation about the play appeared in the press prior to opening, protests surrounding the production became so intense that MTC had to stop selling tickets and audience members were forced to pass through metal detectors upon entering the theatre. When the play premiered in England, a British Muslim group went so far as to issue a fatwa on McNally.

"I'll never know if the chaos was genuine because it was created so artificially," McNally says with a sigh. "It was never intended to be blasphemous. I thought the play would open the experience of the life of Christ, which I find a significant and meaningful life, to gay men and women who have been told they are sinners, to let them hear this story and to feel welcome, and I was very proud of it.

"I had the same thing with my first play, *And Things That Go Bump in the Night*," he continues. "One night somebody pulled an actor off the stage, and started screaming, 'You shouldn't be doing this obscene play!' and another actor jumped off and started fighting with him. I don't like that kind of conflict in the theatre. I want people to be agitated and argue when it's over, but I don't think actors should be pulled off the stage."

McNally hasn't let such incidents affect his work, and somehow the inexhaustible writer doesn't suffer from writer's block. "Usually I figure out what I want to do and do it pretty quickly," he says of his writing method. "At Columbia, I'd stay up all night writing my papers. When I worked at a newspaper, the pressure taught me to write for deadlines. I think newspapers were good training for theatre—it was loud and people were running around. I write in the corner of a rehearsal room, and people ask how I can work there. I could work in a subway if I had to. I don't need a perfect environment."

Another way McNally avoids writer's block is by never sitting in front of an empty screen. "It's masochistic, and I won't do it to myself," he says simply. "If I don't feel like writing or don't have something I want to write, I go to a museum, I go for a walk, I see a friend, I travel."

McNally penned *Deuce* in a few months last year. Interested in people who had earned their living doing physical work and no longer can, such as older athletes or dancers, McNally focused on two women who were once great tennis players. He also wrote it thinking of Seldes, hoping she would want to be in it. McNally frequently has specific actors in mind when writing, such as Kathy Bates for *Frankie and Johnny* or Nathan Lane for *The*

Lisbon Traviata. "Sometimes you write a part for people just hoping you'll have access to what they can bring to it," McNally explains. "It's not line reading, it's rhythms and cadence. You can't teach it, so finding the right people is big part of it.

"I basically hear Nathan Lane in everything I write," he admits after a pause, "man, woman, old, young . . . who was *Master Class* written for? I would say Nathan Lane." Though Lane never played Maria Callas, he did feature in earlier McNally works such as *The Lisbon Traviata, Lips Together, Teeth Apart,* and *Love! Valour! Compassion!* "I believe very much in writing for specific actors, when you find people who share your world view," McNally adds, "because you can't explain to someone why something is funny or sad."

Through the years, McNally also has given voice to characters in musicals and even an opera. He first tried his hand at writing the book for a musical with 1984's *The Rink,* but it was *Kiss of the Spider Woman* that brought him acclaim as a musical writer when he won the 1993 Tony Award for Best Book of a Musical. He won the same award in 1998 for *Ragtime,* the highly praised adaptation of E. L. Doctorow's novel.

"It's a different job of craftsmanship," McNally says of writing a musical. "Theatre is collaborative to begin with, but with a musical, there are three authors: the lyricist, the composer, and the book writer. The musicals I've done are often ones I've cared about very much. But *Ragtime* was Doctorow's baby. I tried to take care of his baby and present it in a new way."

Opera fan since childhood, McNally was well prepared for his operatic venture *Dead Man Walking.* Working with composer Jake Heggie, he wrote the opera version of Sister Helen Prejean's story about visiting an inmate on death row for San Francisco Opera in 2000. The show has been unusually successful for a contemporary opera and is performed around the world.

Thus far, McNally's writing has earned him four Tony Awards, an Emmy Award, and a citation from the American Academy of Arts and Letters. Among his many other accolades and awards, he received the John Jay Award for distinguished professional achievement from the college in 1992 and the inaugural I. A. L. Diamond ['41] Award for Achievement in the Arts from Dean Austin Quigley at a reception prior to a performance of the 110th Varsity Show in 2004. McNally, who penned the sixty-sixth Varsity Show, keeps that statuette on a shelf just below his Tonys in his Greenwich Village apartment.

But at sixty-seven, the scribe is not about to rest on his laurels. In June, there will be a workshop of *Catch Me If You Can,* a musical based on the

2002 Steven Spielberg movie that he is creating with music by Scott Witt-man and Marc Shaiman (creators of the musical *Hairspray*). A musical by McNally, composer John Kander, and lyricist Fred Ebb, *The Visit*, is sched-uled to open in September at the Signature Theatre in Arlington, Virginia, starring Chita Rivera, for whom McNally composed a one-woman musical in 2005.

In the meantime, McNally continues to devour New York theatre at an incredible rate. Attending shows three times a week, if not more, McNally enjoys everything from Broadway to Off-Off-Broadway. He also has begun to listen to more instrumental music later in life, which he confesses to not having enjoyed at the college.

"I ended up being a great proselytizer for Columbia," says McNally. "The program we took was great, two years of Humanities and CC . . . stuff I probably never would have done. Somewhere else, I would have just focused on journalism. In summers, I worked at a newspaper in Corpus Christi as a reporter. I always was interested in writing, from the time I was a student in elementary school, cranking out little things on ditto machines.

"I always knew that I wanted to be a writer, but I was kind of surprised that I ended up writing plays."

Living Life by the Beat of His Own Libretto

Peter Marks / 2010

Originally published in the *Washington Post*, March 14, 2010, E1, E9. © 2010 The Washington Post. All rights reserved. Used under license.

From his aisle seat in the Kennedy Center, dressed in a comfy sweater and corduroy slacks, Terrence McNally is gazing serenely at the Opera House stage.

The production he's immersed in is a Russian company's concert version of the Tchaikovsky opera *Eugene Onegin*, and though he seems thoroughly engrossed, the serious fan in him can't resist breaking the spell with some running color commentary.

"I like the mezzo, but she's going to fall out of her dress," the playwright leans over and says at one point, about a svelte blonde singer with unwieldy décolletage.

"That had a nice snap to it," he remarks at Mariinsky conductor Valery Gergiev's handling of the vibrant ballroom scene in Act Three. About the Russian tenor Sergei Semishkur, whose character is killed in a duel, McNally's even more enthusiastic. "Bravo!" he shouts repeatedly during the curtain call, tilting his head to add: "He *really* hit a note at the end there."

McNally's relationship with opera is a lifelong romance, a passion that was ignited when he was a mere stripling in a Catholic elementary school in Dallas by a nun who brought in a recording of soprano Licia Albanese singing Puccini. "I just liked it right on the spot," he says over a dinner before *Onegin*. "If there were thirty of us in the classroom, I was the one who loved it instantly."

A guiding principle for composing plays is to write what you care about, a dictum the McNally canon has embraced with unabashed ardor. He has made opera a signature motif, a theme springing from a deeply personal place. It shows up in his plays the way other formative kinds of music suffuse the oeuvre of other artists—Gershwin in the films of Woody Allen, the blues in the dramas of August Wilson.

The artistic connection may be even more intense in McNally's case, because the evidence reveals what an abiding influence the musical form has remained for him. Again and again over a long career, the playwright, now seventy-one, has mined opera's dramatic possibilities in plays that variously feature opera buffs, composers, singers, even conductors. And now the Kennedy Center, in a mini-festival running through April 18 that it calls "Terrence McNally's Nights at the Opera," is presenting three of those works, in three of its theatres: 1985's *The Lisbon Traviata*, 1995's *Master Class*, and a new play, *Golden Age*, which is set backstage at an Italian opera house in the mid-nineteenth century.

An accomplished cadre of actors has been recruited for the project, among them John Glover and Malcolm Gets for *Traviata*; Tyne Daly, portraying Maria Callas in *Master Class*; and Marc Kudisch and Jeffrey Carlson for *Golden Age*. (Christopher Ashley, Stephen Wadsworth, and Walter Bobbie are their respective directors.)

"I feel very blessed and I'm enjoying the process," says McNally, a New Yorker spending the better part of a month in Washington, attending rehearsals and playing the tourist; on Monday, he and his partner of nine years, Tom Kirdahy, were given a private tour of the US Supreme Court. "And the Kennedy Center is treating me like royalty," he adds.

The first-class handling is gratifying for McNally, who, despite the Broadway successes of works like *Master Class* and *Love! Valour! Compassion!*—which won him the Tony Award for best play in back-to-back years in the '90s—can speak with some fresh pain about his disappointments. He mentions, for instance, a falling out several years ago with his longtime artistic haven, the Manhattan Theatre Club, which he says made him all but persona non grata after it rescinded an offer to open its refurbished Biltmore Theatre on Broadway with one of his plays [*Dedication*]. And his belief that some of his output, from his libretto for the musical *Ragtime* to a recent play, *Some Men*, has been dealt with roughly by some reviewers can cause a temporary darkening of his mood.

"I've never felt like a critics' darling," he says, quickly summoning a memory from forty-five years ago of the drubbing of his first Broadway play, *And Things That Go Bump in the Night*. It opened April 26, 1965, and closed twelve days later. "I thought the reviews would say 'flawed, uneven, by a vital, talented playwright,'" he recalls. "But one said, 'It would have been better if Terrence McNally's parents smothered him in his cradle.' Actually, two reviews of my first play mentioned my death."

Still McNally persevered: a producer, Theodore Mann, filled the theatre for that first play's short run by charging $1 a ticket, thereby bolstering McNally's faith in his abilities. And he has since faced far, far tougher days: the death of a longtime lover, his own recurring struggle with lung cancer. These days, he says, he is out of the woods and feeling better.

So much better, in fact, that he is using the occasion of the Kennedy Center spotlight to tinker a bit with the plays, even revisiting the twenty-five-year-old script of *The Lisbon Traviata*, an acidly funny tragicomedy revolving around abrasive friends who share an opera obsession. "I've made a few little fixes, a few little changes here and there," he says, adding that once upon a time he wasn't scrupulous enough about proofreading the versions of his scripts published for use by actors.

He was far more vigilant when it came to the casting of the Washington productions. Glover, a McNally favorite who won a Tony for his portrayal of twin brothers in the gay-in-the-age-of-AIDS comedy *Love! Valour! Compassion!*, says the playwright called him last fall to ask if he'd accept the role of Mendy, the hilariously prickly opera devotee of *Lisbon Traviata*, a part that in its original incarnation established the whirlwind comic virtuosity of an actor by the name of Nathan Lane.

When Glover—intimidated by Lane's imprint on the part—failed to call McNally back, the dramatist left him a pointed voicemail. "He was so offended," Glover says. "So I called him up and I said, 'Listen, I'll be honest with you: I'm terrified. I know nothing about opera and Nathan was terrific and I'm terrified to do it.' And Terrence said: 'Doesn't that mean you're supposed to take it on?'"

McNally is an actor's playwright: His best works are filled with caustic wit, a sense of humor that is delectably playable. He even writes funny in *Master Class* about his classical deity, Maria Callas, the singer who for him took opera to a higher level, a performer who didn't hit notes so much as strike nerves. "I loved Callas before I ever saw her," the playwright says, recalling evenings as a teenager in Texas listening to her on radio broadcasts from the Metropolitan Opera House.

"That was my theatre," he explains. "I just fell in love with the sound of her voice. She didn't sound like she was singing. She sounded like she was saying something."

His fascination only deepened after moving to New York to attend Columbia University, where he befriended a classmate and fellow opera lover, a young man named Michael Kahn, who would go on to run the Shakespeare Theatre Company. Together, they waited at the Met box office, sometimes for days at a time, for standing room tickets to Callas performances.

"It was a real obsession," Kahn says. "We'd run off to get every pirated Callas record. We went to everything and listened to everything, to every little piece, playing every note, then playing it back to hear this phrase or that again, and then having heated discussions and fights. *Lisbon Traviata* is very much a picture of those times."

A large chunk of the play is consumed by a tornadic session of opera-world name-dropping and trivia-dispensing, but the banter also reflects a sardonic side to McNally's embrace: "Love and death. That's all they're ever singing about," a character observes. "Boy meets girl, boy gets girl, boy and girl croak. That's all you need to know from *Aida* to *Zaide*."

Kahn remembers being so enveloped in their idol's mystique that he and McNally were provoked to anarchic acts. In the wake of the infamous 1958 firing of Callas by the Met's general manager, Rudolf Bing, the two students marched over to the Met at 2 a.m. and painted two words across the advertising posters: "Viva Callas."

A few mornings after attending *Eugene Onegin*, McNally is on the phone, his memory having been jogged about that long-ago college prank. He laughs warmly, pointing out it was not committed out of anger.

"No, it was done for love. We were teenagers," McNally says, "and that's how passionate we were."

McNally's Aria

Randy Shulman / 2010

Originally published in *Metro Weekly*, March 25, 2010, 24–27. Reprinted by permission.

Three years ago, Terrence McNally's phone rang.

On the line, Michael Kaiser, president of the John F. Kennedy Center for the Performing Arts.

"We'd like to do a McNally festival," said Kaiser.

"My God, really?" replied McNally. "I'm very flattered and honored, but what are you talking about?"

"We'd like to do three plays simultaneously," Kaiser explained, one in the Eisenhower, one in the Terrace, and one in the center's newest venue, the Family Theater, which for years housed the AFI Theater.

Using 1989's potent—and extremely gay-centric—*The Lisbon Traviata* as a starting point, Kaiser and McNally crafted a festival that ultimately celebrated McNally's long-standing passion for opera, including his 1995 Tony-winning masterpiece *Master Class* and a new work, *Golden Age*. The resulting "Terrence McNally's Nights at the Opera"—helmed by power-house stars like Tyne Daly, who plays Maria Callas in *Master Class*, and John Glover and Malcolm Gets in *Traviata*—began its month-long run at the Kennedy Center last week.

"The three plays talk to one another," says McNally. "*Lisbon Traviata* is about fans. *Master Class* is about an interpreter. And *Golden Age* is about a creator. Three very interesting aspects. A triptych."

The seventy-one-year-old playwright has been hands-on during the production process—helping with every aspect from the casting to even rewriting key portions of *Lisbon Traviata*. He and his partner, Broadway producer Tom Kirdahy, have already spent the better part of a month in our city. Concurrently, a production of McNally's brutal, skin-ripping drama *Lips Together, Teeth Apart*, a landmark 1991 work that dealt with homophobia and AIDS, is getting a Broadway run with Megan Mullally and Patton Oswalt in April.

"It's bliss, it's entertaining, it's never, ever, ever boring," Kirdahy says of his life with McNally. "And it's everything I ever dreamed of. If that sounds corny, I'm sorry, but really, every day is a gift."

And the gift will be enhanced in the near future, as the couple plan to take advantage of DC's recent law allowing same-sex marriages.

"To be surrounded by friends in a city that we love, to say 'I do' out loud, holding hands with the man I love," says Kirdahy, "promises to be quite thrilling."

"This is a very significant moment in our lives doing these plays here," says McNally. "So getting married here has resonance. We were up in New York at a rehearsal of *Lips Together* last night, and on the way back to DC, Tom said he feels like we're coming home. And I said, 'I know what you mean.' It felt nice. DC is a real home for us."

METRO WEEKLY: Let's start with your boyhood. You were raised in Corpus Christi, Texas.

TERRENCE MCNALLY: I really enjoyed growing up. We lived in Dallas for a couple of years, but Corpus Christi is where I first had sex—and that's when you start remembering your life. [*Laughs*] At least that's how I remember mine.

MW: When did you come out?

MCNALLY: That happened before I went to bed with a boy. I was attracted to fellow species members. You know, I don't have a big coming out story to tell you. It seemed very natural to me—I never felt it was wrong. I think something as natural as sexual attraction is not to be fought. We so often hear about people feeling great shame, and "I must be the only sinful person like this." Thank God I never had those feelings. I guess I defined God on my own terms—terms that were comfortable to me. I attended Catholic school, and the one message I got from being in Catholic school was that I was created in God's image; therefore, I was okay.

As wonderful as it was growing up in Corpus Christi, I had my bags packed from about the time I was fifteen and went right from my high school graduation to New York. It's not quite as dramatic as it sounds—I had been accepted to Columbia University—but I got to New York when I was seventeen. I always knew I was going to go there partially because I was gay and I knew there must be many other gay men up there, and partially for the culture, too. I knew there would be theatre. But it was opera as much as anything that made me want to go to Columbia.

I'm fortunate that I had the *smarts* to get out of Texas, to get out of a hostile environment and live life openly as a gay man. There are people who do not relocate. But I don't want to live in an environment where I'm embattled every time I go out the door.

MW: How did you develop an affinity for opera?

MCNALLY: I didn't. I just liked it the first time I heard it. I have friends who don't like opera to this day, and my only analogy for it would be I don't like calves' liver. People always say, "Wait till you taste *my* calves' liver," or "There's a restaurant I'm going to take you to and you will really change your mind about calves' liver." I've had calves' liver maybe forty-five times in my life, and I just don't like calves' liver. Some people just don't like opera.

People will say "Who can like an art form where someone drinks poison or is stabbed and then sings for another ten minutes?" But what can I say? It doesn't seem unnatural to me. It seems an artistic expression of maybe what it's *like* to die. Opera is not a realistic art form. But I don't think *art* is realistic. A Rembrandt or a Picasso . . . —it's not real life as we see it with our own eyes, but it's how these people interpret it. I don't think you learn to love opera—and that's fine. You can have a full, happy life and not give a shit about Maria Callas or Giuseppe Verdi. But opera enhanced my life.

MW: When did you experience your first opera?

MCNALLY: I was in Catholic school, and the nun came in one day and said, "I'm going to teach you about something called opera." She put on some Puccini love duets and I just loved it. And the first record I ever bought was a recording of *Tosca* because she played *Tosca* that day. It cost $11.44. Records cost $5.72, and I had a job after school in a cafeteria carrying trays for older patrons, and I was working just to get $11.44 together to pay for these records because every album I owned was two sets—you know, *La Bohème*, *Tosca*, *La Traviata*, they were all two LPs and they were all $11.44. Now I don't have a single record. Now I shop on the internet.

MW: Everything's a download.

MCNALLY: Yeah. I kind of miss the booklets and all that, but I think the sound is pretty good. And to think you can download the "Ring Cycle" or Beethoven's nine symphonies in under a minute—something these men spent a lifetime composing—it's like *zoooop* and there's Act I of *Parsifal*. Kind of mind boggling.

MW: By and large, some of your renowned works—*Love! Valour! Compassion!*, *Lisbon Traviata*—are exclusively gay in terms of their content.

MCNALLY: This high school English teacher of mine—Mrs. Maurine McElroy—said, "Write what you know about." And one of the things I do know a little something about is gay men. So it seems very natural to write about them.

I had gay men in plays as sexual people long before it was okay to. There have been gay men [in plays] I'm sure before mine, but they were always the swishy next-door neighbor, comic relief, or the tormented young man who committed suicide. I was maybe the first not to have anything like that. I [included gays] . . . from my very first play in *Things That Go Bump in the Night*, which had two gay men in it, and these gays were not stereotypical in any way. All the seeds of everything I've written since are there.

The play was done on Broadway in 1964, and I was pilloried for it—"the play was obscene, it was dirty, not fit for human consumption." I was an innocent when I wrote it in the sense I thought maybe it's not the greatest play in the English language, but [critics] certainly will see me as talented, someone to be encouraged. Instead I got infamously bad reviews. They were more than negative—they were vicious. Things like "The American theatre would be better if Terrence McNally's parents had smothered him in his cradle." How do you invoke such hatred?

MW: Did the critics close it?

MCNALLY: I thought we might close in one night, but the producer— Ted Mann of Circle in the Square—said, "I want to try an experiment. I can run the show for two weeks if we can sell tickets for $1 on weekdays and $2 on Friday and Saturday night." I said, "Well, Ted, that's a great idea but I don't think anyone is going to show up even at those prices after reading these awful reviews."

It sold out for the two weeks we ran. The theatre was packed every night. And there were people who like it, so I felt my work does speak to some people. There were people who are clapping, people going "Bravo." There were people going "boo," too, but I was reaching people.

I've often said that if Ted Mann had not done that, I might have very easily not written another play. If it had run for one night only, I don't know if I ever would have had the courage to put another blank white sheet of paper into my typewriter.

MW: Many of your works were groundbreaking from a gay perspective. With 1975's *The Ritz*, for example, you set a comedy in a gay bathhouse. *Nobody* set a comedy in a gay bathhouse.

MCNALLY: I thought it was very political and subversive to do. I said, "Here's a Broadway audience paying top dollar to see a French sex farce that stands the tradition totally on its head." I was very proud of myself for doing that. Sex is only threatening to straight audiences, I think, if it's sexy. But there is nothing un-sexier than a French sex farce—you are laughing at what fools we make of ourselves trying to get laid. I think that's one reason *The Ritz* worked. No one sort of said, "Hey, wait a minute, what's going on here? We shouldn't be laughing at this. We're supposed to be appalled."

MW: At the other end of the spectrum, your controversial 1998 drama *Corpus Christi* stirred up a tremendous amount of vitriol.

MCNALLY: I didn't think it was controversial in this day and age to suggest that Christ and his Apostles could be imagined as gay men. I was naïve because I thought the message that we're all created in God's image had been more accepted than it has been. I thought people would at least say, "Yeah, this world *should* be about love and acceptance and tolerance, about love of our family and fellow man, and that we all have divinity. And when we recognize the divinity in each other, we become truly complete people." But it was all dismissed as a sacrilegious, dirty blasphemous play. I really didn't see that coming.

The reception to *Corpus Christi* revealed how much homophobia still exists in polite society. In New York there's not a lot of gay bashing, but there's a lot of insidious stuff said at dinner parties when gay people leave the room, I have a feeling, and I think we have to address that. I wouldn't be writing half the plays I did if I didn't think homophobia still existed. The reaction to *Corpus Christi* just shows how strong it is. You can say Christ was a woman, you can say Christ was black, but if you suggest that Christ might have been a gay man, then you're suddenly a blasphemer.

MW: You have an interesting resume in that you've traveled extensively between play and musical formats. The list of musicals you've written books for is impressive—*Kiss of the Spider Woman, The Rink, The Full Monty, Ragtime....*

MCNALLY: When I work on a book for a musical, I make sure it's a story I really want to tell with collaborators whom I want to be working with. And I take it every bit as seriously as I do my own plays. I think the mistakes some of my peers make is they think musicals are "Playwriting Lite." You write a scene and put a parenthesis "Song Here." I write them as a play, and if my collaborators, composers, and lyricist can't find a song in a scene, then I've failed, and I rewrite that scene.

Writing a book for a musical is really leaving your ego behind and just working through craft and technique, still with personal emotion and integrity. You're adding to the fodder for music, and if your ego is saying, "No, no, I love that line, you can't have it," you're not going to be a good collaborator.

But a musical has to be about the music. If someone comes out saying, "God, what a great book, but I thought the score was mediocre," well, I don't want to see that musical. Why should anyone want to see it? Go see a play.

MW: Looking over the credits for the Kennedy Center production of *Lisbon Traviata*: you're gay, at least two of the main actors are gay, the director is gay, the play's content is gay. Can you get a production that's more gay?

MCNALLY: [*Laughs*] No, I don't think so. But remember, gay doesn't necessarily mean good. It used to be it was enough just to be a gay play, it was enough to be a gay restaurant. Now it's got to be a *good* gay restaurant and a *good* gay play, so the bar has been raised considerably. And *that* is good.

MW: You've gotten to the point where you are a legend in the theatre industry. How does that resonate with you?

MCNALLY: It doesn't in that I think of myself as somebody that has to go do the laundry in a few minutes. [*Laughs*]

MW: Speaking of your home life: your partner of nine years is Tom Kirdahy.

MCNALLY: I feel blessed. I have the best spouse in the world.

MW: How did you and Tom fall in love?

MCNALLY: Oh, for me, at first sight. I met him and just said I want to be with this man. I was one of the founders of a gay group on Long Island—an organization called EEGO, East End Gay Organization. And I got a call from them saying they were doing an evening of panel discussion on gay theatre, and I said, "Okay, I'll be on it." I got there sort of on the early side, and there was this incredibly attractive, sexy, smart, funny man there—Tom—and I just said, "This is a corny line but I'd like to see you again, but I'm leaving for Machu Picchu in the morning." I went off to South America for about six weeks. And the first person I called when I got back was Tom. He accepted a date, and we've been together ever since. He's a remarkable person, a man of great intelligence, courage, and passion.

MW: Any marriage plans on the horizon?

MCNALLY: Actually, we're going to try to get married here in DC. We're going to have a meeting with LGBT people who know exactly what we have to do since we don't live in the District. We were civilly united [in Vermont] seven years ago, but it's not the same. We want to be married. And this city has become so important to us because of the Kennedy Center festival. Wouldn't it be nice to say we got married here?

MW: Do you think the act of getting married will change the nature of your relationship with Tom?

MCNALLY: The thing that really changed our relationship for the better was the civil union, simply because we didn't just sign a certificate; we stood up and said "I love you" with witnesses and said the words "in sickness and in health." It was powerful and ennobling. I mean, what a profound thing it is to commit your life to another person. So in my mind we are married. I just want it as a citizen in writing that we *are* married. We want "The M Word."

A Playwright's Status Report: McNally's *Mothers and Sons* Gauges a Changed America

Patrick Healy / 2014

Originally published in the *New York Times*, March 2, 2014, AR6. From the New York Times.

The sky over Central Park was always full of white balloons. At least, that's how Terrence McNally saw New York City in 1988, when he wrote a short play for an Off-Broadway revue about life in the age of AIDS.

He set *Andre's Mother* at one of the countless memorial services in the park, when loved ones released balloons as symbols of souls floating to heaven. It would be the first of his plays about gay men and AIDS. While later ones like *Love! Valour! Compassion!*, the winner of the Tony for best play in 1995, injected bitchy humor to leaven the pathos, *Andre's Mother* is all rage: a harangue by Cal, who has just buried his lover Andre, directed at the title character, a nameless stand-in for homophobic parents everywhere.

"God, how many of us live in this city because we don't want to hurt our mothers and live in mortal terror of their disapproval," Cal tells her in a monologue that drew praise from reviewers.

The mother, alone at the end, kisses her balloon and lets go. Yet we don't know her mind; Mr. McNally keeps her silent.

No longer. Mr. McNally has given Andre's mother a name, Katharine, and a voice full of bitter and politically incorrect opinions—supplied by the Tony winner Tyne Daly—in his new Broadway play *Mothers and Sons*, now in previews at the John Golden Theatre. Set in the present, Katharine has returned to New York to seek out Cal (Frederick Weller) for the first time since Andre's memorial, and finds that he has a husband, Will (Bobby Steggert), and that they are raising a six-year-old son, Bud (Grayson Taylor).

Mothers and Sons is less a sequel to *Andre's Mother* than an ambitious attempt to dramatize the head-spinning changes in gay America since that earlier play, affecting not only same-sex couples but also people like Katharine, who tells Cal that homosexuality "still sickens" her in spite of happy nuclear families like his.

"While society has changed a great deal, a lot of individuals like Katharine haven't, and I wanted to show them as real, complicated people," said Mr. McNally, who, at seventy-five, is back to his prolific self with recent Off-Broadway plays as well (*And Away We Go, Golden Age*) after recovering from lung cancer.

"The characters from *Andre's Mother* have stayed with me for twenty-five years, partly, I suppose, because there's a little of Terrence and Dorothy K. McNally in there," he added, referring to his mother, who, like Katharine, grew up in Port Chester, New York, then married and moved to Texas.

Asked if his mother came to accept his sexuality before her death, at the age of eighty-six in 2001, Mr. McNally sighed during an interview in the comfortable duplex apartment in Greenwich Village that he shares with his husband, Tom Kirdahy, a lawyer and theatre producer.

"That's a long story," said Mr. McNally, who has an impish, open face and blue eyes that still twinkle invitingly. "Things were good when she came to New York, and I won Tony Awards. She would turn on the charm. It was not so good when I traveled back to Corpus Christi in Texas. Then it was, 'Please come alone.' I went down with one guy, and she literally acted like she forgot his name."

Like Andre, Mr. McNally grew up in Texas and fled as quickly as he could. He received scholarships to Yale and Columbia; he ended up in New York on the flip of a coin. He quickly felt Columbia was a mistake, he recalled, but before he could transfer to Yale, he fell in love with seeing theatre and opera. Staying put provided entrée that he might have missed at Yale. In his senior year, for instance, Mr. McNally moved in with playwright Edward Albee (who was a decade older), and their relationship continued as Mr. Albee was writing *Who's Afraid of Virginia Woolf*?

Their years together were marked by heavy drinking, Mr. McNally said, which impaired his writing. His first Broadway play, *And Things That Go Bump in the Night*, in 1965 when he was twenty-six, was savaged by critics; while notable for rendering one of the first same-sex romances onstage (between a bisexual man and a cross-dresser), it was regarded as a three-hour mess with unlikable characters. Mr. McNally stopped writing after reviews like one he still quotes easily (though he does not recall its author): "The

American theatre would be a better place this morning if Terrence McNally's parents had smothered him in his cradle."

His life and career began to change course in 1980, at Stephen Sondheim's fiftieth birthday party, where Mr. McNally—in his cups as usual—spilled a drink on Lauren Bacall, who was not amused.

"Then someone I hardly knew, Angela Lansbury, waved me over to where she was sitting," he said. "And she said, 'I just want to say, I don't know you very well, but every time I see you, you're drunk, and it bothers me.' I was so upset. She was someone I revered, and she said this with such love and concern. I went to an A.A. meeting, and within a year, I had stopped drinking."

While Mr. McNally's playwriting quickly shifted from satires and political polemics to more serious work—the first play he wrote in sobriety was *Frankie and Johnny in the Clair de Lune*—a clear head also led him to write forcefully about the lives of gay men during the AIDS crisis, he said. Looking back on those plays, he believes that the opera-loving Mendy in his play *The Lisbon Traviata* and the soul-searching gay friends of *Love! Valour!* hold up as characters today, "even though they weren't remotely thinking about gay marriage or parenting or civil benefits like today's generation," he said. "All these characters had enormous feelings of longing and loneliness that are still very real today, but I wanted to write a new play that explored those feelings in the generations that followed mine."

As with his 1995 play *Master Class*, which he wrote for Zoe Caldwell (who won a Tony as Maria Callas), Mr. McNally wrote *Mothers and Sons* for Ms. Daly, whom he came to know when she starred in a *Master Class* revival that reached Broadway in 2011. Mr. McNally had promised a play to Bucks County Playhouse, in Pennsylvania, and in Ms. Daly he felt he had found an ideal performer to become Andre's mother. Ms. Daly showed she has a way with strong-willed, hardheaded characters in her Broadway turns as Callas and as Rose in *Gypsy*, and her touch was in evidence during a rehearsal this winter for *Mothers and Sons*.

"I'm grateful you don't use many exclamation points in your writing, Terrence," Ms. Daly said as the other actors and the director, Sheryl Kaller, sat at a square table and rehearsed scenes, Mr. McNally occasionally typing notes on his laptop. "I don't always appreciate scripts that tell actors which tone to take."

Later, in a telephone interview, Ms. Daly added: "I like working with Terrence because he's a grown-up. I've worked with a lot of babies in the theatre." She declined to name names. "But theatre is grown-up work. And this play is a serious, grown-up work." (The original *Andre's Mother* was adapted for public television and shown in 1990, winning Mr. McNally an Emmy.)

At another rehearsal, a read-through of the script reduced several of the play's producers to tears, including Roy Furman, a usually poised investment banker.

"At first, I turned this play down, because I had so many shows in the works, but I read it a second time and felt such passion in the writing," Mr. Furman said. "You don't feel that passion a lot."

Selling sizable numbers of tickets to a serious-minded Broadway play lacking celebrity-level stars, especially in a season with audience draws like Denzel Washington (*A Raisin in the Sun*) and Bryan Cranston (*All the Way*), poses a significant challenge for *Mothers and Sons*. Ms. Kaller's last Broadway drama, *Next Fall*, which also focused on gay relationships, was a commercial failure, but she was optimistic that this play will "sell like gangbusters" because it has wide appeal.

"It's a play about family, about how do we love our children, about how we love our parents, and it's very, very current," she said.

The play's lead producer, Mr. Kirdahy, said *Mothers and Sons* would offer low-priced tickets to young theatregoers and use marketing strategies like an online photo album where "audiences could take and share pictures of their families to show how people define family today." Mr. Kirdahy, who has produced several recent McNally plays, said that he and Mr. McNally—who jokingly refers to Mr. Kirdahy as "management"—avoid talking about bringing the play to Broadway. "We've set up good boundaries, like not talking about the show after 10 p.m., because one of us might not sleep if we have arguments," Mr. Kirdahy said.

The two do speak frankly, of course; after the play's premiere in Bucks County last summer, they agreed that Cal needed to be fleshed out further. The character now has a powerful new monologue about the devotion of same-sex couples and their love for their children.

Bud, the six-year-old in *Mothers and Sons*, is an especially critical character at the play's end, which takes a turn toward optimism: the possibility that Katharine might come to know the family better. The child actor, Grayson, has some heart-tugging dialogue, but Mr. McNally responded sharply to the suggestion that he was using Bud as a device to draw tears.

"Not at all," he said. "That thought would only occur to someone who doesn't like the play and is looking for reasons to explain their dislike."

"Think about it for a moment: we now live in a time when same-sex couples are having children and being good fathers," he said. "I wanted to write about how the last twenty-five years have transformed us. And wonderfully so. I like what I see now."

Break Down the Barriers:
An Interview with Terrence McNally

Raymond-Jean Frontain / 2018

Printed with permission.

This interview took place on May 11, 2018, at a restaurant near McNally's Manhattan apartment. Two weeks earlier, on April 23, a documentary titled *Every Act of Life* (Floating World Pictures, dir. Jeff Kaufman) premiered at the Tribeca Film Festival and was followed by a panel chaired by former chief drama critic for the *New York Times* Frank Rich that included actors F. Murray Abraham, Tyne Daly, and Nathan Lane, as well as actor-director Joe Mantello. Two weeks later, on May 20, McNally was inducted into the American Academy of Arts and Letters, where he joined Eric Bentley, John Guare, Tony Kushner, and David Mamet as one of only five playwrights in that 250-member body. The honors arrived in advance of McNally's turning eighty in November, a milestone that colors some of his reflections below.

Raymond-Jean Frontain: Two thousand-eighteen is proving a banner year for you. *Fire and Air* premiered at the Classic Stage Company, *Anastasia* celebrated its one-year anniversary and is going strong, and you've been elected to the American Academy of Arts and Letters, one of only five playwrights to be currently a member of that body. Congratulations also on the premiere of Jeff Kaufman's *Every Act of Life*, the bio-documentary about you that was screened at last month's Tribeca Film Festival. Tell me, was it overwhelming not only to see your life magnified on the big screen, but to hear so many colleagues testify to the formative influence that acting in or directing one of your plays has had on their career?

Terrence McNally: Yes, overwhelming, enriching, very positive. For somebody who doesn't like to hear his voice on the radio, watching myself was not without its squirming moments. But, for the most part, I survived.

I've seen it twice now, and I'm very pleased with it. I don't feel it's a biographical study of me, but a tribute to the playwrights of my generation, to all of us that work in the theatre, to—you were at the premiere—Murray, Tyne, Nathan, Joe, to all the people who were there. All of us celebrating our life in the theatre, why we believe in art. Still, the experience was overwhelming. I'm going to be eighty in November. And it's nice to have the milestone marked somehow. I have an ego like everybody else, and mine was very nicely stroked at the premiere.

It's been a really wonderful year. The election to the Academy is something I'd dreamed about, and it's an occasion that I take very seriously. I'm very proud of it. I've already done an event for them. I did a tribute to Pete Gurney [playwright A. R. Gurney] because every year the Academy celebrates members who have died, and they asked me to do a speech about him.

RJF: I've been wondering if the election brought obligations, like the Forty Immortals of the Académie Française who meet regularly to vote on usage issues and monitor the evolution of the language.

TM: Well, I'm not officially a member yet. That's about two weeks off. This event was like a preview. But they said, "Since you're a playwright and you're about to be inducted, and we lost Pete this year, would you speak on him?" As you said, there are only five playwrights, so if I get more involved with the Academy, I'd work to increase the number of playwrights who are considered authors of literature as well. I think that playwrights are tainted with the brush of show biz. Too often we're seen as entertainers, not serious writers.

But "overwhelmed" is not the right word. I'm very proud, but overwhelmed is not the right word. Overwhelmed means you can't deal with it. What overwhelmed me recently was the opening night of a wonderful new play in London called *The Inheritance*, which is by a young American playwright, Matt Lopez. It's a two-part, seven-hour play about gay men in America, in New York City, pre- and post-AIDS, with the ghost of E. M. Forster running through it talking to him. At the opening the author said this play could not have been written without the influence of Terrence McNally's lifetime's work. And that's the highest honor I've ever been paid. I was totally unprepared for it. What a lovely way to be rewarded.

RJF: Did you have a prior connection with Lopez, like comment on an early draft of his play or have him in a class you conducted at the New School or at Juilliard?

TM: No, he was my assistant on *A Man of No Importance* [in 2002], although I can't say I remember talking much with him about his intentions then. But I do remember that he sent me a play and asked, "Could you please tell me if you think I'm a playwright?" I remember reading his play, although I don't remember now what it was about. He said I left an eleven-minute message on his answering machine, telling him very much he was a playwright and that I thought he was going to write some wonderful plays; he'd chosen the right craft. And then I didn't see him or hear from him for fifteen years.

So, while I appreciate being celebrated, honored, remembered, thanked, whatever word you want, the greatest honor is for Matt to acknowledge me at the end of his play like that, a play that I thought was so moving, that devastated me. I was full of gratitude, and you know the theme in most of my plays is mattering—"Am I noticed? Am I heard?" I feel very heard, very noticed, very, very much appreciated as I turn eighty.

But the movie [*Every Act of Life*] doesn't really celebrate me. Look at the friends and talents that I've worked with. No playwright does it alone. *Master Class* has been performed around the world because Zoe [Caldwell] created it, not because Mary Smith did. I've said this to you before: I think Shakespeare must have had very good actors to write for. You don't write *Hamlet* and *King Lear* for bad actors; you write them for actors in your company who hear your voice, understand your concerns. And I knew that when I started out. Fortunately, most of the voices and faces of the people I've worked most closely with are in this movie. So it's kind of a celebration of what we've all done together, not a celebration of my life.

RJF: I was impressed by the way Frank Rich led off the panel discussion following the film by calling attention to the number of people who acknowledged your having taken a chance on them. Like Joe Mantello, who said that you had to fight to have him put in as director of *Love! Valour!*, or Tyne Daly saying that she didn't imagine that she could play Callas [in the revival of *Master Class*] and your not only insisting, "Trust me, I see you in this part," but going on to write *Mothers and Sons* specifically for her. The audience responded warmly to Nathan Lane's recalling how despondent he was to be appearing in a play he didn't like, and your coming up to him out of the blue and telling him what a fine actor you thought he was, and then not only inviting him to audition for Mendy in *Lisbon Traviata*, but fighting to cast him when others thought him too young for the part. I'm sorry that the story of your writing the part of Googie Gomez in *The Ritz* for Rita Moreno after hearing her riff at a party as a Puerto Rican actress who mangles her adopted language didn't make it into the film, inasmuch as her performance won her a Tony and the story's become Broadway legend.

TM: Well, I like to think I have good taste in other people's talents. I go to the theatre, I think, an average of five nights a week, which introduces me to a lot of new talent. I go to shows on Broadway, I go Off-Broadway. I don't "discover" these people; I simply go out to theatre and see the work they're doing. You don't "discover" great collaborators by staying at home waiting to see just Tony-nominated plays. You've got to be a little more adventurous and go downtown, or to Brooklyn, or see something that wasn't well reviewed, perhaps, but has an interesting actor in it. The play Nathan talks about was a big flop, but I thought he was wonderful in it. I understand that because this is such a collaborative business, it's part of the job knowing who are the rising directors, who are the new acting talents I may want to work with sometime. You have to be willing to use an actor in a role that you'd be surprised to see them do. Part of being a playwright, I think, is finding the right collaborators and then fighting to use that talent. The only reason I had to fight for Joe was because at that time no one had heard of him as a director. But I'd seen a scene he'd done at a workshop for new directors, and after talking with him I knew that he understood the play [*Love! Valour! Compassion!*] better than anyone else we were talking to. There were other candidates for the job who'd won Tony Awards, and in the theatre, prize winners tend to get hired over non-prize winners. But that doesn't always mean they're good, you know. If the collection of Tony Awards in any given production was a sure sign it was going to succeed, then what the hell happened to *Catch Me If You Can*? I think we had, like, between us—the authors, the director, and the choreographer—seventeen Tony Awards, and I still ended up withdrawing the credit from my resume. It won no awards [. . .]. But on paper. . . .

RJF: It had one win, for a supporting role.

TM: Oh, right. Norbert Leo Butz won a Tony for Best Actor. Well, that's for an actor. You know what I'm saying: who wouldn't invest in the show with this pedigree on paper? And then you get it in the room, and you find they're not the right people to do this show. That's why I keep saying the big void in the American theatre is producers. We need people who don't just raise money but are smart about putting this director with that script, with that designer, with that actor. I feel like there are people who can raise fifteen million dollars to produce a show, but they don't necessarily get the right ingredients to put in the pot.

RJF: You said something similar in response to Frank Rich in the panel discussion after the documentary, and you got a significant amount of applause from the audience, which apparently included quite a few ardent theatregoers. You complained that too often we hear of a director-driven production, a text-driven production, or an actor-driven production, when we should be talking about a communally conceived production. I think this is why I find *It's Only a Play* to be one of the richest things you've written. Too often it's classified as a farce, the suggestion being that it's a slighter effort than *Lips Together* or *Ganesh*. But the point of the play seems to be that after all the recriminations as to what went wrong in that evening's performance of *The Golden Egg*, this group of theatre people pick themselves up and start reinventing themselves as a community. It's a *combined* creative effort in which even the acid-tongued theatre critic becomes involved.

TM: Well, you know, theatre is the original pick-yourself-up-and-start-all-over-again business, and if you can't pick yourself up, you're not gonna last very long in it. I would say the trick is to develop an elephant hide to protect your delicate soul and humanity, and feel peace within that. It's a balancing act and some people aren't very good at it, but that's how you survive in this business.

But I think you're right. *It's Only a Play* is a much more complicated play about theatre, the mystery of it, the agony of it, and also the big joy it can be when it all works. It's much more than some funny lines about theatre people. I think it's a much more serious play than people notice when they just hear some of the name-dropping and some of the bitchy lines; there's a lot of heart in that play too. And I think that sometimes gets lost.

I think in general right now my work is probably being more appreciated or better understood than it was originally. I don't know, suddenly a lot of my plays are being done. *Ragtime* is probably right now the most produced musical in America. *Frankie and Johnny* is suddenly being done a lot again, *Master Class* was just redone on Broadway. I've had very few plays that have completely disappeared. I've had my fair share that have sort of died until some director comes along and reinvents it, puts a new spin on it. But I've had a fairly successful career. Maybe I have been kind of turning plays out, I'm not sure. To me, being in rehearsal for a play is like a great party, and I'm always wanting to go to a party. And you have to write a new play to go to the next party.

RJF: I think the title *It's Only a Play* is double-edged. I think of those two moments in your *Puccini* film script when Puccini and Toscanini are frustrated that something is not going right with an opera. The one looks at the other and says, "Ah! It's only an opera," and the other replies, "Yes," and then they stare at each other and laugh uproariously at how ridiculous that proposition is. On the one hand, as an artist you have to keep things in perspective; but on the other, the play or opera is the most important thing in the world to you at this moment.

TM: It's life and death, you know. I guess by this period of my life I'm more reflective than I used to be. Turning eighty is a milestone, and with the combination of the Arts and Letters induction and the movie. . . . The morning after *Fire and Air* opened, I realized that for the first time in decades I have no outstanding obligations—no first draft due, no auditions to attend, no previews—and I realized that this is the beginning of my third act and I want to write it. *I* want to write it. I don't want it to be written for me. I'm thinking that right now I'm a free agent. If I want to go up and see the Tennessee Williams exhibit [at the J. Pierpont Morgan Library and Museum], which I hear is terrific, I can. I can't say "I'd love to go but we have auditions, or that rewrite has to be done by 5 o'clock." It's only been two months [since *Fire and Air* opened], so I'm kind of new to all this freedom, but I'm enjoying it.

Still, I've been doing a lot lately. I've done a lot of speaking and things. People say "We'd like you to talk only ten, fifteen minutes." Ten to fifteen minutes to address people who would rather be eating their dinner, or want to get home and watch television. Tough audience. I keep saying to people that they're asking a lot of me because it's never only ten or fifteen minutes. I can't wing it, I have to write something, and that takes some time. Then you see one person eating and one person looking at their watch and uhh . . . I'm losing them. You have to work to engage the audience.

So, not exactly loafing yet, but I have three ideas for plays I think I want to write. But I don't owe them to anybody, you know? No one's waiting to read them but me. It's a very strange feeling after sixty-odd years of always a deadline to be met, a commitment to be honored. I'm looking forward to maybe some travelling. I don't think I've been in Italy in ten years, and France is a country that I really don't know. I very much want to go back to India. I shock myself to think how little I've been reading since I began writing plays. After a long day of rehearsal and rewrites, the last thing I want to do is read a book. And unfortunately, there is the curse of CNN and MSNBC, and it's so easy to just turn that on and start watching. I've become a bit of a news junkie, although you feel like you're watching the same thing night after night, a president [Donald Trump] who's done something outrageous. We rail against him until the next day when he does something more outrageous.

So, maybe I'll reread *War and Peace*. Or Proust, which I was much too young to have read when I did.

RJF: I'm surprised that you can imagine taking a respite from writing, Terrence. So many of your plays deal with our need to connect with other people. Johnny says "We have to connect, or we die," and I've always assumed that writing plays was one of your primary ways of grounding yourself in the world, was a satisfying way for you to connect with other people. I'm surprised that you can imagine yourself not writing.

TM: I want to reflect for a little while on what I really, really, really want to do next. You know, consider what's the one thing that, as a human being, will cause me to be dissatisfied with my life if I don't finish. I have ideas for three plays, but I'm glad they're not promised to someone so I don't feel I have to work on them right away. We'll see. This is all very new to me, and I may be blowing hot air and soon be right back in the galleys. You know, one of my heroes is Verdi, and he referred to them as his galley years when he felt like he had to turn out an opera per year for these theatres. I don't have to do that. There are some very nice revivals coming up that I look forward to, but that's very different. Actually, they're not going be revivals because they're plays I want to fix. They're being redone because interesting directors have some excellent new ideas about how to approach them.

And also the film [*Every Act of Life*] does not go into my involvement with opera, and I'm very proud of my work there. One date to blaze into my mind is 2021 when the Met premieres *Dead Man Walking*. To have it done at the Met is thrilling, and it was just done in London. I wasn't sure the British would get it at all. It's so emotional, and I just loved it there.

So there are things I'm looking forward to, but a new production of an opera that's twenty-two years old is not the same participation as [composer] Jake [Heggie] and I sitting together and writing the opera in the first place.

RJF: I'm not trying to argue with you about your not feeling the need to write a new play or opera, but you've given us so many powerful moments, like Bellini at the end of *Golden Age*, when, even as he's standing backstage at the premiere of what we know is his last great opera . . .

TM: And I think he knew it was his last.

RJF: . . . he's still thinking of the music he hasn't gotten down on paper yet, he's thinking of making an opera of *King Lear*. Composing is an existential act for him, his way of connecting with the world, as writing plays has seemed for you. I've assumed that you'd always have one more play that was percolating in the back of your mind, have another set of characters emerging in your consciousness. . . .

TM: Well, they are already. But whether I have the willpower, the stamina. . . . I used to be able to write eight hours, twelve hours a day. I can't do that anymore. I physically can't. And I know when to stop.

I've never been one who believed in staring at a blank page or, now, a blank screen trying to get an idea. Go out and take a walk. Go to the museum, read a book. I don't mean to sound as though I'm pontificating that this is a new chapter. But I'm very curious what I'm going to do next. And I hope it's more interesting than just writing another play. Or, rather, that I'm writing my *King Lear*. We'll see.

It's just so interesting how theatre keeps changing. You know, I came to New York just as "the golden days" of Broadway were in decline. It didn't seem like it then, but Broadway was no longer the only place to be and Off-Broadway was just beginning. This was before Edward [Albee]'s *Zoo Story*, even. Really interesting things were going on down in the Village, like that production of [O'Neill's] *The Iceman Cometh* and [Brecht and Weill's] *Threepenny Opera*. I saw the decline of one kind of theatre and the birth of another.

But now all these not-for-profit theatres that used to do new American plays—like Manhattan Theatre Club, where you could see the majority of my work in the '80s and '90s—now they don't necessarily do new American plays. Now they're doing [George Bernard Shaw's] *Saint Joan*, and that was not in their original mandate, to do revivals of British classics. Playwrights Horizons, they've carried the torch the longest. It's very hard to just do brand-new plays. Suddenly people have discovered that women can write plays too, and we have a lot of very interesting women. Maybe they were always there; they just weren't getting produced. But now, last season I think all the Playwrights Horizons' plays were by women, so that's huge. You know, that used to be such a novelty: "Oh, I'm gonna go see a play by a woman tonight." And now you don't even think twice about it or about women directors. And I think that color-blind casting is finally happening. That was one of the biggest fights you would get into with people. "There's no way that I will do that play with an interracial cast," and you'd say, "But it's not interracial; it's color-blind."

You know, I was on a campaign for James Earl Jones to play Big Daddy [in Tennessee Williams's *Cat on a Hot Tin Roof*]. I said he would be magnificent. I said, "At this time I think we know that Big Daddy as written by Tennessee Williams was a patriarchal white male, but now when the history of the play is established, wouldn't a great force of nature like James Earl Jones embody that?" I'm just so glad this has happened. And I think *Hamilton* really just smashed those doors down. So now it's no novelty that an African American actress [Condola Rashad] is playing St. Joan. Yeah, she's either good or she's not. The story is not whether she's black or white.

RJF: You've spoken about actors who "hear" you, like Nathan Lane automatically finding the voice of Mendy when he did a cold reading of *Lisbon Traviata*, or Zoe Caldwell explaining that she had no difficulty with those long speeches of Maria Callas because she simply followed your punctuation.

TM: Punctuation is like musical marking. Too many American actors are trained to disregard what the playwright says. "If we don't feel like a comma there, we won't take it." Well, you know, if you're doing a musical score and the composer wrote a rest or set a tempo of andante time, you wouldn't do it three-quartertime. But even getting verbal accuracy is a bit of a challenge with some very talented American actors who think paraphrasing is okay. To me punctuation is help from the playwright. Why is there a comma there . . . assuming the playwright himself understands the difference between a comma and a semicolon and a dash and a period? But Zoe said, "Terrence's Maria is easy. I just follow the punctuation, as I do in Shakespeare." The breaks are written for you. I wish more actors had that respect.

RJF: What is it like to sit in a theatre watching a production of one of your plays when the actors haven't heard the script?

TM: Painful. I don't have perfect pitch when it comes to music, and someone will audition for a musical I've worked on and they leave the room and I say, "God! They were sensational," and the composer will look at me and say, "They were a quarter tone flat with our song." I don't hear that, but that's how I feel when I don't hear my "music," my words, on stage. My words are my music. And Nathan and Zoe and Kathy Bates and Christine Baranski and Murray Abraham and all the wonderful actors I work with, they just get it. And if they don't hear you, I'm never going to be happy with their performance. People have had great successes in plays of mine and I've never really loved their performance, because music is not just observing punctuation, it's sharing your sensibility, why something is funny or why it's sad, and they don't get why a line is funny or why a line is ironic or tragic. If you have to explain, if they don't hear my voice and get my humor, then you've taken all the fun out of it. [*Laughs*]

And then . . . with a new play you just pray you get the right cast, the perfect actor, the perfect director, and perfect decor. Because when they do a later production of *Master Class*, whoever is playing Maria is being judged; I'm not. And that's because we got it right the first time. If you don't get it right the first time, you may not get a second. Go back to Chekhov's first play bombing because he was writing in a new rhythm, from a new point of view of theatre, and the old classically trained Russian actors didn't get it. They were still declaiming. That's why afterwards he'd go to every rehearsal and have a say in the casting of a new play. Yes, you have to be totally responsible for everyone in your original cast, or your play may not get a second production.

The buck finally stops with me as to whether it's a good play or not. But the way our not-for-profit theatre is set up today, they announce in a year in advance, "We're gonna do this play September 11th to December 12th," and that becomes inflexible. If the actor you want is not available, the theatre is not going to cancel; they've got to find someone who will do it those dates. And the available person may not be the best actor. That's the downside of institutional theatre. The Met has to do *Tosca* tonight at eight whether or not they have the best, most suitable woman to sing the role. The curtain has to go up on something called *Tosca* because people paid a year in advance to see it.

RJF: Yet over the years you've worked with so many actors who seem to have heard your voice perfectly. Even at the start of your career. I'm sorry to have been too young to have seen the original productions of *Things That Go Bump in the Night* and *Bad Habits* because I cannot read them without hearing Eileen Heckart's voice and Doris Roberts's. It leaves me wondering whether Heckart invested Ruby with the astringent tone and wide-eyed mockery she'd patented as an actress, or you wrote Ruby's condescension to suit Heckart's performing style? Or whether you constructed the two roles that Doris played in *Bad Habits* specifically for her tone, the quiver in her voice, her pregnant hesitations, her anxious hysteria? I'd rush to see a good production of either of those plays with any good actress in it, but in my mind's ear I suspect that I'll always hear Eileen Heckart's and Doris Roberts's voices.

TM: Well, Doris was someone I knew from my Actors Studio days, and I always thought she was terrific. I thought her a somewhat underappreciated actress and wrote those parts specifically for her. But *Things That Go Bump* was my very first play. It almost happened in London first because I wrote it for Irene Worth.

RJF: Really?!

TM: That's who I wrote it for because I'd seen the Peter Brook *King Lear*, and she was Goneril or Regan, and I just thought she was the most commanding figure. I mean, I was twenty-three, and I wrote a play for Irene Worth because she had so blown me away. She got sent the script and she expressed interest, so I went to London and we read it aloud in her garden apartment. I heard her read it, but it was not to be.

But you know who Doris is, so you can hear her as Dolly Scupp or Becky Hedges [in *Bad Habits*]. Other people today would be hearing Marie [the part that Roberts played on the long-running television sitcom *Everybody Loves Raymond*] in those parts, and really that character is not much like Doris, who has a whole other side to her as an actress. But walking around these streets with Doris . . . I mean, we've sat in this restaurant in this same booth before, and people just come up and talk to her as Marie. She's not Doris, she's Marie to them, and they want her autograph even in the "sophisticated" restaurants.

RJF: I've got just one more question and then I can let you enjoy your lunch. In past interviews—usually after the opening of a new musical—you've commented that you have a sign on your desk "No More Musicals," yet you're invariably pulled into the creation of another musical. Why is it that every time you're done with one musical you're certain it's going to be the last, yet when a new opportunity comes along you dive right into it? It's not that you have a love-hate relationship with the musical, but . . .

TM: No! I love musicals. It's, frankly, I have to ask if it's a project that interests me, number one, because when writing the book for *Ragtime*, for example, I'm at the service of Doctorow. So I have to really love the source material. And musicals are slower to get written than a play because of the collaboration involved. There are very few composers I'm eager to work with. I admired [*Ragtime* collaborators] Stephen Flaherty and Lynn Ahrens's work when I first heard it, when they were new Off-Broadway. David Yazbek [with whom McNally worked on *The Full Monty*] was a very talented young composer who'd never done a theatre score, but I'd heard his music, and it was so quirky and unique. I think the score for *Monty* is amazing. And [John] Kander and [Fred] Ebb [*The Rink, Kiss of the Spider Woman, The Visit*] were a whole other thing. They were people whose work I deeply admired and whom I was very excited to work with. I thought I'd learn something working with them, and I did.

So, I say "no more musicals" simply because of the amount of time they take. Sometimes it takes three days just to set up a work meeting, unless you do what [Betty] Comden and [Adolph] Green did. Supposedly they met every day except for, like, Christmas, Thanksgiving, and New Year's Day. And they met regardless until eventually they had to get with a composer. Steve [Flaherty] and I live so far apart that there are logistics of whether I want to spend the next few years going up to 59th Street and Tenth Avenue, all the way over to the West Side, to Stephen's place, or try to get Steve and Lynn to come down here [the East Village]. That's why I say no more musicals. Musicals are written by committee. Choreographers have a lot to say about the book, and directors do as well. Meetings with all these people are time-consuming. I think one of the reasons *Hamilton* is so good is that it feels like one person alone wrote it. It's totally Lin-Manuel Miranda's vision, and with a lot of musicals you feel too many hands were in it. Sometimes it can be to the musical's advantage, but a lot of the time not.

I'm fiercely proud of what we came up with for *Ragtime.* I think it's one of the classics, frankly. It's being received as a classic by many people now, but it was a good two or three or more years in the making. I didn't have to work on it every day, no, but my involvement didn't leave any time between meetings with the creative team, rehearsals, and previews to write a new play. It's a very time-consuming process. That sounds bad because I spend a lot of time on my own plays, but with a musical you have to have a consensus. When I'm writing a play like *Fire and Air*, I don't have to be in agreement with anyone but myself. When the writing's done, I want a director who appreciates it and a producer who supports it, but during the actual writing I only have to please myself. In a musical, if I write a scene and the composer and lyricist can't hear a song in it, I've let them down.

And then I've got to go back after I receive the songs they've written, and argue that the character of Mother I've created would never say a word they've given her to sing, or ask why Father is singing a jazzy song here? It's a lot of give and take, which is why I say "no more musicals."

RJF: Is the renewed popularity of *Ragtime* a result of the Black Lives Matter movement, do you think?

TM: I think the movement makes the musical seem more relevant, but theatre companies usually schedule things two years in advance, so most of the productions taking place now were decided before the Black Lives Matter movement really got its momentum. A production opened in Sarasota just last week, in fact, and people asked me, "Did you rewrite the show to make it more relevant?" I said "No, what do you mean, it's history." Well, Act I ends with the police clubbing an African American woman to death because they think she's got a gun at a political rally. The police guarding the politician say, "I thought she had a gun." But the Sarasota audience thought we'd changed the musical to make it more contemporary. Clearly, they had never read Doctorow's novel.

I'm not in favor of taking the N-word out of Mark Twain. I don't know what that accomplishes. You know, in *Ragtime* the N-word is used quite often, and there was a high school in New Jersey that forbade the drama club's use of that word, and the students who were in the show rebelled. The cast was easily half black and they said, "This is historical. Don't call me that word now or we've got a real problem, but I can live with the word in a piece that takes place in 1907." It was the students who demanded the original text.

RJF: That's a nice note to close on since it reminds me of what I find so moving about your plays in general: their determination to seek connection, whether among the characters on stage or between the characters and the audience.

TM: Theatre is collaborative, but life is collaborative. We all deal with a wonderful weave and bond together, if we remember to. I think the arts have been trying to do that since Aeschylus back in the early days of theatre. I don't know who the first composer was, but Aeschylus is our first playwright, and I've tried to follow in that tradition as best I can by showing what connects us, what makes us human beings. Art is important to remind us that we're not alone, that this is a wonderful world and we can make it more wonderful by fully embracing each other. And I think that's the message of art, finally. I don't know why it's so hard to remind ourselves sometimes, but thank God we've had great artists who don't let us forget. And thank the audiences who support them because I think that their [artists'] true mission has been to bring the barriers down, break them down, not build walls, tear them down.

Index

Abraham, F. Murray, xvi, xliv, 35, 117,
    126, 146
Albee, Edward, xiv–xv, xxxix, 5, 8, 55,
    67, 80, 85, 97, 100, 115, 143; *Who's
    Afraid of Virginia Woolf?*, 32,
    46–47; *The Zoo Story*, xvii
Arcena, Loy, 65, 94
Ardent, Fanny, 117

Bacall, Lauren, 144
Baitz, Jon Robin, xvi
Baranski, Christine, xvi, xxiii, xliv, 13,
    50, 90, 102, 105, 154
Bates, Kathy, xvi, 14, 35, 36, 39, 49, 50,
    117, 154
Beaser, Robert, xxx
Becker, Randy, 95
Bellini, Vincenzo (*I Puritani*),
    xxxii–xxxiii
Bentley, Eric, xvii, 87
Bonasorte, Gary, xv, xxiv, 61, 71, 106
Burrows, Abe, 46
Busch, Charles, 111

Caldwell, Zoe, xvi, 55, 58–59, 72, 90, 92,
    93–94, 111–12, 115, 116, 117, 148,
    154
Callas, Maria, xiv, xxxi, 21, 58–59, 72, 74,
    110, 133–34
Cheever, John, xli, 71
Chekhov, Anton, 35, 77, 83, 154

Clurman, Harold, 18
Coco, James, xvi, xxiv, xl, 6, 9–10, 15, 33,
    49, 75
Cohn, Ruby, xxxviin17
Comden, Betty, and Adolph Green, 156
Crowley, Mart (*The Boys in the Band*),
    xxii, 80, 98
Cuskern, Dominic, xv

Daly, Tyne, xvi, xliv, 132, 142, 144, 146, 148
Daniele, Graciela, xliv
Devlin, Barry (*A Man of No
    Importance*), xxix, 108
Diaghilev, Sergei, xxxiii
Doctorow, E. L. (*Ragtime*), xxix, 105, 113
Drivas, Robert, xiv, xvi, xl, 5, 10, 55
Durrenmatt, Friedrich (*The Visit*), xxix,
    105, 113

Falco, Edie, 117
Fierstein, Harvey (*Torch Song Trilogy*),
    18
Finn, William, 58
Fisher, Jules, and Peggy Eisenhaur, 93
Flaherty, Stephen, and Lynn Ahrens,
    xxix, xliv, 101, 105, 156
Foglia, Leonard, 92

Garland, Judy, xiv
Gershwin, George, 54, 82
Gets, Malcolm, 132

Glover, John, xvi, xliv, 132, 133
Guare, John, xvii, xxxviin8, 63

Hart, Moss (*Act One*), xxxviiin30
Heald, Anthony, xvi
Heckart, Eileen, 5, 155
Heggie, Jake, xxx, xliv, 101, 114, 129
Hickey, John Benjamin, xliv
Horowitz, Israel, xvi

Innaurato, Albert, xxviii

Johnson, Lyndon Baines, xiv, xxxv, 16, 31
Jones, James Earl, 153

Kahn, Michael, xiv, 31, 53, 86, 88, 110,
    125, 133
Kander, John, and Fred Ebb, xxviii–
    xxix, xxx, xliv, 101, 105, 112, 156
Kaufman, Jeff (*Every Act of Life*), xvii,
    xxxv, xliv, 146–47
Kazan, Molly, xxxix, 7, 31–32, 88, 110,
    111, 119
Kerr, Jean, 95
Kirdahy, Tom, xv, xliii, 123, 135–36,
    140–41
Kirkland, Sally, 6, 15
Kleban, Edward L., xiv, 31, 86, 110, 125
Kramer, Larry (*The Normal Heart*),
    xxvii, xxxiii
Kukla, Fran, and Ollie, 84–85
Kurtz, Swoosie, 13, 35, 39
Kushner, Tony (*Angels in America*), xii,
    xvii, xxvii, 80, 98

Lane, Nathan, xvi, xliv, 13, 16, 35, 41,
    50, 90, 94, 102, 103, 106, 111–12,
    128–29, 133, 146, 148, 154
Lansbury, Angela, xvi, xxix, 122, 144
Lawrence, Gertrude, xiii, xxxix, 30, 73,
    124
Lear, Norman, xx, xl

Lopez, Matthew (*The Inheritance*), xliv,
    147–48
Ludlam, Charles, 19
LuPone, Patti, 117

Maizie, Marin, xvi
Mamet, David, xvii
Mann, Ted, 33, 138
Mantello, Joe, xliv, 65, 94, 100
Maslon, Laurence, 55–56
May, Elaine, xl, 6, 33, 43, 75
McDevitt, Bryan, 93, 100
McDonald, Audra, xvi, xliv
McElroy, Maurine, xiii, xxxix, 74, 87,
    124, 127, 138
McGarty, Michael, 92
McNally, Terrence: as actor, 32, 67,
    88, 125; and actors, 89–90; and
    AIDS, xxiii–xxiv, xxviii, xli;
    awards and honors, 107, 146–47;
    education, xiii–xiv, 124–25;
    family relations, xii–xiii; and gay
    theater, 17–18, 37, 60–61, 68–69,
    76–77, 78–81, 96–99, 120, 140,
    144; and homosexuality, xvii–
    xviii, 136–39; illness and death,
    xvi, xvii; and Manhattan Theatre
    Club, xvi, 12–13, 70, 75–76, 102,
    126–27; and opera, xii, xiii, 22,
    24, 42–43, 52, 53, 73–74, 85–86,
    131–32, 137; personal relation-
    ships, xii, xiv–xv; and producers,
    47, 114–15, 149; and stage nudity,
    71, 95, 97–98; and theatrical
    multiculturalism, 39–40, 153;
    thoughts on theater, 13, 17, 19,
    27–28, 34–35, 41–42, 43, 46–48,
    61, 76, 84, 90–100, 108–9, 112,
    114–19, 121, 158
    Works: *Anastasia*, xxix, 146; *And
    Away We Go*, xxxii; *And Things
    That Go Bump in the Night*, xi, xv,

xviii, xix, xx, xxxi, xl, 3–5, 8, 15, 18, 20, 25, 26, 32–33, 48, 57, 67, 75, 80, 82, 89, 97, 103, 110, 126, 128, 132–33, 138, 143; *Andre's Mother*, xxiv, xli, 14, 16, 63, 142; *Apple Pie*, xiii; *Bad Habits*, xv, xxi, 6, 20, 49, 58, 67; *Botticelli*, xi, xviii, 20; *Bringing It All Back Home*, xviii; *Catch Me If You Can*, xxix, 129–30, 149; *Corpus Christi*, xvi, xxvi, xlii, 84, 91, 96, 102, 104–5, 116, 128, 139; *Crucifixion*, xlii, 120; *!Cuba, Si!*, xviii; *Dead Man Walking*, xix, xxx, xlii, 101, 107–8, 114, 129, 152; *Dedication or The Stuff of Dreams*, xi, xvi, xxxii, xli, 132; *Deuce*, xxvii, 122–23, 128; *Dusk* (in *By the Sea, By the Sea, By the Beautiful Sea*), xvi; "The Education of Young Henry Bellair, Esq.," xx, xl; *The Five Thirty-Eight*, xli; *The Food of Love*, xxx; *Frankie and Johnny in the Clair de Lune*, xi, xiii, xxiv, 14, 15–16, 18, 20, 23, 26, 34, 36–37, 38, 39, 41, 50, 63, 66, 89, 101, 102–3, 107–8; *The Full Monty*, xxix, 101, 105, 107, 114; *Ghost Light*, xxx, xli; *Golden Age*, xi, xvi, xvii, xxxii, 135, 152; *Great Scott*, xxx, xxxii–xxxiii; *Here's Where I Belong*, xxviii, xl, 9; *Hope* (in *Faith, Hope and Charity*), xvi; *House* (with Jon Robin Baitz), xvi; *Immortal Longings*, xi, xxxii, 151, 157; *It's Only a Play*, xi, xxii, xxiii, xl, 13, 20, 23, 50, 54, 58, 76, 82, 102, 150; *Kiss of the Spider Woman*, xxviii, 14, 63, 98, 108–9; *The Lady of the Camellias*, 8; *The Last Mile*, xli; *Let It Bleed*, xix, xxvii; *Lips Together, Teeth Apart*, xi, xxv, 13, 14, 16, 18, 20, 34, 48, 60–61, 63, 64, 66, 89, 90, 95, 103,

135; *The Lisbon Traviata*, xvii, xxv, xxxi, 14, 16, 18, 20–23, 34, 38, 48, 63, 64, 74–75, 80–81, 83, 95, 103, 133, 134, 135; *A Little Bit Different*, 7, 25, 31, 86, 110, 125; *Love! Valour! Compassion!*, xi, xxv, xxviii, xli, 55, 58, 60, 62, 63, 64–65, 69–70, 81, 84, 94, 95, 103; *A Man of No Importance*, xxix, xxx, xlii, 101, 105, 107, 109, 117–18, 147; *Master Class*, xi, xvi, xvii, xxviii, xxx, xxxi, 58, 60, 63, 72, 83, 89, 90, 96, 104, 115–16, 117, 135; *Mothers and Sons*, 142–43, 145; *Next*, xi, xix, xl, 6, 15, 20, 25, 58, 63, 75, 83; *Noon* (in *Morning, Noon and Night*), xvi, xx, 9–10, 17; *A Perfect Ganesh*, xi, xxv, xxxii, 13–14, 53, 59, 63, 64, 66, 83, 84, 109, 118; *The Playwright*, xxxi, xxxviiin30; "Positively Tenth Street," xx; *Prelude & Liebestod*, xv, xxxii, 14, 23, 84; *Puccini*, 150–51; *Ragtime*, xxviii, xxix, xxxviiin27, 79, 89, 104, 113, 129, 150, 157–58; *The Rink*, xxvii, 14, 15, 20, 43–44, 63, 112; *The Ritz*, xi, xv, xxi–xxii, xl, 6, 15, 20, 24–25, 36, 38, 48–49, 58, 62, 80, 82, 94, 108, 138–39; *The Rollercoaster*, 111, 119; *Some Christmas Letters*, xxiv, xli; *Some Men*, xiv, xxvi, 122–24, 127, 132; *The Stendhal Syndrome*, xxxi; *The Sunday Times*, xvi; *Sweet Eros*, xv, xix, 6, 15; *Teachers Break*, xvi; *This Side of the Door*, xii, 26, 88; *Tour*, xviii; *Unusual Acts of Devotion*, xi, xx, xxvii; *Up in Saratoga*, 48; *The Visit*, xxix, 101, 115, 130; *Where Has Tommy Flowers Gone?*, xv, xix, 20, 48, 68, 91; *Whiskey*, xvi, xxi; *Witness*, xv, xviii; "XXIII Skidoo," xx

Meadow, Lynne, 102, 126, 127
Melfi, Leonard, xv, 17
Mercouri, Melina, xviii
Merman, Ethel, xiii, xxxix, 30, 73, 111
Merrick, David, 47
Miller, Arthur, 22, 100, 115
Minnelli, Liza, xxviii
Miranda, Lin-Manuel (*Hamilton*), 157
Mitchell, Brian Stokes, xvi
Monroe, Marilyn, 111
Moreno, Rita, 148

Pacino, Al, 14, 103
Page, Geraldine, xxii, 41, 50
Papp, Joe, 47
Parsons, Estelle, xii, 88
Pfeiffer, Michelle, 14, 35–36, 103
Pintauro, Joe, xvi
Polanski, Roman, 117
Prejean, Sister Helen (*Dead Man Walking*), xxx
Prince, Faith, xvi, 105
Puccini, Giacomo, 26–27, 108
Puig, Manuel (*Kiss of the Spider Woman*), xxviii

Rae, Charlotte, xvi
Rashad, Condola, 153
Rees, Roger, 105
Rich, Frank, xvii, 102, 146, 148
Rivera, Chita, xvi, xxviii, xliv, 15, 43, 101, 118
Roberts, Doris, xvi, 111, 126, 155–56
Roos, Don, xliv
Rubin, Jerry, 87

Seldes, Marian, xvi, 122–23, 128
Shaiman, Mark, and Scott Whitman, xxix

Shakespeare, William, 12, 42, 50, 87, 148; *Antony and Cleopatra*, xxxiii; *Hamlet*, 93; *King Lear*, 68; *The Merchant of Venice*, 81
Shepherd, Sam, xi
Sherwood, Madeleine, 3–5
Sondheim, Stephen, xx, 144; *A Funny Thing Happened on the Way to the Forum*, 25
Steggert, Bobby, xvi, 142
Steinbeck, John, xxxviiin25, xxxix–xl, 7, 55, 109–10; *East of Eden*, xxviii
Stevens, Robert, 47
Stock, Micah, xvi
Storey, David (*The Changing Room*), 71
Strasberg, Lee, 93

Thomas, Richard, xvi

Urie, Michael, xliv

Verdi, Giuseppe, 108
Vogel, Paula (*How I Learned to Drive*), 96–97

Wasserstein, Wendy, xv, 37, 53, 71
Weller, Fred, xvi, 142
Welsh, Kenneth, 35, 117
Whitehead, Robert, 47, 115
Wilde, Oscar, xxix
Williams, Tennessee, xii, 28, 83, 97, 100, 153
Wilson, Lanford, xi, xvi
Worth, Irene, 155

Yazbeck, David, xxix, 114, 156

About the Editor

Raymond-Jean Frontain is an independent scholar who has published eight books and over a hundred scholarly articles on the Bible as literature, gay literature, Renaissance poetry, the Indian novel, and modern drama. His previous works on Terrence McNally include *The Theater of Terrence McNally: Something about Grace* (2019) and an edition of McNally's writings about theatre, *Muse of Fire* (2021). He is currently at work on a study of Tennessee Williams's sexual ethic.

Made in the USA
Las Vegas, NV
12 February 2023

67382050R00121